Arthur James Balfour

A Defence of philosophic Doubt

Being an Essay on the Foundations of Belief

Arthur James Balfour

A Defence of philosophic Doubt
Being an Essay on the Foundations of Belief

ISBN/EAN: 9783337054090

Printed in Europe, USA, Canada, Australia, Japan

Cover: Foto ©ninafisch / pixelio.de

More available books at **www.hansebooks.com**

A DEFENCE

OF

PHILOSOPHIC DOUBT

A DEFENCE

OF

PHILOSOPHIC DOUBT

BEING AN ESSAY ON

THE FOUNDATIONS OF BELIEF

BY

ARTHUR JAMES BALFOUR, M.A., M.P.

London

MACMILLAN AND CO.

1879

'As, to the religious, it will seem absurd to set forth any justification for Religion; so, to the scientific, it will seem absurd to defend Science. Yet to do the last is certainly as needful as to do the first'

HERBERT SPENCER

'A doctrine is first received as an intuitive truth, standing beyond all need of demonstration; then it becomes the object of rigid demonstration; afterwards the demonstration ceases to be conclusive, and is merely probable; and, finally, the effort is limited to demonstrating that there is no conclusive reason on the other side. In the later stages of belief, the show of demonstration is mere bluster, or is useful only to trip up an antagonist'

LESLIE STEPHEN

PREFACE.

It is not necessary to preface this Essay by any precise account of its scope and design. It may be sufficiently described by saying that it is a piece of destructive criticism, formed by a series of arguments of a highly abstract character. The reader who is not deterred by this description from reading the work will find, I think, no difficulty in understanding its plan.

It may be convenient to mention that the first and sixth chapters and the Appendix have already appeared in 'Mind'; and that the thirteenth chapter was published in the 'Fortnightly Review.' In each case there have been some verbal alterations, but nothing deserving the name of an alteration in substance. The sixth chapter elicited a short reply from Professor Caird, which will be found in the number of 'Mind' for this month. For reasons which I there gave I have not thought it necessary to make any important changes in consequence of his remarks.

I must not omit to acknowledge the great and unvarying kindness which my brother-in-law, Mr. HENRY SIDGWICK, has shown in criticising the various portions of the Essay as they were written. His interest in the work, and his suggestions for its improvement, have both been invaluable ; and I have the more reason to be grateful for them, owing to the fact that, in many respects, his point of view differs widely from my own.

WHITTINGHAME :
    January 1879.

*** The original title of this book was ‘ A Defence of Philosophic Scepticism,’ and it was even for a short time advertised under this name. It was, however, pointed out to me that, considering the nature of its contents, the number of people who would read the book would probably bear an infinitely small proportion to the number of people who would read only its title, and that most of those who read the title without reading the book would assume that by Scepticism was meant scepticism in matters of religion. As I could deny the accuracy neither of the premises nor of the conclusion of this piece of reasoning, I substituted the present for the original title, in the hope that, though it is, as I think, less accurate, it may at all events prove less misleading.

CONTENTS.

PART III.

APPENDIX.

A

DEFENCE OF PHILOSOPHIC DOUBT.

Errata

Page 67, last line but one, *for* the *read* this
 ,,   99, line 14, *for* transcendentalist *read* transcendentalists
 ,, 153, heading of page, *for* Natural *read* Popular
 ,, 156. line 6, *after* self-evident *insert* beliefs
 ,, 228. ,, 21, *for* to all *read* at all
 ,, 274. ,, 14, ,, their .. this
 ,, 303. ,, 11, ,, the   ,. this

named thus : Science, Metaphysics, Ethics, and
Philosophy. By Science is meant here, not only what
commonly goes by that name, but also history, and
knowledge of particular matters of fact ; so that
'knowledge of phenomena and the relations subsisting between phenomena' would be a more accurate,
though less convenient, expression for what is
intended. In Metaphysics is included, not only Theology and all doctrines of the Absolute, but also (and
this is not necessarily the same thing) all real or
supposed knowledge of entities which are not phenomenal.

PART III.

A

DEFENCE OF PHILOSOPHIC DOUBT.

PART I.

CHAPTER I.

ON THE IDEA OF A PHILOSOPHY.

EVERYTHING that we know, or think we know, may be classed under one of four heads, which, without departing very widely from ordinary usage, may be named thus: Science, Metaphysics, Ethics, and Philosophy. By Science is meant here, not only what commonly goes by that name, but also history, and knowledge of particular matters of fact; so that 'knowledge of phenomena and the relations subsisting between phenomena' would be a more accurate, though less convenient, expression for what is intended. In Metaphysics is included, not only Theology and all doctrines of the Absolute, but also (and this is not necessarily the same thing) all real or supposed knowledge of entities which are not phenomenal.

B

What is meant by Ethics I have shown at length in the Appendix which will be found at the end of the volume. Here it is only necessary to say that it includes, not only what are commonly called moral systems, but also some analogous systems not usually so described.

Multitudes of propositions, all professing to embody knowledge belonging to one of these departments, are being continually put forward for our acceptance. And as no one believes all of them, so those who profess to act rationally must hold that there are grounds for rejecting the propositions they disbelieve, and for accepting those they believe. The systematic account of these grounds of belief and disbelief makes up the fourth of the classes into which possible knowledge is divided, and is here always called Philosophy.

If it be objected that this is not the common meaning of the term, I reply that it would be difficult to point out what the common meaning is. It has been used, perhaps, most frequently in England, as being equivalent to Psychology, which is properly a department of science. But researches after the absolute are also called philosophical, and these belong to ontology. Ethics is sometimes called moral philosophy, as science is sometimes called natural philosophy; while Logic, which a very common usage regards as a branch of philosophy, would, as I shall presently explain, be included in it also by my definition. So that there cannot, on the whole, be much harm in using the term to represent a definite subject of investigation for which there is no other word.

It follows directly from this definition, that however restricted the range of possible knowledge may be, philosophy can never be excluded from it. For unless the restriction be purely arbitrary, there must be reasons for it; and it is the systematic account of these reasons which is here called philosophy. So that even if it should turn out that Metaphysics is an illusion, and only 'positive' knowledge is attainable, this discovery would be so far from destroying philosophy that it is only by philosophy that it could be established.

If mankind was in the condition of believing *nothing*, and without a bias in any particular direction, was merely on the look-out for some legitimate creed, it would not, I conceive, be possible, *à priori*, to name any of the positive characteristics which the philosophy corresponding to that creed must necessarily possess. But since this is by no means the case, since everybody has a certain number of scientific beliefs, and most people have a certain number of ethical and metaphysical (theological) ones, it may be possible to describe some of the attributes which should be found in a philosophy professing to support these provisional conclusions.

For example.—Since no one supposes that all

the propositions we believe are self-evident, it may be assumed that the greater number of them are legitimate inferences from propositions which *are* self-evident. And from this it follows that philosophy must consist of two main departments, one of which deals with these ultimate, or self-evident propositions, the other with modes of inference.

I do not forget that some writers have held that the truth of a system is to be inferred, not from any self-evident propositions lying at its root, but from the consistency and coherence of its parts, though each of these taken by itself is by no means self-evident. Of such a system it would apparently be incorrect to say that one part is ultimate and another derivative; it ought rather to be said, that the truth of the whole is an inference from the consistency of the parts, while the truth of the parts is an inference from the truth of the whole. But even on this theory the formula above stated holds good, for such systems, so far from being self-contained (as it were) and sufficient evidence for themselves, are really, as a little consideration will show, dependent for their validity on some such proposition as this—'all that is coherent is true.' Which is itself again either ultimate or derivative.

This double function is an important characteristic of a complete philosophy; let me now mention another which, though it would seem sufficiently obvious, is continually ignored. It may be stated thus: 'The business of philosophy is to deal with the grounds, not the causes of belief.'

There is no distinction which has to be kept more steadily in view than this between the causes or antecedents which produce a belief, and the grounds or reasons which justify one. The enquiry into the first is psychological, the enquiry into the second is philosophical, and they belong therefore (according to the classification just announced) to entirely distinct departments of knowledge.

No doubt, in constructing a philosophy, a previous psychological enquiry may be required. It may be necessary to acquaint ourselves with the various modes by which we arrive at conviction, before we can select those which are legitimate. But what we must not do, and what we are very apt to do, is to suppose that by performing the first operation satisfactorily, we absolve ourselves from performing the second at all. In the face of modern discovery we have continually to recollect that no progress made in tracing the history of opinions, no development of the theory of association of ideas, no application of the doctrine of evolution to mind, however much they may prepare the ground for a philosophy, add, or can add, one fragment to its structure.

Thus, it is never a final answer to philosophy to say of a particular belief, it is innate, connate, empirical, or, *à priori*, the result of inheritance, or the

product of the association of ideas. Psychology is
satisfied by such replies, but to make psychology the
rational foundation for philosophy, is to make a department of science support that on which all science
is by definition supposed to rest. It is strictly impossible that any solution of the question ' How
came I to believe this ?' should completely satisfy
the demand 'Why ought I to believe it ?' though,
especially in the case of derivative beliefs, it may go
some way towards it. In the case of what profess
to be ultimate beliefs, discussions as to their origin
are either philosophically irrelevant, or else prove to
demonstration that they are not ultimate. This will
perhaps be clearer if we take a concrete case. Let
us suppose that the result of a particular psychological investigation is that a certain judgment, *e.g.*,
' Everything has a cause,' is '*à priori.*' The psychologist who makes this discovery is apt to trespass
on the domain of philosophy, and add, ' it is therefore true.' Now if ' everything has a cause ' is to be
accepted as true, because it is '*à priori*,' then for
that very reason it is not ultimate ; two propositions
at least must be accepted before it : 1st, all '*à priori*'
judgments are true, and, 2nd, this is an '*à priori*'
judgment. Both of which are assertions both dis-
putable and disputed. So in loose philosophical
discussion it is very common to advance some principle as being self-evident, neither requiring nor
possessing any justification, and immediately after-

wards to adduce in its support some such argument as that 'it is common to all men,' or that 'it has been implanted in our nature by a benevolent and all-wise Creator.' In such cases it is clear either that the principles in question are not self-evident, or that the arguments used to support them are super-fluous.

It is by the consideration of such fallacies as these that I have been induced to use the word ultimate, when the expression ' *à priori* ' might appear the most natural. ' *À priori* ' means indepen-dent of experience ; but ' independent of experience ' is ambiguous. It may mean either that experience has not produced the judgment in question, or that it furnishes no grounds for believing it. The first meaning is quite beside the purpose ; philosophy has no direct concern with the origin of beliefs, which, as before stated, is part of the subject-matter of psychology. The second meaning, on the other hand, while it excludes experience as a ground of belief, and so far expresses the desired idea, does not express the full ' differentia ' of ultimate beliefs ; viz. that we require *no grounds for believing them at all.* On the contrary, it sometimes seems to suggest itself directly as a reason for accepting a judgment (as if the fact that experience did not prove any-thing was a ground for believing it), and sometimes mediately, as showing that the constitution of our mind when in a healthy condition impels us to believe it, or that it was implanted in us by the Author of our being;—which reasons, whether good or bad, show, by the very fact that they are given as reasons, that the judgment called *à priori* is not ultimate.

While, then, it is evidently not the business of philosophy to account for ultimate axioms and modes of inference, it is also clear (though it may be hardly necessary to make the remark) that it is not its business to *prove* them. To prove any conclusion is to show that it legitimately follows from a true premiss ; so that if we were obliged to perform this operation for our axioms and modes of inference before they were to be received as ultimate, we should be driven either to argue in a circle or to an infinite regress. Indeed, this will sufficiently appear if we reflect that all we mean by ultimate is 'independent of proof.'

But if philosophy is neither to investigate the causes nor to prove the grounds of belief, what, it may be asked, is it to do ? Its business, as I apprehend it, is to disengage the latter, to distinguish them from what simulates to be ultimate, and to exhibit them in systematic order.

What is meant here by disengaging the grounds of belief in contradistinction to proving them, will appear more clearly if we consider what is done by deductive logic. Deductive logic, apart from the practical rules with which it is encumbered, is (according to the terminology here employed) neither an art nor a science, but a systematic account of an ultimate mode of inference by which it may be distinguished from all other modes, whether legitimate or illegitimate, whether ultimate or derivative : it is therefore by definition a branch of philosophy.

Now when deductive logic says that any three propositions which can be reduced to the form, ' All A is B, all C is A ; .·. all C is B,' are legitimately connected as premises and conclusion, whatever may be their content, it is by no means meant that such pieces of reasoning derive their validity from the fact of their corresponding with the formula.   It simply means, to distinguish and mark off a certain mode of inference by giving a general description of it ; each particular example of such inference being in itself the witness of its own validity.

This example explains the procedure of Philosophy with regard to *inferences*—the axioms of mathematics furnish an illustration of its procedure in the matter of ultimate *principles*.   ' Two hundred and forty pence and twenty shillings, being each equal to a pound, are equal to one another,' is one of an indefinite number of similar self-evident propositions, which are described by saying that ' things which are equal to the same thing are equal to one another ; ' but which do not require to be deduced from such general description in order to make them certain.   Such a deduction is, no doubt, possible.

I may, if I please, say, 'things which are equal, &c.' 'Two hundred and forty pence and twenty shillings are things which are equal, &c.,' 'therefore they are equal to each other.' But such a syllogism would be as frivolous as Mr. Mill supposes all syllogisms to be ; and for this reason, viz. that the conclusion is quite as obvious and certain as the premiss which is introduced to prove it.

It is conceivable, of course, that the axioms at the basis of knowledge are incapable of classification ; that no two of them have anything in common except the fact that they are ultimate. In such an event the business of philosophy will be to enumerate, instead of describing them. But this can hardly be the case with modes of inference. The philosophy of deduction is already, comparatively speaking, complete ; and though the same cannot be said of any other mode of inference, it is difficult to believe that the bond connecting premises and conclusion differs in every case, so as to exclude the possibility of classification. Something very distantly approaching this state of things would exist if each department of knowledge had a mode of reasoning peculiar to itself, as some have supposed, *e.g.*, theology to have.

To classify inferences is to exhibit what is called their common form. And it is plain that if of two inferences, which by classification have the same form, one is false and the other true, the classification which connects them is philosophically worthless. There would be no use in deductive logic, for instance, if some syllogisms in 'Barbara' were trustworthy and others not.

It follows from this very obvious remark that every kind of logic, if it is to be philosophical, must be formal. The whole object of a philosophy of inference being to distinguish valid and ultimate inferences from those which are invalid or derivative, this can only be done either by exhibiting the common form or forms of such inferences, or (on the violent hypothesis that they have no common forms) by enumerating every concrete instance. To enunciate a form of inference which shall include both valid and invalid examples, can at best only have a psychological interest; philosophically, it is only misleading. These remarks will be found of importance when we come to consider theories of inference other than syllogistic ones.

The same remark applies, *mutatis mutandis*, to any classification of ultimate propositions.

There is no ground '*à priori*' (*i.e.* following from the idea of a philosophy) for supposing that ultimate judgments are all general or all particular. Of course, if they are the latter, there must be some legitimate mode of reasoning from particulars without the help of general propositions.

I have now, shortly and incompletely, but I hope at sufficient length for my purpose, sketched out the form to which any reasonable system of belief must be capable of being reduced. What I desire to do in the remainder of this essay is to examine how far —not certainly every creed current among mankind, nor even those which are accepted by educated and civilised men, but—the vast system of modern physical science conforms to this standard. This is only a fragment of the whole subject; but even this, if pursued in detail, would demand volumes for its complete treatment, not to speak of an author intimately acquainted with the methods and results of every one of the sciences. I need not say that nothing of the kind is aimed at here. I propose to deal only with the roots, so to speak, from which all sciences, however far they may spread their branches, ultimately spring;—roots which are special to no science, but common to all; and even of this subject, so limited and doubly limited, I shall not attempt a complete treatment, though I trust it may be sufficient for the end in view.

Now, there are several ways in which the subject so sketched out might be attacked ; all of them, so far as abstract reason is concerned, equally legitimate. We might begin, for example, by taking science as it stands, and tracing back each particular thread of argument till we arrived at the unproved and unprovable belief on which it must ultimately depend. Such a method would be complete, but to carry it out would require a writer with a great deal of knowledge and a reader with a great deal of time. Again, we might attempt to find, by a process of mere casual exploration, all the axioms which are really self-evident, and all the processes of inference which are obviously sound, and then see how far a dogmatic structure resting on them could be made to harmonise with the received body of the sciences. This method of procedure is, however, too unsystematic to be likely to produce good results, even if it could be made to produce any results at all : I therefore incline to the more convenient, though less ambitious plan, of starting with the clearest and most plausible statement of the most ordinary view of scientific philosophy, and seeing how far this will carry us towards the goal we desire to reach. When this fails us, it will then be time to examine what help can be derived from other and less popular systems.

Now, the most ordinary view of scientific philosophy I take to be this : that science, in so far as it consists of a statement of the laws of phenomena, is founded entirely on observation and experiment ; that observation and experiment, in fact, furnish not only the occasions of scientific discovery, but also the sole evidence of scientific truth,—evidence, however, which is considered by most men of science not only amply sufficient, but also as good as any which can be well imagined. Considering, however, what a large number of persons there are who suppose themselves to derive all their knowledge from these sources, it is somewhat remarkable that we should have so little information respecting the precise method by which this feat is to be accomplished. At first sight, indeed, the problem may not seem a hard one. We are constantly drawing inferences from experience by methods which do not appear to be very abstruse; and all that it may seem necessary to do is to extend the operation of these methods to the utmost limits of knowledge—to prove, in other words, the most general propositions respecting the course of Nature in exactly the same manner as we are accustomed to prove the more limited truths by which we guide our daily life.

Whether this is possible or not is the point which I propose to examine in the next section. And in doing so I cannot pursue a more convenient course than to take as my text Mr. Mill's 'Logic,' which professes to solve this initial problem in an affirmative sense.

CHAPTER II.

EMPIRICAL LOGIC.

THERE are two points of view from which any system
of logic may be criticised. We may consider, first,
how far it gives a satisfactory account of those
methods of inference with which it professes to deal ;
and, secondly, how far it is complete in the sense of
dealing with all methods of inference. The first of
these conditions, of course, every logic which is worth
anything must satisfy. Mr. Mill challenges criticism
under the second head also. He considers not only
that he has told us all about some modes of inference,
but that he has told us all about all—all, that is, of
course, which are legitimate ; so that if we only
master his book, we shall be acquainted with every
method by which mediate truths are or can be derived
from those which are immediate.

This completeness of range is not attained, however, by adding on new methods to those which have
already been reduced to system, but rather by bringing forward one single method, and announcing that
all others are either modifications of this or are not
concerned with inference at all. It is in this last way

that Mr. Mill disposes of the syllogism.   I have too
great a regard for him, and attach too great weight
to the formidable list of authorities whom he quotes
as witnesses to its truth and importance, to treat his
celebrated speculation on this subject in anything but
a serious spirit.   At the same time, I must confess
that it appears to me to originate in a misuse of language, and to end in an important philosophic error.

This doctrine, discovered by Mr. Mill and ap-
plauded by Sir John Herschel and Professor Bain, is,
on its negative side, this : There can be no inference
from the premises of a syllogism, because in the
major premiss there is already asserted what is
afterwards asserted in the conclusion.

Now, when a logician puts any mode of inference
on its trial, he has to decide two questions concerning it, and, so far as I can see, only two. First, does
it involve a progress from what is known to what is
not known ? (the answer to this question decides
whether it is or is not a mode of inference). Secondly,
if there is a progress from the known to the unknown,
is that progress justified ? (the answer to this question decides whether the mode of inference is legitimate). The first question is, so to speak, a question of
Fact ; the second question is one of Law. Now, taking
in the case of the Syllogism the second question first,
no one has ever thought of denying that *if*, in that form,
there is any inference at all, it is legitimate.   The
conclusion may not be inferred from the premises ;

but, at any rate, if *these* are true, *it* is true.   So that
the only question that remains to be decided is the
question of fact.   Do we, as a matter of fact, when
we employ a syllogism, ever proceed from what we
do know or think we know to what we do *not* know ?
This question can certainly only be answered in the
affirmative ; and, indeed, it is so answered by Mill
himself,—at least by implication.[1]

But, says Mr. Mill,[2] are we warranted in 'asserting a general proposition without having satisfied ourselves of the truth of everything which it
fairly includes ?'   Supposing we give the expected
answer, and agree that we are *not* warranted,
then Mr. Mill would go on to say—this is equivalent
to allowing that we ought not to assert any major
premiss unless we are already acquainted with the
conclusion, because the conclusion is undoubtedly
something 'fairly included' in the major premiss ;
and it is absurd to say that a truth which we must
know *before* we can assert another truth can be concluded from it.   To this I reply, that even if it be
true that we have no right to assert the major premiss unless we previously believe the conclusion,
that is not a matter with which logic has any concern.
So long as, in point of fact, we *do* assert the major
premiss without first believing the conclusion, so long
will the latter be an inference from the former, and
so long will the syllogism be the formal statement of

<hr>

[1] *Logic,* vol. i. p. 206.   [2] *Ibid.* vol. i. p. 207.

that inference. Granted that a major premiss arrived at by any process which does not independently prove the conclusion is illegitimate, still, if it *is* arrived at, it is in no way prevented by the illegitimacy of its origin from being the basis of a real inference, and of one which, in relation to its premises, is correct.

So far, then, it appears to me that on his own data Mr. Mill uses misleading language about the functions of the syllogism ; but if this was all, I should not so long have troubled the reader about the matter. If the controversy turned simply on whether we should use the word 'infer' or the word 'interpret,' whether we should talk of 'drawing a conclusion from' or of 'drawing a conclusion according to,' a formula, the matter might be left to professed logicians, with only this recommendation—that if they decide in each case on the second alternative, it would be well to revise the common definition of the word 'infer.'

The really important thing which gives a certain amount of plausibility to Mr. Mill's theory of the syllogism is the doctrine that all inference is from particulars ; and this is mixed up in such a manner with the general argument which I have been discussing above, that careless readers carry away, I am convinced, a sort of general idea that it follows from taking the correct—by which they mean Mr. Mill's — view of the functions of the syllogism.   The truth is that Mr. Mill's criticism of the ordinary theory of the syllogism, where it is not merely verbal, so far from proving this doctrine, depends on it for its whole effect. *Supposing we know any general proposition with the same immediate certainty that we know any of the particular propositions which serve as a foundation for Induction, then, if it is formally possible to make any deductions from it at all (which will not, I suppose, be denied), one of these things must be true—either by the mere act of knowing the general proposition we know 'everything which it fairly includes,' so that the deduction, though possible, is superfluous; or else we can proceed by the syllogistic process from something we know to something we do not know, and which, it may be, can be arrived at by no other method.*   Now, the first of these alternatives certainly cannot be proved, and I think I may affirm without exaggeration that it is extravagantly absurd ; we are, therefore, reduced to the second alternative, which in effect amounts to this : that, on a certain supposition respecting the nature of our ultimate premises, the syllogism would not only be *a* mode of inference, but would be a formal statement of the *only* mode of inference which it would be in our power to use.

The substantial part, in short, of Mill's attack on the syllogism amounts to this,—that in every case where we deduce a conclusion from a general proposition, the ultimate grounds for our believing that conclusion is a process of inference by which both the general proposition *and* the conclusion can be co-ordinately proved; and this again is founded on the doctrine that all inference is from particulars.

Before following out this important philosophic doctrine, as held by Mr. Mill, to some of its results, I have three general remarks to make on it. Firstly, whether it be true or untrue, it does not lie within the province of Logic either to prove it or to assume it. As Mr. Mill himself very properly remarks :— ' With the original data or ultimate premises of our knowledge ; with their number or nature . . . logic, in a direct way at least, has, in the sense in which I conceive the science, nothing to do. These questions are partly not a subject of science at all, and partly that of a very different science.'[1] In the second place, whether the doctrine be true or untrue, it is impossible in any general way to prove it. It is possible no doubt for a man to go over all his beliefs in turn, and find to his own satisfaction that whenever they are not imme- diate, they are ultimately inferred from particulars ; but he can hardly show that this is a necessary cha- racteristic of all conclusions. Something would be done in this direction if it could be proved that there was no satisfactory method known by which infer- ences could be drawn from general propositions : unfortunately, it seems at present easier to show this of particular ones.

<hr>

[1] *Logic*, vol. i. p. 6.

My third remark is, that if the views on ethics expressed in the Appendix are correct, the whole of our morality must be deduced from general propositions which are not, and which cannot be, themselves inferences from particulars. To ethical inferences, therefore, Mr. Mill's theory is altogether inapplicable.

Let us, however, assume with Mr. Mill that all our knowledge springs ultimately from particular experiences, and that there is therefore but one fundamental type of inference—namely, inference from particulars by ‘ simple enumeration ’—what rules has he to give us by which we may judge how far in any given case the operation of inferring is legitimately performed ? We should expect beforehand that in a work on logic, consisting of two large volumes, and founded on this particular view of inference, the systematic account of such rules would form a considerable part. This is not so. What Mr. Mill has to say on the subject is scattered up and down his book, chiefly in connection with certain concrete examples, and must be collected for purposes of criticism from these ; so that we have the singular phenomenon of a work professing to treat mainly of inference, in which the universal type of inference is treated of only incidentally !

How this comes about most of my readers are probably already aware : it is well known that the mode by which, according to Mr. Mill, we arrive at

a law of nature is by discovering, through one of the
' Four Methods,' that A is causally connected in a
particular instance with B, and then, by virtue of the
law of universal causation, extending this discovery
to other times and other places :—the general proposition expressing the law of causation being thus
the major premiss of the syllogism by which the
discovery is established.

Omitting the case of mathematical truths, we
have, therefore, hardly any cause to employ the
' universal type' of reasoning, except for the purpose of proving the law of universal causation. But
since this is not only the most important but also
the most perfect example of its application, we
cannot do better than follow Mr. Mill's (from some
points of view rather singular) course, and examine
it chiefly in this connection.

The first important thing to note is that the
legitimacy of this sort of reasoning does not depend
on its form. Without going the length of Mr. Mill,
and asserting that inference from particulars never
can be formally cogent, we may safely say that as yet
neither Mr. Mill nor any one else has shown how it
is to be made so.

Now, to say that the legitimacy of any piece of
reasoning does not depend on its form is the same
as saying that, if you want to know if it is correct,
you must determine the fact by means of extraneous
considerations.   If (to put the matter in a more

concrete way) a particular mode of reasoning gives me A as an inference from B, and a precisely similar mode gives me C as an inference from D (both B and D being supposed to be true), then, if I find that A is not true, or, at any rate, is not proved, I must have some other reason for believing C to be true than that it is inferred from D in exactly the same manner as A was from B. So much is plain. Now let us apply these general remarks to the particular case of the Law of Universal Causation.

The Law of Universal Causation is an inference from particulars ' by simple enumeration.' It has been found a certain number of times to be true ; it has never (I allow this for the sake of argument), it has never, I say, been known to be false. This is the statement, and as far as I can judge the complete statement, of the inductive argument on which it rests.[1] But if we trust as a rule to this same inductive argument, 'we shall,' says Mill, ' in general err grossly.' It is clear therefore that we must distinguish the correct argument by which the Law of Causation is proved from the incorrect arguments which it exactly resembles ; and this it is equally clear can only be done by means of considerations to be found outside of the argument itself. What are these considerations ? They can be seen on page 102 of the second volume of the ' Logic,' and may be paraphrased somewhat in the following way :—

---

[1] Vol. ii. p. 102.

Certain sequences may be observed to be constant and invariable within limits which, compared with the total range of time and space open to human observation, are restricted. It is hazardous to assume that these sequences will obtain much beyond the sphere in which they have been observed to be true, because they may be the result not of direct causation but of an arrangement, or ' collocation ' of causes; and this arrangement, and consequently its effects, may only exist within the limits where it has been observed. If, however, we suppose the sphere in which we have observed such a sequence to be gradually extended, then, in proportion as it approaches to the total range open to human observation, in that proportion will the observed sequence approach the certainty and universality of a law of nature, until ultimately the two become indistinguishable. This is the case with the Law of Causation.

Now the objection that has to be made to this method of proof is that it assumes the whole question at issue. The distinction between sequences which are the result of direct causation and sequences which depend on the collocation of causes, has no meaning unless we assume a universe governed by causation; and the existence of such a universe is the very thing we want to demonstrate. Grant all that Mr. Mill or Mr. Bain could desire—and a great deal more than could be proved—grant that at every

time and in every place throughout that very limited
portion of time and space open to human observation
every event has had a cause, and every cause has
been always followed by the same event, we should
still be no nearer proving that an inference founded
on these particulars was more likely to be accurate
than an inference founded on any other particulars, so long as the only distinction between the two
assumed a universe of the very kind we wished to
prove. And this is precisely what Mr. Mill's distinction does assume. It is dangerous in an ordinary
way (he says) to infer from particulars ; but we may
do so safely if our induction is sufficiently wide. And
why ? Because we shall then be sure that what we
have observed is not due to chance or the accidental
collocation of causes, but to the direct operation of
causation. This is doubtless a most excellent canon
of criticism, and one which may enable us to judge
of the worth of many inferences ' by simple enumeration.' There is, however, one such inference which
it can never enable us to judge of, and that is the
Law of Causation itself.

This expedient for placing the empirical argument in favour of the uniformity of nature on a sure
basis may seem rather clumsy, but the truth is, that,
though not good, it is as good as any other which it
was possible for Mr. Mill, with his views about the
sources of knowledge, to suggest.

For in a general way we may lay it down that

since by informal inference we mean inference of which the truth cannot be discovered from the form, any attempt to prove a conclusion by means of such inference, can only be made even apparently effective in one of three ways : Firstly, we may distinguish the legitimate from the illegitimate application of the method by means of some principle which is itself arrived at by that method. This is Mr. Mill's device, and involves a more or less obvious argument in a circle. Or, secondly, our principle of distinction may be given either *à priori*, or by some other mode of inference. This plan, though common enough, is of course inconsistent with empirical philosophy, at any rate as conceived by Mr. Mill. Or, thirdly, we may adopt no extraneous principle of distinction at all, but simply affirm that of two similar cases of inferences we perceive one to be cogent and the other not.

I am not aware that any philosopher has formally adopted this last expedient. In reality, however, it is hardly to be distinguished from those theories according to which particular experiences are the *occasions* of our forming 'intuitive' judgments. It is true that in the one case the particular experiences are called 'reasons,' and in the other 'occasions,' and that a system founded on the first would be called 'empirical,' and one founded on the second 'intuitional.' But except in the names there is no important difference between the two. For why are we to accept the conclusion supposed to be proved by the 'reasons'? Because of the cogency of the reasoning? Not at all. Precisely similar reasoning from equally true premises frequently leads to 'gross error.' We accept this example of reasoning, if we do accept it, in exactly the same way as, by the theories I allude to, certain judgments are accepted ; in the one case it is the reasoning which is known to be valid by a special intuition, and in the other it is the judgment.

It would not, therefore, have been open to Mr. Mill to take this view of the proof by which the Law of Causation is established. It is in reality, though not in form, an 'intuitional' proof ; and so anxious is he to be free from any taint of 'intuitivism,' that of the chapter nominally devoted to proving the law, he has thought it expedient to devote a quarter to disproving the 'intuitive' proofs of other people ; and if the reader will refer to the early part of that chapter he will see that Mr. Mill's dialectic would be quite as effective against the particular intuitional doctrine, which, as I have explained above, lies concealed under an empirical disguise, as it is against those more usual and orthodox theories with which we are familiar.

In the foregoing attack on Mr. Mill's view of inference, in so far, at least, as it is applied to the proof of the law of universal causation, I have said nothing which, as I imagine, has not, in one shape or another, suggested itself to many students of his logic. But I am anxious to explain that the fact of singling him out for criticism implies a recognition of his merits even more than of his defects. If his empirical view of the universe is peculiarly easy to attack, it is not because his method of proof is less satisfactory than that of other empirical philosophers, but because he saw more clearly, or at any rate allowed his readers to see more clearly, what it was that had to be proved, and the only method by which, on purely empirical data, even the semblance of proof was possible. If he failed (and I think he failed completely), it was because he attempted what, in the present state of our knowledge, cannot, I believe, be accomplished.

It is impossible to deny that science is only possible if we assume the law of universal causation ; that, if observation and experiment be the sole foundation of knowledge, the law of universal causation must be proved from particulars ; that Mr. Mill has stated (or, if you please, has avoided stating) the method of proof from particulars as ingeniously as can well be imagined ; and that his statement (or want of statement) cannot in reality stand for a moment against hostile criticism. The most important of these points I have proved, as I think, in the course of the preceding remarks, the rest of them I hope the reader will admit without proof; and I now, therefore, go on to show, in a few words, that even if legitimate inference from particulars were possible, and the law of causation were proved, it is by no means the adequate foundation for the superstructure of science which Mr. Mill, and those who accept Mr. Mill's general line of thought, appear to imagine.

CHAPTER III.

INDUCTION.

ADMITTING then that the course of nature is regular, and that every event has an antecedent upon which it invariably follows, and a consequent which invariably follows *it*, the question still remains, how are the real members of these sequences to be discovered? How can we single out the causes which produce any given effect and the effects which are produced by any given cause? Mr. Mill would say (and it will again, I think, prove a convenient course to begin the discussion by examining his opinion) that the discovery must be made by the employment of one of his well-known 'Four Methods.' To see how far the assertion is correct, it will only be necessary to quote two of them—the first and the second. They run as follows : 'If any instance in which the phenomenon under investigation occurs, and an instance in which it does not occur, have every circumstance in common save one, that one occurring only in the former ; the circumstance in which alone the two instances differ is the effect, or the cause, or an indispensable part of the cause of the phenomenon.' And 'if two or more instances of the phenomenon under investigation have only one circumstance in common, the circumstance in which alone all the instances agree is the cause (or effect) of the given phenomenon.'

For the first of these methods—the method of difference—Mr. Mill claims that a single instance of its application is sufficient to prove a general law of nature ; and in a certain sense no doubt the claim may be allowed. It would certainly prove a general law of nature—if it could be applied ; but then it unfortunately never *can* be applied. The state of the universe is never the same at two successive instants in every particular but one. Simultaneously with the change falling under the special notice of the observer, or (if it be a case of experiment) introduced into the phenomena by the experimenter, there occur countless changes which he neither knows of nor produces, and which, for anything that the canon tells us to the contrary, may each or all of them be the cause of the subsequent effect. A parallel objection may be brought against the second method—that of agreement. As Mr. Mill himself explains at length, this method can never by a single application prove a case of causation, owing to the fact that the same effect is often produced by more than one cause ; so that, even if two 'instances of a phenomenon' *have* only one circumstance in common, there is a probability, but only a probability, that that circumstance is the cause (or effect) of that phenomenon.   But has it ever occurred that two instances of a phenomenon have only one circumstance in common?   We may safely reply, never. As in the case of the method of difference, the reasoning is vitiated by the fact that the universe never differs in two successive moments in only one particular, so the method of agreement fails, not only for the reason given by Mr. Mill, but because the universe, at two successive moments, never agrees in only one particular.   And neither the one canon nor the other shows us any grounds for selecting from among the countless points of difference or agreement that one which is the cause or the effect of which we are in search.

I have stated this objection as against Mill, but it must not be supposed that it has only weight against Mr. Mill's statement of the law of induction. It is equally applicable to the ordinary version of the means whereby we obtain knowledge by experiment and observation, of which view, indeed, Mr. Mill merely attempts a systematic exposition.   If we see a man swallow the contents of a phial, and immediately fall down dead, we conclude that his death is the consequence of what he has drunk ; and we do so undoubtedly on the grounds stated in the canon of the Method of Difference.   All other circumstances seemed to remain the same except these two—his drinking the liquid and his death ; we therefore pair them off as cause and effect. The smallest reflection, however, shows that there must have been an indefinite number of events which, like the drinking of the liquid, immediately preceded the death of the man ; what is not so plain is the principle which may justify us in assuming, that though they are antecedents of the effect, they are no part of its cause.

Now there are two ways in which this difficulty or ambiguity in the ordinary version of inductive reasoning may be met. It may, in the first place, be asserted, that by previous observation or experiment we may, and commonly do, arrive at some conclusions which enable us with more or less confidence to select from among the phenomena which precede an event the one which produced it. For example, we know that there are many drugs which taken even in small doses produce instant death ; and this is a consideration which materially influences us in affirming, in the case I have just used for illustration, that the drinking of the contents of the phial, and the sudden death of the man, were not mere coincidences, but were events connected by causation. But though it may be admitted that in fact we do thus habitually use our knowledge of the general laws of nature to guide us in the interpretation of particular observations or experiments, this is no justification of inductive methods in the abstract, since these general laws of nature must, on any empirical theory, in the first instance themselves have been arrived at by induction. It is therefore plain that, unless we are doomed to wander in an endless logical circuit, some inductions must be valid which derive, or at all events require, no support from any extraneous authority.

We turn then to the second possible solution of the difficulty, which might be stated perhaps somewhat in this way :—' Mr. Mill (it might be said) is in error when he supposes that one properly conducted experiment can prove a law of nature, even if the method employed be the " Method of Difference." In all cases of induction we can do no more than prove a certain law to be *probable*. If our observations or experiments be numerous and successful, the probability proved may be a very high one ; if they are few and ambiguous, it may be a very slight one ; but in either case what we prove is probability and probability alone. This, however, need cause us no uneasiness. If demonstrative certainty is denied us, we may still by this method obtain that practical certainty which is all we require to guide us in the affairs of life.'

This, I imagine, is the opinion of Professor Jevons, elaborated at some length in ' The Principles of Science.' That work has no pretension to be a complete philosophy of science, since, if I understand it rightly, the uniformity of nature is assumed in it without proof, as a necessary condition of inductive enquiry ; but, this assumption once granted, the further steps by which we arrive at a knowledge of the laws of nature from the facts of nature are given in detail, so that it is directly concerned with the subject-matter of this chapter.

Now it can hardly be doubted that Professor Jevons is correct in saying that by induction we can arrive at nothing better than probability ; and that in consequence a study of the theory of probability is a necessary and most important part of the philosophy of science. But his enthusiasm for this branch of the subject carries him perhaps rather further than sober reason warrants. Because, apart from the logic of chance we can do little, he seems to suppose that, aided by the logic of chance, we can do everything. The universe appears to him like a gigantic ballot-box, from which the scientific observer occupies himself in drawing and replacing black and white balls ; and because the resources of the calculus would enable the drawer to determine, after any number of draws, the chances of the next ball being black or white, even when the number of the balls in the box is infinite, he appears to suppose that a similar procedure will enable the experimenter to foretell the probability of a future event from a study of the sequences and co-existences of phenomena in the past.

It may be doubted, however, how far the universe can be fairly assumed to resemble a ballot-box, even though the size of the hypothetical ballot-box be infinite. And it is still more open to question whether a legitimate application of the theory of probability will permit us to hold scientific beliefs with anything like the certainty which men of science attach to them, even granting all the premises which they are in the habit of claiming.

Let us, in order to make this perfectly clear, examine a hypothetical case of induction, which we may make as favourable as we choose. Let us imagine that two phenomena, A and B, are of very frequent occurrence; that whenever A has been observed B has invariably followed it, and (if you please) that whenever B has been observed A has invariably been found to precede it. Let us further suppose that the connection between the two has been proved both by the 'method of difference' and 'the method of agreement,' with as much completeness as anything can be proved by these means. Then, granting the principle of the uniformity of nature, what probability is there that when next A shall occur B will be found to follow it? It is evident that unless this probability be very high, amounting indeed almost to practical certainty, then, either the confidence with which we commonly regard the laws of nature is greatly exaggerated (since no law can have *better* experimental evidence than that which connects A and B), or else some considerations not supplied by the principle of the uniformity of nature, or the logic of induction, have been omitted from the proof.

It may be admitted at once that, in a world which we assume to be governed by law, the invariable sequence of B on A is a proof that there is probably some causal link, direct or indirect, between them. In other words, it is very unlikely that this constant coincidence is the work of chance. What the precise numerical value of this probability may be it is not easy to determine, but undoubtedly it would be very large ; and as we are at liberty to imagine as many coincidences as we please, we may consider it as practically infinite. This being granted, it would seem to follow that, in a uniform world, the most confident expectation might be entertained that when next A appeared, it would be succeeded by B, and this is, as I understand it, the opinion of Mr. Mill and Mr. Jevons, as it certainly is the opinion of ordinary common sense. It is not, however, a conclusion which can be legitimately drawn from the premises provided for us by inductive philosophy, as the following considerations will show.

The fact that in our experience A invariably precedes B gives a certain probability in favour of A being causally connected with B. But it gives no probability at all in favour of A being the *whole* cause of B. Every cause that we are acquainted with is complex. But there is no process whatever by which we can show how complex it is. Mr. Mill says somewhere that induction is a process of elimination ; but he gives no method, and there is no method, for eliminating all the phenomena which do not co-operate with A when it produces B. Of course it is easy to take two cases of A and B occurring, and to say that the circumstances in which the two cases differed cannot be necessary for the production of B by A. But this assertion must be carefully qualified before it is accepted. If we could conceive the second case of A occurring to be precisely similar to the first case except in certain particulars, then, since B follows both times, it is plain of course that these particulars are not necessary for the production of B. But no such inference can be made if the first case of A occurring has some circumstances which the second has not, while the second has some which the first has not. It may be that these exceptional circumstances, though different in each case, were in each case necessary, and that without them B would in neither case have followed.

This piece of reasoning will perhaps be clearer if put in a more symbolic form :—(1) A happens twice, and is each time followed by B. The first time it happens it is accompanied only by a, b, c; the second time it happens it is accompanied only by x, y, z. It is impossible to infer from this that a, b, c, x, y, z were not essential factors in the production of B. (2) A happens twice and is each time followed by B. The first time it happens it is accompanied only by a, b, c.   The second time it happens it is accompanied only by b, c.   From this it may be inferred with certainty that a is *not* necessary to the production of B.   Now it is evident that the canon of elimination which could be deduced from these two examples, though logically perfect, can never be applied in practice.   It is like **Mr. Mill's** 'method of difference' —admirable if only it could be used.   Unfortunately we know only an infinitesimal fraction of the phenomena which accompany any cause, and even to this fraction the above canon can never be made to fit. It invariably happens that the second time A occurs it will be accompanied by some things which did not co-exist with it before, and will not be accompanied by some things which did co-exist with it before.   It therefore occurs under the circumstances mentioned in the first of the above formulas, and no inference is possible respecting the share which any of its accompaniments have in the production of B.

But it may be said, 'though it is impossible to assert positively which of the phenomena accompanying A are *not* necessary for the production of B, still if we find one of these phenomena only occurring once in conjunction with A out of the many times in which A occurs, we may surely assert that in all probability it was on that occasion no factor in the production of B.'

It is not necessary for my purpose to dispute this ; whether it could be successfully disputed or no.

For it leaves altogether unsolved the further problem of how we are to dispose of these phenomena which are always to be found in company with A—the fixed stars, for example. On what principle are we to say that these are not necessary to A in order that B may be produced ? What is to be our method of elimination here ? It cannot evidently be experiment, because in this respect every experiment is identical. For the same reason it cannot be observation. It can be no deduction from the theory of probability ; the ballot-box gives us no assistance ; and common sense, which quietly ignores the difficulty, furnishes us with no hint as to the principle on which it does so.

Now if it be admitted, as in theory I think it must be admitted, that every phenomenon which has always accompanied A is as likely as not to .be an essential part of the cause of B ; it appears to follow that our expectation that B will in the future follow A must depend in part on our expectation that each of the phenomena which have always accompanied A will do so again. But these phenomena are in number infinite. We know, or might know, thousands of them ; yet those we know are entirely lost in the vast multitude of those which we do *not* know, but which we have every reason to believe exist in the infinity of space. Because, therefore, we are unable to eliminate the accompaniments of A which are not necessary for the production of B, we have now to

face the further difficulty of determining the probability that these accompaniments of A will co-exist
with it in the future. But this problem puts us back
precisely into the position from which we were
trying to escape. In order to solve it, we have to
traverse exactly the same ground as we had when we
were enquiring into the methods by which the causes
of B were to be discovered. For a case of *persistence* (and of course still more obviously of *recurrence*)
is in reality a case of *causation*. The persistence of
the planet Mars, for example, through another year
depends upon causes of which its existence at this
moment is only one. What are these other causes?
and what is the probability of their being in operation
for another year? These are the very questions we
asked when we were trying to determine the method
by which the antecedents of B might be discovered,
and for which we could find no answer. The continued existence of the planet Mars may, for anything we know to the contrary, depend upon the
continued existence of the moon,—a phenomenon
which, as far as our experience goes, has always co-
existed with it. What then is the probability of the
moon's continuing to exist? About this precisely
the same series of questions may be asked, meeting
with precisely the same series of unsatisfactory
answers. So that we find ourselves finally in this
position.—Experiment and observation, if conducted
under favourable circumstances, can determine with

a probability approaching to certainty, that a phenomenon A is causally connected with a phenomenon B. But neither experiment nor observation can give us the smallest information as to whether any of the infinite multitude of phenomena which accompany A whenever B is produced, are or are not necessary parts of the cause of B; nor can they tell us—and for exactly the same reason—anything about the probability of a single one of these accompaniments of A, however well we may be acquainted with it, continuing to accompany it in the future; still less can they assist us in computing the chances of the recurrence or persistence of those essential parts of the cause of B which may exist in indefinite numbers, but of which we know absolutely nothing. In other words—granting that the course of nature is uniform, no scientific methods, by the help of this principle alone, can give us any assurance that the laws of nature, which we suppose ourselves to have discovered, will continue to operate in the future.

What additional principle, then, must be established in order that this assurance may be obtained? It is evident in a general way that the principle, whatever it may be, must be a *principle of elimination*; that is, it must enable us to eliminate from among the innumerable antecedents of a phenomenon those which we may be certain have nothing whatever to do with its occurrence. But I confess myself altogether unable to formulate such a principle, much less to prove it. There is, no doubt, a practical instinct, common both to the unscientific and to the scientific observer, which induces men to ignore as much as possible the share which either very remote or very permanent phenomena may have in the production of the effects for which they are trying to account. Nobody, for example, seriously imagines that the existence of a star in the Milky Way is a necessary concomitant to a spark before it can explode a barrel of gunpowder. On the other hand, this instinct, though it is so strong that it is not easy gravely to discuss any theory flagrantly inconsistent with it, can hardly be accurately defined, and certainly cannot always be trusted. The most distant object that has ever been perceived has had some appreciable effect on the affairs of this planet—since its perception is in itself such an effect ; and if we consider permanence,—the sun, which has accompanied every phenomenon ever experienced, is an essential and not very remote link in the chain of causes, by which all the events that occur on the surface of the globe are produced.

It is evident, therefore, that the difficulty of proving the uniformity of nature, and the law of universal causation, is not the only obstacle which stands in the way of a satisfactory empirical philosophy. Even granting the truth of these great principles, it is not easy to frame with their help an inductive logic, which shall really enable us to argue to unobserved instances ; and, I shall show in the next chapter, could we prove such laws, it would, to say the least, by no means be sufficient by itself to justify us in holding the complete scientific creed in its ordinary shape.

CHAPTER IV.

HISTORICAL INFERENCE.

THE proper classification of the sciences is a subject
which has of late engaged the attention of scientific
philosophers, and is, therefore, it need not be said,
one about which there is some difference of opinion.
Into the minutiæ of this controversy, the importance
of which is, perhaps, not very great, I do not propose to enter ; but one broad division, not of the
sciences, indeed, but of science (for it runs across the
lines separating the particular sciences), it is necessary that I should recall to the reader, since it has
an important philosophic bearing on the subject in
hand, and must be constantly kept in mind throughout the following discussion.

Every statement concerning phenomena—in
other words, every scientific proposition—is of one
of two kinds :—It expresses either a *law* or a *fact.*
That anarchy ends in despotism is a law (whether
true or not is of no moment) ; that the French Revo-
lution gave birth to the power of Napoleon is a fact.
That accidental variations, which are of use to the
individual in the struggle for existence, are likely to
become permanent is a law ; that existing species are

produced by natural selection is a fact. That all forms of energy tend to resolve themselves into heat at equal temperatures is a law; that the earth will become an inert mass, containing no energy that can be turned into work, is a fact.

Now, in so far as science is founded upon observation and experiment (and on the most extravagantly *à priori* theory these must form an essential part of its groundwork), it is plain that all the propositions stating *laws* (which I will call, the abstract part of science) must ultimately be, to a certain extent, founded on the propositions stating *facts*—i.e. on the *concrete* part of science. What is perhaps less plain, but what is no less certain, is, that almost the whole of our knowledge of concrete science is in like manner founded upon abstract science. As regards facts that are still in the future, this is sufficiently obvious. Leaving supernatural prophecy out of account, our sole means of foretelling what is to come depends upon our knowledge of natural laws ; and this indeed is, according to some people, the chief reason which makes natural laws worth investigating. A little reflection shows that it is equally true of facts that have already occurred, whether those facts be what are ordinarily called scientific, as, for example, the existence of the glacial epoch, or whether they are what are ordinarily called historical, as, for example, the death of Julius Cæsar.

Massing these together under the common name

'historical,' we may say generally that a law of nature is an essential part of every inference whatever by which we arrive at facts which are occurring or have occurred, other than those of which we are immediately informed by perception or memory ; from which it may be deduced that every principle which is required to establish a law must be required to establish a historical fact, though it does not follow, of course, that these principles will be *sufficient*. In order to determine this latter point, we ought in strictness to have before us a complete list of these principles, in order that we might apply them to cases of historical inference. But it will be more convenient to assume that our knowledge of the laws of nature, as taught us by science, is to be trusted, and that the only general principle required for arriving at this knowledge is the law of universal causation. On this assumption (which is sufficiently in accordance with current philosophy) the problem before us would be as follows :—Given as premises (1st) some knowledge of existing and recent facts obtained immediately by perception or memory ; (2nd) a knowledge of the abstract laws of phenomena as set forth by science ; (3rd) the law of causation—can we deduce from these the ordinary version of history, and, if not, what additional principles will be required to enable us to do so, and what is the evidence on which they rest ?

The first of these kinds of premises—some knowledge of existing and recent facts—is not necessary, as might at first appear, because it is required to establish the laws of phenomena; for these are already assumed. It is necessary, rather, because without it nothing concrete could be inferred from the abstract propositions contained under the second and third of the above-mentioned heads. The existence and distribution of phenomena at any given period cannot be arrived at by a mere knowledge of the *laws* of phenomena ; it requires also some knowledge of the existence and distribution of phenomena at some other period ; ultimately, therefore, our mediate knowledge of the existence and distribution of phenomena, both in the past and the future, must depend on some immediate knowledge of them, and we have no such immediate knowledge, except concerning the present and perhaps the recent past.

Now, although a knowledge of the laws of phenomena—that is, of causes and their corresponding effects—is a necessary element in every inference about concrete science, there is a most important difference in the way in which these laws are employed, according as we are dealing with the future or with the past. For whereas every inference about the future necessarily involves at least one argument from cause to effect, so every inference about the past necessarily involves at least one argument from effect to cause, a distinction which, curiously enough, is all in favour of that department of knowledge concerning which we suppose ourselves to know the least—namely, the future. It seems, indeed, clear enough that the ordinary view is correct, and that *if* we knew all existing causes, and all the laws binding them to their consequents, and *if* we had infinite powers of calculation, then, assuming the law of universal causation to be true, and that no new cause came into operation, we could forecast the whole future of the universe. The 'ifs' here are somewhat too large, perhaps, to make this very substantial comfort, but, as the reader will at once perceive, it is by no means obvious that even on similar terms we could give a complete account of the past, because it does not appear to be inconsistent with our assumptions to suppose that *more* than one set of causes could have produced existing effects;[1] in other words, that more than one version of history is equally possible.

This reflection, then, points out very clearly what is the first question we have more particularly to examine—namely, whether a knowledge of natural laws such as we possess, combined with the principle of causation, is sufficient to enable us to overcome the apparent ambiguity introduced into historical inference by the possible plurality of causes ; and, if this question be answered in the negative, we shall then have to determine whether any valid principle can be found to fill up this gap in our ordinary reasoning. The enquiry, it may be observed, is of

---

[1] See note on p. 63.

some importance, since no issue less than this has to be determined—namely, whether a branch of science of the greatest speculative interest, which has grown in not very many years from an ill-considered history of a few nations for a few centuries, to an account, in outline at least, of the history of the whole human race, of the organic world, of the planet on which we dwell, and of the system to which it belongs— whether (I say) this vast department of knowledge deserves to retain its position, or should be considered as a mere collection of illustrations, by imaginary, though possible, examples, of how natural laws work or may work in the concrete.

In order that we may attack the problem with the best hope of success, let us begin by considering it as simplified by certain arbitrary limitations. The possibility of history, as we have seen, rests on the possibility of eliminating all sets of causes but one of existing effects; let us then at first take into consideration only *one* effect, and let us suppose that it *must* have been produced by one of two causes, but *might* have been produced by either. Under these conditions, what we have to determine is the ground which may justify us in asserting, as we so often do assert, that one of them was the actual historical cause rather than the other. To fix our ideas, let us take a concrete case. A collection of flints broken into shapes rudely resembling arrow-heads is found during the course of some excavation. No human being (who need be considered) doubts under these circumstances that one of the causes of this striking effect was the will and intelligence of man, though at the same time it is not to be denied that each one of these arrow-heads, and therefore all of them, *might* be the product of that unknown collection of mechanical causes which in this case, for convenience, we may call accident. Why do we unhesitatingly reject accident in favour of intelligence? The answer is ready. The probabilities are infinitely in favour of the latter—that is, the chances against accident are enormously, if indefinitely, greater than the chances against intelligence. This answer, which certainly commends itself to common sense, suggests, however, a further enquiry. On what grounds do we form this estimate of the comparative probability of the two causes? It is plain that we ought to have *some* grounds. The particular value that we assign to the chance of one or other of any two possible causes being the actual cause cannot be determined by mere abstract speculation, but must be derived from some theory respecting the conditions under which these causes were likely to have acted. It is not difficult to see that in the example before us these conditions are supposed to be, on the whole, similar to those which obtain now. It is assumed that an arrow-head shape *was*, as it *is*, merely one of an indefinite number of other forms, all of which are produced, in equal or greater numbers, by mechanical causes, and that it *was*, as it *is*, a form which man in a state of savagery finds useful, and is therefore likely to manufacture ; and on this hypothesis it is quite true that the chances in favour of a human origin are enormous.   But it is no less evident that this hypothesis is itself the statement of a historical fact ; that it must, therefore, involve an inference from effects to causes ; that these effects may again be conceivably due to more than one set of causes ; that we must again select one set of causes rather than another on grounds of probability, and again be obliged, in order to establish that probability, to make a new inference from effects to causes.   If, now, we imagine this process carried on indefinitely, we may suppose ourselves at last to arrive at the deduction of the totality of causes from the totality of effects.   Supposing, as seems likely enough, that the totality of effects might conceivably have been produced by more than one selection or arrangement of causes, on what principle are we now to choose between these conflicting possibilities ?   Most of them, perhaps all except the one we commonly select, would, it can scarcely be doubted, seem in the highest degree extravagant and improbable. But their extravagance is merely the result of the manner in which they strike on our imagination ; and as for their improbability, I am altogether at a loss to see how, from our principles, any estimate of their probability at all like what we require can be founded. Since we are dealing with the totality of effects, it cannot clearly be founded on any *further* inference from effect to cause, and no other foundation seems to me possible, except by the intervention of some new scientific axiom.

I am afraid that this speculation may seem the mere extravagance of scepticism ; and the illustration I am about to give may, perhaps, strengthen the prejudice against my view, though I hope it may make the grounds of it more clear and intelligible.

Let us suppose, then, that our only source of information respecting the past was derived from written documents—that, with the exception of what each man remembered, he knew absolutely nothing of times gone by beyond what he read in books or MSS. professing to have been written at the various periods of which they spoke. Let us further suppose that from such materials a more or less consistent and plausible history has been constructed, and then let us try and determine the sort of grounds we have for estimating its probable truth.

The effects here are the books and MSS. ; the causes inferred from these effects are—various writers having access to information about different periods, who have taken care to place this information accurately upon record. Since there are, however, other possible causes, for example, the invention by one or more persons of a story, and the forgery of the documents required for its support, it becomes necessary to find a principle which may enable us to choose between the rival hypotheses.

It is commonly said that the authenticity of any document may be shown by two kinds of evidence— the external and the internal; and since internal evidence would be defined as evidence drawn from the document itself, it might seem natural to conclude that such evidence really exists, and that it might provide us with the principle of which we are in search.   In strictness, however, this is not the case. From the character of any document *alone* no conclusion can be drawn in favour of its genuineness, provided the bare possibility of its forgery be admitted. Supposing, for example, it is said that the style and character of thought of some book show it to have been the product of a certain age and country—this implies a knowledge of that age and country which, if it is to be admitted as evidence, must clearly be derived from some other source than the book it is intended to vindicate; and this is equally true of any possible characteristic which can be adduced either for or against any theory respecting date of composition or authorship. It would appear, indeed, at first sight, as if the contents of a book might be so unlike the sort of things people invent, or so difficult to make self-consistent if they were invented, that its genuineness could be concluded from the mere consideration of these peculiarities. But even this inference involves some hypothesis respecting the condition of the world at the supposed date of authorship. It supposes that the ability to invent and the desire to invent existed at that time in such degrees as to make invention of this sort highly improbable; but since this estimate cannot be founded on the document itself without a *petitio principii*, it must be founded either on some hitherto undiscovered axiom, or on other documents, or on other non-documentary phenomena. The first of these possibilities I reserve for discussion later on. The last is excluded by hypothesis. There remains, therefore, the second. But the smallest consideration will show that all the remarks just applied to a single document apply equally well to any number of documents taken together. Once admit the possibility of their forgery, the improbability of such an event can only be deduced from facts which are themselves deductions from all or some of these documents, and which consequently cannot in this matter be used as a basis of inference at all. It may be stated, therefore, generally that if we start from the arbitrary hypothesis with which I began this illustration, then, first, it is quite as probable that all history should be fictitious as that some of it should be true; and, secondly, as a necessary corollary, if two versions of it are mutually exclusive, it is impossible to say which is the more likely.

The general principle from which this is a deduction seems to me, indeed, almost self-evident when clearly stated.   It would run thus :—' If more than one cause can produce a given effect, it is impossible, by the mere contemplation of the effect, to say by what cause it was probably produced.' The same is true of ' groups of effects,' and ' groups of causes.'   It is also true of the ' totality of effects,' and the ' totality of causes.'   Now, if the ' totality of effects ' means existing effects, the ' totality of causes ' is, if not history, at all events the necessary foundation of history.   Therefore, the chances against any particular version of history being true is simply as the number of *possible* versions of it is to one.[1]

It will be a fitting transition to the next stage in this discussion if I here notice the interesting effect which the existence of one particular cause has on the validity of all historical inferences—I mean the universal first cause, whether that be the unknown x of certain philosophers, or the personal God of the theologians.

It is of the essence of this idea of a First Cause that everything which exists—in other words, the whole of the premises on which we found our knowledge of history—is produced by It directly

---

[1] Strictly speaking—as the number of possible versions of it *minus* unity are to one.

or indirectly.   Moreover, it is clearly impossible to shew that, while It could produce one set of phenomena directly, It was only able to produce another set indirectly, *i.e.*, by means of some phenomenal cause intervening.   From this it follows that there is no period of history at which creation might not have taken place; nor am I able to see that, if it did take place, it would do so at one period more probably than at another.   In other words, whatever date in the past we select, there are always two causes which are equally likely to have produced the phenomena then existing : the one is the group of phenomena which might have produced them according to known laws ; the other is the First Cause.   It may be worth noting that these remarks are true not only of the metaphysical substance, whether personal or not, which is the origin of all things, but also of any phenomena which may be assumed to have produced the present order of nature, but of whose laws we are ignorant. Supposing, for example, it was shown that, by tracing back the course of events through time, we arrived at a point where the recognised laws of nature failed us,[1] and where we were in consequence compelled to assume a new, and, of course, unknown set of antecedents acting in unknown ways ; in that case we should not be justified in supposing that the

---

[1] This speculation was suggested by certain physical theories respecting the distribution of heat.

point where the known causes failed us was the point where the unknown causes came into operation. The probabilities, in fact, are infinitely the other way. For since these causes *are* unknown, we clearly cannot say that their properties are such as to make their appearance more probable at one time than at another. That they must appear at some period or other is shown, according to our hypothesis, by the insufficiency of established laws when followed up beyond a certain point ; but since, also by hypothesis, we can predicate nothing of these unknown causes, except their existence and their power to produce the present order of nature, it would seem that they are quite as likely to have exercised that power at any one instant of time as at any other.

The reader acquainted with the elements of geometrical optics will see clearly the point which I am attempting to establish, if he will consider the distinction between a ' real ' and a ' virtual ' image. A spectator whose position is fixed is contemplating (let us suppose) what appears to him to be the flame of a candle. He believes it to be a candle because the rays of light reach his eye precisely as they would do if they emanated from a candle placed where he sees the image of the flame. Nevertheless, in forming this very natural conclusion, he may be altogether in error. Since the rays would reach his eyes in precisely the same manner, whether they came from a real flame or the virtual image of a flame produced by some optical contrivance, and since the manner in which the rays reach his eye is (we may suppose) the sole ground on which he can found any inference at all, it is perfectly plain that he can have no reason for believing the one rather than the other to be the true object of perception. So it is with us and our inferences about the past, if we substitute time for space, the facts immediately presented to us for the rays striking directly on the retina, and the history of the past, as given to us by science, for the image of the flame. If we are fortunate we may be able to point to an imaginary condition of the world at some given period, and say, ' Trace out the consequence of these causes according to the known laws of nature, and you will arrive at the state of things you now see around you,' just as some one might say, ' On the supposition that a candle flame exists, your actual perception is fully accounted for.' But just as in the second case a virtual image would have precisely the same effect as the real image, so in the first case other combinations of phenomena obeying known laws, or a metaphysical first cause, or phenomena obeying unknown laws which the failure of known laws compels us to believe in, might all of them result in the existing universe. But whereas in the second case the rays from the image would not generally be the only available means of forming a judgment respecting the real nature of their origin, and we have usually some other independent grounds for deciding in favour of one hypothesis rather than another, in the first case, so far as at present appears, it is not so.   Existing facts are our sole (particular) evidence for historic facts, and if our general principles can get nothing definite out of them, science at all events has nothing further to suggest.

All the cases we have so far considered have these characteristics in common—that in each we have to choose between two or more causes, or sets of causes, which are the possible historical antecedents of the world as we see it ; that in each the causes between which our choice lie are *actual*[1] causes, that is, are (by hypothesis) known to exist or to have existed ; and that in each we have as yet discovered no reason for preferring any one possible alternative to any other.   But at this point an interesting question suggests itself.   Why should we retain the limitation (originally adopted in order to simplify the investigation) stated in the second of the preceding propositions ?   On what principle do we confine our attention to actual causes ?   Why should we not admit causes about whose existence or non-existence now, or in past times, we know absolutely nothing as possible historical antecedents, and if

---

[1] This use of the word 'actual' is clumsy and not very accurate : but as its meaning in this connection is clearly defined, its employment will, I hope, lead to no confusion.

we do so admit them, what effect will the admission have on the validity of our ordinary historical inference ? The last question, at all events, does not seem hard to answer. If we are to admit, as elements in the historic problem, an indefinite number of such possible causes on the same footing as we now admit actual causes, then (if we are limited to our initial assumptions) all inference with regard to the past becomes impossible. We may, if we please, amuse ourselves by showing how actual causes may be a sufficient explanation of the facts as we see them, but we must at the same time admit that the chances are infinitely against that explanation being the true one, and for this obvious reason :—since every historical belief must be founded in the last resort on an inference from effect to cause, it follows that if there are an infinite number of causes, so far as we know, all equally possible, the chances against any one of them—therefore against any *actual* one of them—being the real cause are also infinite. If, therefore, history is to exist at all, it will be necessary to show that the *actual* causes are the only possible ones, or, at all events, that there is a very great presumption in their favour.

We have now considered historic inference in the light of four separate suppositions. We have supposed that our choice lay—1st, between different sets of phenomenal causes whose laws are known ; 2nd, between a ' noumenal ' cause and phenomenal causes ; 3rd, between phenominal causes whose laws are known, and phenomenal causes which are known to have existed, but whose laws are *not* known ; 4th, between causes which are known to exist, or to have existed, and causes which, for anything we at present know to the contrary, may have existed in indefinite numbers.

In all these cases there are two alternatives presented to us ; in each of them science unhesitatingly accepts one and rejects the other, and in, at all events, most instances common sense endorses the choice.   Nevertheless, the preceding discussion has, I hope, made it plain that this course derives no justification from our supposed knowledge of the abstract laws connecting phenomena, even when taken in connection with the law of universal causation. It is necessary, therefore, to supplement these grounds of belief by some other principle or principles, which it now becomes our business to find out, and, if possible, to justify.

We turn first, as is natural, to the ' Uniformity of Nature.'   But a little reflection shows that it scarcely gives us that of which we are in search, since, according to one of its meanings, it is insufficient, while, according to another, it is not only insufficient, but untrue.   If it be taken to mean, as it usually is, that the past, the present, and the future are uniform in *this*, that the same antecedent is always followed by the same consequent, then it is, of course, one of the very assumptions with which we started, and which have left us with all these unsolved problems on our hands. If, on the other hand, it means that the same consequents are always preceded by the same antecedents, we could, no doubt, from this, in theory, construct a history of the past precisely to the same extent and with the same fatal limitations as from the converse proposition we can in theory now construct a history of the future. But then, unfortunately, this is opposed to the practical teachings of the very science in aid of which we appeal to it, and is in apparent contradiction both to 'observation' and to 'experiment.' [1]

A third meaning, according to which the Uniformity of Nature would imply that no supernatural interference with the Order of Nature, *i.e.*, with the succession of natural causes and effects, was possible,

---

[1] This may be a convenient place at which to touch on an objection which the reader accustomed to regard the universe from a mechanical point of view may be tempted to raise. He may say, ' I utterly deny the possible plurality of causes, on the existence of which depends so much of your argument. I hold that the world may be regarded as a system of particles obeying mechanical laws, that it is therefore quite as possible to reconstruct the past, as it is to construct the future, from the present ; and that both operations may, in theory, be carried out with absolute certainty.' Since, however, this theoretical possibility can never by any accident be realised in practice, it may, for my purposes, be neglected. I write for human beings with human powers of calculation. But besides this, it is by no means proved, I believe, to the satisfaction of the men of science that the world *is* a purely mechanical system. I am, therefore, justified in assuming, with the majority of scientific philosophers, that while one kind of cause can only have one kind of effect, one kind of effect may have more than one kind of cause. The attentive reader will see that, even were this otherwise, still, so long as it is so for our powers of observation and calculation, the main argument of the chapter remains entirely unaffected.

would give a solution of the second problem, but of the second problem only.   I know of no proof of such a principle, nor can I conceive any.   Hume's argument against miracles, I need not say, is inapplicable.

Another general principle is suggested by a phrase that is sometimes used—' The Simplicity of Nature.'   Let us examine how far it is possible to extract from this the premiss of which we are in search.

When we speak of Nature being ' simple,' it is not, I presume, meant that its laws are easily understood, that is, are ' simple ' relatively to our faculties of comprehension.   In the first place, it is not the case ; in the second place, if it were the case, we should derive no assistance from it in our present difficulty, since every one of the alternatives we have been weighing is as easily understood as every other ; and in the third place, it would involve the hypothesis of a pre-established harmony between the ' cosmos ' and the ' microcosmos ' which men of science at least would be slow to admit.   Nor, for this same reason, can it mean that the most ' simple ' or ' natural ' explanation—that is, the explanation which, when understood, seems, in some vague way, especially to commend itself to the investigator— is always the true one—more particularly as different investigators take very different views as to what *is* ' natural.'   It is clear, indeed, that if we are to get any assistance out of the Simplicity of Nature, it must be because the Simplicity of Nature is something 'objective,' something that can be stated in terms which have no reference to the mind of the observer, something which merely expresses the manner in which natural phenomena occur. That Nature employs the fewest possible number of causes, or rather kinds of cause, to produce her results (which corresponds to the maxim, ' that causes are not to be multiplied without a reason ') is a proposition which conforms to these conditions, and which seems to assert a kind of simplicity. Will this serve our turn ? So far as the fourth problem (which requires us to decide between known and unknown causes) is concerned, it apparently will. It practically tells us that if we know of causes that might have produced a given result, that these causes, or some of them, did actually do so. It therefore unquestionably affords a solution of this problem exactly in accordance with the ordinary scientific view.

If, however, we examine its bearing on the first and third problems, this does not appear to be altogether the fact. In these two cases we are required to choose between kinds of cause which are by hypothesis known to exist : so that the principle of ' Simplicity ' leaves us very much where we were. While, with regard to the second problem, since the alternative there lies between natural and supernatural causes, a principle which (in so far as it says anything) gives us information only about the former, cannot be of much assistance.

I may add that, though philosophers never hesitate to appeal to the Simplicity of Nature when it suits their convenience, I am not aware that any of them have thought fit to supply us with a proof of its reality.

Though there seems, then, to be no obvious or recognised principle which will exactly serve our purpose, there must nevertheless be some—perhaps unformulated—notion which lies at the root of existing historical judgments, and which on analysis may furnish us with the principle of which we are in search.

Now I take this notion to be that there is a sort of continuity in the course of Nature through the past which *discourages* (so to speak) violent changes and the interference of unknown causes. But such a statement as it stands is, it need hardly be observed, far too vague to have any philosophic value, and requires a good deal of analysis before even we come to the question of proof. To begin with, what is violent? It cannot, of course, mean merely *startling*, as it would then refer solely to the effect produced on the imagination, and could hardly be made the foundation of a canon by which to judge the course of Nature. It must, therefore, have some objective meaning attached to it, though at the same time it is clear that no such meaning can be given to it which shall have any absolute value. It is, I mean, impossible to say what is or is not objectively a violent change, except by taking some particular change as a standard of comparison. Now, what is this standard change? It cannot evidently be a fixed or permanent rate of change to which all others must conform, because if so it must either be one of which we have immediate knowledge, or one we have arrived at by historical inference. It cannot be the second, as this (since we are looking for a basis for historical inference) would involve a very obvious argument in a circle. It cannot, again, be the first, because recognised history supplies us with many more violent changes than those of which we have immediate experience, so that it is impossible both that history should be true and that historic changes should conform to the standard.

A meaning which promises better results, because it does not at first sight appear to suggest a fixed standard, would be as follows :—‘ If there are two possible causes for any effect, that one is to be chosen which involves the least violent change.’ But this, it must be observed, is not a statement respecting Nature, but a maxim intended to guide the judgment of the natural philosopher. It must, therefore, derive its authority from some fact in nature, exactly as the ordinary rules of induction derive their authority from the law of universal causation. Now what is the fact? Our guesses (according to this maxim) become more accurate as they approach a certain limit. The smaller the change required by the conclusion, the more likely is the inference on which that conclusion rests to be sound. But the limit here implied is a condition of things under which there would be no change at all, a supposition which is absolutely incompatible with history and everything else.

It must also be remarked that 'rate of change,' or 'amount of change,' is itself an expression to which it is only now and then possible to attach a precise meaning ; in fact, only in those cases in which we are dealing with *quantities*, mass, velocity, force, and so forth. Science is, however, so far at present from being purely quantitative (whatever it may some day become), that those notions are far indeed from being sufficient to cover the necessary ground.

Since, then, it does not seem easy even to formulate the axiom or axioms which are required in addition to the law of causation to justify our ordinary historic judgments, the second step in the philosophy of the subject, by which we seek to prove or classify them (according as they are derivative or ultimate), cannot be attempted. The truth of the matter appears to be that history rests on a kind of scientific instinct, none the less healthy because it is not very reasonable. This, fortunately, is quite vigorous enough to resist the attacks of any merely philosophic scepticism, as any one anxious to try the experiment may discover for himself provided he will ask the next man of science he meets, whether (say) 4000 B.C. is not as likely as any other assignable date for the commencement of this Earth as a separate planet. If the enquirer is fortunate enough to get any answer at all to so absurd a question, he will probably be told that no known causes are adequate to the production of existing effects in so short a time. To which it may be replied, that there is no particular reason for supposing that known causes have been the only ones in operation. On this the man of science may not improbably rejoin that gratuitous suppositions ought to be avoided—that the *deus ex machinâ* is to be excluded as much from science as from art. If he were further asked the grounds of this canon, I do not know exactly what would be his answer, though I know that whether he could find an answer or not, the strength of his convictions would not be in any way diminished.

From certain assumptions, then, which seem reasonable enough, we have arrived at a very negative result. Before concluding, it may be as well to point out certain ways in which the nature of this conclusion reacts on the premises. It will be recollected that we started with the supposition that, in addition to the law of causation, we were to accept the teaching of science so far as particular abstract laws were concerned. But it will be seen at once that the evidence of many of these laws is itself historical—*i.e.*, depends on the truth of the current version of his-

tory.   Of how many this may be said I do not enquire, but it is obviously true of those which in any
way depend on a series of observations carried
through many years, such as parts of astronomy and
sociology (if this is to be considered a science).
It is also true of all laws which are direct deductions
from the historic facts which alone are supposed to
exemplify them, such as parts of geology.   What,
however, is of perhaps more interest is the bearing
which some of the points brought out in the preceding discussion have on the empirical evidence of the
law of universal causation.

The nature of the process of inference by which
this great principle is proved from experience has
been discussed, and, I think, shown to be invalid, in
a previous chapter ; but one remark concerning the
premises of that inference may be made appropriately
now.   It was pointed out at the commencement of
the chapter that, though our knowledge of the laws
of nature must be founded, in part at least, on our
knowledge of particular matters of fact, that nevertheless all our knowledge of particular matters of fact
other than those of which we have immediate experience, must in their turn be founded upon our
knowledge of the laws of nature.   Now, it is commonly admitted that a law of nature depends for its
generality upon the law of universal causation, in
other words, is extended to unobserved instances
solely by means of that law ; from which it follows,

that the law of universal causation is a necessary
premiss in every inference by which we arrive at
historical facts. What I have been hitherto attempting to show is, that even assuming this premiss to be
true, there is an inevitable ambiguity in the inference ;
what I now wish to insist on is, that whether those
views be true or false, this at any rate is certain, that
if the law of universal causation be founded on experience at all, that experience must be extremely
limited. Empirical philosophers, dilating on the
accumulated evidence we have for this law, are in
the habit of telling us that it is the uncontradicted
result of observations extending through centuries ;
but they have omitted to notice, that unless we first
believe in the law, we can have no reason for believing in the observations. Turn the matter as we
will, the fact that mankind have been observing or
doing anything else for centuries, cannot be to any
of us a matter of direct observation or intuition. It
must, therefore, be an inference ; and if an inference
from experience, the only experience it can be inferred from, is the immediate and limited experience
of each individual ; this, therefore, either at one remove or two, is the only possible empirical foundation for the law of causation, or any other general
principle.

This argument does not show, of course, that
empirical philosophy is false ; but it does show,
beyond question, that it is not plausible. What

ever be its philosophic value, there is certainly something consolatory to common sense in the idea that our convictions rest on a broad basis of experience. There is something practical in the very sound of a phrase which implies a method of judging that most satisfactorily distinguishes us from the pre-Baconian philosophers. But when it becomes evident that this 'broad basis' itself rests on the exceedingly narrow basis of individual experience, when it is once understood that what I perceive, and remember having perceived, is my sole ground for believing that people in past ages perceived anything at all, empiricism certainly loses much of its dignity, though its philosophic value remains, perhaps, very much what it was before.

PART II.

CHAPTER V.

INTRODUCTION TO PART II.

In the three preceding chapters I have discussed empirical reasoning concisely, but I hope sufficiently, from three different points of view. I showed, in the first place, that whereas, according to this philosophy, all our knowledge is derived from particulars, that there was nevertheless no method, or at all events no method hitherto discovered, by which inference from particulars was possible; and that Mr. Mill's theory on this subject will in no sense bear minute examination. From this reasoning it necessarily follows that pure empiricism is not at present a tenable system; but there is a kind of mixed or spurious empiricism, which, taking for granted (on no very explicit or intelligible grounds) the principle of universal causation, assumes that by the help of this alone we can argue from particular matters of fact to the general laws of phenomena. This I imagine to be a not uncommon view among men of science, and to be that formally put forward by Mr. Jevons in his 'Principles of Science.' The assumption required by this theory is evidently a large one—so large, indeed, as to make it, philosophically speaking, nearly worthless ; but, even granting that assumption, I showed in the next place, in the third chapter, that no experience, however large, and no experiments, however well contrived and successful, could give us any reasonable assurance that the co-existences or sequences which have been observed among phenomena will be repeated in the future. This is as much as to say that inductive logic (even granting the uniformity of Nature) is worthless, since it can do no more than find a rule according to which all known instances of an event have occurred, without giving us any right to extend this rule to instances which are not known.

It appears, then, that neither the mixed and incomplete empiricism considered in the third chapter, still less the pure empiricism considered in the second chapter, affords us any satisfactory method for inferring the laws of nature from particular observations or experiments ; but even this does not exhibit the full weakness and inadequacy of scientific logic, for in the fourth chapter I showed that, *granting* that we possessed a knowledge of the laws of phenomena, and *granting* the truth of the law of universal causation—in other words, granting the truth of that which it was shown in the two preceding chapters could not be proved—it was impossible, even on these terms, to arrive at any knowledge of historical facts, taking this expression in its widest sense as including all that has occurred outside our individual sphere of immediate experience.

I have therefore stated three distinct objections that may be taken to the ordinary proof of current scientific beliefs. Empirical philosophy, so far as I can see, gets over none of them ; though every one of them must be got over by any system which has pretensions to being an adequate philosophy of science. This being so, it is not necessary, I suppose, to dwell longer on this part of the subject, even if by so doing other difficulties might be started equally hard of solution. It will be convenient rather to proceed at once to the next branch of the enquiry.

The reader will recollect that in the first chapter philosophy was divided into the philosophy of inference and the philosophy of ultimate premises. The three preceding chapters may be described as dealing in the main with the first of these divisions ; and we still require therefore to give a more particular consideration to the second. How is this subject to be approached ? On the whole, perhaps, most conveniently by taking the premises which, if not ultimate from a philosophic point of view, are at any rate ultimate from a scientific point of view—*i.e.*, those on which science depends, but which do not depend on science—and trying to find out the proof, or kind of proof, of which they are susceptible.

Now these premises consist (so far as I can judge), in the first place, of certain unknown principles, shown in the third and fourth chapters to be necessary to the validity of science, but which, since they *are* unknown, need no longer detain us. In the second place, of the Law of Universal Causation ; which, as was shown in the second chapter, cannot be proved by induction ; and, in the third place, of individual or particular experiences, which (as will be shown in the ninth chapter, though it is here assumed) must be supposed to refer to a persistent universe.

It is the evidence of these last two premises or kinds of premiss which will now chiefly occupy us ; but as the discussion of this matter will oblige me to deal with a great many dissimilar and disconnected systems, a change of method will be necessary. I shall make henceforth no attempt to link each chapter to that which precedes and follows it by an argumentative chain. On the contrary, each chapter will contain a discussion as complete as seems necessary of one subject, and it will only be related to the other similar chapters inasmuch as it proceeds from the same basis and leads to the same conclusion.

Before entering, however, into this more extended examination of the various methods by which philosophers have attempted to establish the existence of a persistent universe governed by causation, I shall perhaps be asked whether this is a matter which really requires proof at all. Is not the belief (it may be said) in the reality of such a universe one of those truths which lie at the root of all knowledge, for which proof is impossible, or, if possible, still unnecessary? I reply that this is a question the true answer to which may be suggested, but, from the nature of things, cannot be demonstrated. Each person must, in the last resort, decide for himself whether or not any given proposition is to his mind of the kind I have described in the first section as 'ultimate.' In this particular case all that can be said is that, as a matter of fact, the law of causation does not appear to be accepted in its integrity by the greater part of the human race, and that those who do accept it seem to feel the necessity of founding it upon some kind of proof: either upon experience, which, as I have already shown, can furnish no proof at all; or upon some of the philosophical principles which it will be my business to examine in the sequel. With regard to a persistent universe, the case is somewhat different. Everybody practically believes in it, even those who speculatively question it: but at the same time the verdict of all philosophy seems to be that the dogma asserting its existence is one which *can* be speculatively questioned, and must therefore, if it be true, be capable of some speculative defence. So many demonstrations of it have been offered, that it may well be assumed that, in the judgment of those qualified to decide, some demonstration is required. If, however, anyone still thinks that this is a matter which those interested in the rational foundation of science may be permitted to neglect, the following considerations may perhaps induce him to alter his opinion.

If an immediate knowledge of a persistent world is given us at all, it will be admitted, I think, that it is given us in perception; if its existence is an ultimate fact which cannot and need not be proved, it is a fact of which we are assured by what is somewhat absurdly called the 'direct evidence of the senses.' In other words, we know that there is a persistent world much in the same sort of way and with the same absolute assurance as we know that we feel hot or cold. The first question, therefore, which has to be asked is, What do we know immediately and with certainty by means of perception ? The answer suggested by the psychology of Berkeley and Hume in effect amounted to this. The only things we know and can know immediately are our own sensations and ideas. Objects are merely groups of sensations. Imagined objects are merely groups of ideas; and as these pass and vanish away, so do the *things*, of which they are in truth the only real constituents, cease to have any but a nominal existence. While they were real they were 'affections of the mind,' and when they ceased to be affections of the mind, they ceased to be anything.

The soundness of this psychology, which, if true, would completely dispose of any immediate knowledge of a persistent world, is, however, open to question.   It is maintained by thinkers of a different school[1] that in perceiving objects we cannot properly be said to perceive either sensations or related sensations, or even facts of sensation, but only qualities of objects ; qualities which are constituted not by sensations but by relations, and which are therefore *thought* but cannot be *felt*.   If this theory of perception be sound, it is evident that the argument of the psychological idealist cannot be maintained in the shape in which I have just stated it. If the world, as it is immediately perceived, does not consist of sensations, it need not evidently be transient merely because sensations are so.   We therefore have again to ask ourselves whether in perception we gain an assurance, both immediate and reflective, of the existence of persistent objects ;[2] and to this question, though without subscribing to all their views, I answer, as the psychological idealist answered, No.

---

[1] Cf. Mr. Green's edition of Hume, and an article, published after the greater part of this essay was written, in the *Contemporary Review*, March 1878.

[2] The reader may, perhaps, be inclined hastily to imagine that an assurance cannot be both immediate *and* reflective. This combination is, however, not only possible, but it ought to be found in all ultimate premises, and is actually found in the axioms of mathematics. A proposition of which we have immediate reflective assurance, is one which, after reflection, is seen to be certain without proof.

I must here guard against a possible misconception which may be suggested by the word 'immediate.' In one sense of the term all the knowledge, real or supposed, which is obtained by perception alone may be called immediate : since knowledge obtained through any conscious process of inference is *ipso facto* mediate. Nevertheless, we cannot properly be said to have an assurance, both immediate and reflective, of the truth of all the facts we immediately perceive. Our real or supposed knowledge of the facts is immediate ; our reflective assurance of the truth of these facts is certainly not immediate. If, for example, I see an object in space, my knowledge of its real shape and size is obtained by no piece of conscious reasoning, and cannot therefore be appropriately described as mediate or derivative. Nevertheless, the reflective assurance that the thing seen is actually that shape and size, and not merely shaded and coloured so as to look as if it were, can only be arrived at by a more or less elaborate process of inference, and must undoubtedly therefore be looked on as mediate. In harmony with this explanation our original question would therefore run thus :—Conceding that we immediately perceive the existence of a persisting universe, is the reflective assurance that such a universe exists immediate, or is it legitimate (if it be so at all) only in virtue of a process of inference ? To my thinking, the bare consideration of the problem so stated is sufficient to show that the latter alternative should be accepted. It appears to me that the immediate belief which the majority of mankind certainly have in the reality of such a universe is of the same kind as that which they had in the apparent motion of the sun and stars ; and that, on reflection, speculative doubt is not only possible and legitimate, but is hardly to be avoided.

If anyone disagrees with this statement, I would ask him how he deals with the admitted occurrence of optical or other (so-called) illusions of the senses ? In such cases the judgment respecting the persistence of the object perceived is as immediate, and is given in perception precisely in the same way, as it is when perception is normal. The only difference is that on reflection it is seen to be incorrect. And by what method is its incorrectness shown ? By showing its inconsistency with the order of nature as revealed to us by science. But unless there exists a persisting universe, the order of nature, as revealed to us by science, is a dream. If therefore the existence of such a universe is given us merely in perception, we can assert that a particular object is transient only by a mediate inference from an authority whose immediate verdict is that it is persistent. ' True,' it may be replied, ' but this is a fact which presents no difficulty. We are constantly correcting one observation by means of another, without concluding from this, that observation is a means of acquiring knowledge unworthy of credit.   This shows that two authorities of precisely the same kind may qualify without destroying each other, and without giving rise to any suspicions of latent contradiction. In what lies the distinction between this case and the one stated above?'   The distinction lies in this : that in the second case the scientific observations correct and can correct each other only on the presupposition which it is the business of the perceptions in the first case to establish.   We can extract a single truth out of a series of observations only on the supposition that they all deal with a single object, and they can only deal with a single object if that object persists through at least the whole period over which the observations extend. If perceptions can correct each other only on similar terms, it would seem tolerably plain that they cannot correct each other when the question in dispute is whether the object perceived has, or has not, the attribute of persistence.   If there be a persistent world, the fact that the 'evidence of our senses' occasionally misleads us as to its true character may be of small importance.   But if our whole ground for believing in the existence of a persistent world be derived from the evidence of the senses, the fact that they deceive us, though only occasionally, casts a suspicion over all the rest of their testimony.

Reverting to the remarks on the psychology of perception made a few pages back, the reader may perhaps say—'If objects are constituted by relations which are *thought*, not *felt*, may not one of the relations by which they are constituted be that very persistence whose reality you tell us has to be inferred? May not the assurance that objects persist be thus given in the process of sense perception, though not, strictly speaking, derived from the evidence of the senses?'

Now I do not at present deny that such assurance may be legitimately attained by reasoning on the basis of the psychology which offers us this analysis of the perceived object. But without at present going into this question, it is safe, I suppose, to assert that to think an object as persisting cannot make it persist. Whatever may be the truths of which we are immediately assured in perception, that the object perceived actually has any qualities we choose to attribute to it, cannot be one. To suppose the contrary is to fall into an error similar to that according to which the existence of God was demonstrated from the fact that existence was part of His essence. Grant that everything which is real is thought, it cannot be the fact that everything which is thought is real, since if it were so, mistakes as to the true nature of any object would be impossible; a doctrine as subversive of science as any form of idealism ever devised.

These preliminary remarks have, of course, not been intended as even a proximate solution of any philosophic problem.   Their object has been to suggest doubt, not to establish scepticism.   They have aimed at convincing anyone inclined to an easy acquiescence in his natural convictions, that the reality of the subject-matter of science is not a thing that should too readily be taken for granted.   Our natural convictions may be right, but they must be shown to be right.   Proof of some kind is necessary; and where proof is necessary, scepticism is possible. All that I here contend for is that a preliminary examination of what perception tells us—no assumption being made as to the truth of any particular psychological theory, and no use being made of the words 'subjective,' 'objective,' or 'external'—fails to show that scepticism is *not* possible.   So that if ever this is to be established it must be by the help of systems which, whatever be the nature of their conclusions, cannot be accepted without criticism.   I pass now to the most important, the most elaborate, and the most difficult of these systems, which, in harmony with the terminology it employs, I venture to call 'Transcendentalism.'

CHAPTER VI.

THAT the pure empiricism still in fashion among scientific philosophers leads naturally to scepticism is a fact which has been familiar to certain schools of thought ever since Hume presented it to the world stripped of its plausibilities. It is hardly to be believed that so subtle a thinker did not himself perceive the ultimate consequences of his reasoning. He must have been perfectly aware that on his system a philosophy of science was impossible; nevertheless, his ' Essay on Miracles' and occasional announcements, such as that with which he ends his ' Enquiry concerning the Human Understanding,' appear to have quite convinced natural philo sophers that his scepticism merely undermined religion—a result which to most of them was a cause of very moderate uneasiness. If, however, they ignored, and still ignore, the wider reach of that engine of destruction, it has not been for want of telling.

Hume himself makes no effort to conceal it, and the sneer with which he informs the students

of science that theirs is the only kind of knowledge
worth pursuing, is scarcely less obvious than that
with which he tells the theologian that the most
solid foundations of religion are 'faith' and 'divine
revelation.'   But Hume's own view of his position
is not the only, nor even the main, evidence for
the sceptical nature of the conclusions to which his
theories necessarily lead.   On that scepticism, as
we have been informed with sufficient iteration, is
founded the whole imposing structure of modern
German philosophy; and modern German philosophy, whatever be its value, is not a phenomenon
which easily escapes notice.   If it gives little light
it is not because it is hidden under a bushel.   In
all probability, however, its very magnitude has prevented it from materially influencing the course of
scientific philosophy in this country ; and I believe
I may almost say from permanently influencing
scientific philosophy even in Germany.   A man
may be forgiven if, before seriously attempting to
master so huge a mass of metaphysics, composed of
several inconsistent systems, difficult of comprehension from their essential natures, still more difficult
from the extraordinary jargon under which the ingenuity of man has concealed their import—he may
be forgiven, I say, if he pauses and considers whether
the time may not be better spent in reading something he is more likely to understand.   It is, however, unfortunate that this pardonable, and even

laudable, caution should have prevented so many people from trying to comprehend the exact diffi culty which Kant and Kant's successors saw in the empiricism of Hume, and the extremely ingenious method which they adopted in order to avoid it ; for when these are understood, it becomes at once plain that the difficulty is a real one, and that the solution offered of it, at any rate, deserves consideration.

The relation in which Kant stands to Hume is not a topic which it is necessary for me to discuss ; nor, if it were, could I, it need hardly be said, add anything to what Professor Green and Professor Caird, not to mention previous commentators, have already written on the subject.

What more directly concerns my purpose is to examine the answer which, as I suppose, a transcendentalist would make to the scepticism of the preceding chapters, on the only two points where his defence of the grounds of science and my attack really meet on common ground. I mean 'causation' and the ' existence of a persistent and independent world.'

Now the usual way in which the transcendental problem is put is, ' How is knowledge possible ? ' and, taking transcendentalism as an answer to Hume, this, the usual way, is also the most natural, because it was Hume's theory of the *origin* of knowledge which led necessarily to scepticism. As, however, in this essay I have put forward no theory of the origin of knowledge, from my point of view the question should rather be stated, 'How much of what *pretends* to be knowledge must we accept as such, and why?'   My business, therefore, is to extract from the answer which the transcendentalist gives to the first enquiry, an answer which shall, if possible, satisfy the second ; and for this purpose it is necessary to make a slight, though only a slight, change in the usual mode of stating his doctrine.

The reader will recollect, that in the first chapter I insisted on the obvious truth that every tenable system of knowledge must consist partly of premises which require no proof, and partly of inferences which are legitimately drawn from these.   What, then, on the transcendental theory, are our premises, and by what method do we derive from them the required conclusion?

If we were simply to glance at transcendental literature, and seize on the first apparent answers to these questions, we should be disposed to think that the philosophers of this school assume to start with the truth of a large part of what is commonly called science,—the very thing which, according to my view of the subject, it is the business of philosophy to prove.   'Respecting pure mathematical and pure natural science,' says Kant,[1] 'as they certainly do exist, it may with propriety be asked *how* they are

---

[1] *Critique*, p. 13. Tr.

possible; for that they must be possible is shown by the fact of their really existing.'

'The question, How is knowledge possible? is not,' says Professor Green, 'to be confused with the question upon which metaphysicians are sometimes supposed to waste their time, Is knowledge possible? .... Metaphysic is no superfluous labour. It is no more superfluous, indeed, than is any theory of a process which without theory we already perform.'[1] Passages of this sort would almost lead one to conclude that the business of transcendental speculation was not to justify beliefs, but to account for their existence; to tell us how we do a thing, not whether we ought to do it: a view by which, apparently, philosophy is regarded as dealing with the laws of thought much as physiology deals with the laws of digestion. If this were so, transcendentalism might be an important and useful department of science, but it could have nothing to do with the subject of this essay. It would answer no doubt, it would solve no difficulty. But, in truth, the language often used by Kant and echoed above by Professor Green, if not incorrect, is certainly misleading. Transcendentalism *is* philosophical, in the sense in which I have ventured to use the term; it *does* attempt to establish a creed, and, therefore, of necessity it indicates the nature of our premises and the

---

[1] *Contemporary Review*, Dec. 1877.

manner in which the subordinate beliefs may be legitimately derived from them.

On the first point its statements are not, indeed, explicit and categorical; but this is simply because, for historical reasons, the philosophic problem has not been presented to it exactly in the shape which makes such statements necessary. Nevertheless, all I suppose that a transcendentalist would postulate in the first instance, or rather all that each man who studies his system is required to postulate, is that he knows, and is certain of, *something*; he is conscious, for example, or may be conscious, that he perceives a coloured object, or a particular taste ; in other words, he gets some knowledge, small or great, by *experience*.

This very moderate concession, then, being granted, as it must be granted, by the sceptic, the next question that arises is, How can any knowledge worth speaking of be inferred from such premises ? It is in the answer to this that such force and originality as there may be in transcendentalism is really to be found; and it is here that the full meaning of the question which is placed at the head of that philosophy becomes manifest. 'You allow,' we may suppose a transcendentalist to say, 'You allow that experience is possible; you allow that some knowledge, though it may only be of the facts of immediate perception, can be obtained by that channel. I therefore ask you " how that experience is possible"—in what it essentially consists? and whatever fact or principle I can show to be involved in that experience—whatever I can prove must be, if that experience is to be—of that you must, in common consistency, grant the reality.' A principle so proved is said to be 'transcendentally deduced,' and it is the validity of that deduction in the cases of causation and the existence of a persistent world, that it is my business more particularly to examine.

The whole value, then, of the transcendental philosophy, so far as the questions raised in this essay are concerned, must depend on its being able to show that the trustworthiness of these far-reaching scientific postulates is involved in those simple experiences which everybody must allow to be valid. If it cannot prove this, it may still be a valuable contribution to a possible philosophy; it may still show by its searching analysis all that is implied in the existence of nature, as we ordinarily understand nature, and of the sciences of nature as we are taught to accept them; but more than this it cannot do : it cannot show either that such a nature exists, or that our accounts of it are accurate; it cannot, in other words, supply us with a philosophy adequate to our necessities.

Before going on to consider the general value of this method, or the success of its application in particular instances, it may be well to give some examples of its reasonings by which its precise character may be more clearly understood. Here, for instance, is one taken from Kant's proof of the principle of substance : 'Change cannot be perceived by us except in substances, and origin or extinction in an absolute sense, that does not concern merely a determination of the permanent, cannot be a possible perception, for it is the very notion of the permanent which renders possible the representation (perception) of a transition from one state into another, and from non-being into being, which consequently, can be empirically cognised only as alternating determination of that which is permanent. . . . . Substances in the world of phenomena are the substratum of all determinations of time. . . . . Accordingly, permanence is a necessary condition under which alone phenomena, as things or objects, are determinable in a possible experience.'[1]

Now the point of this demonstration lies, as the reader will see, in showing, or attempting to show, that experience of change is not possible unless we assume unchanging substance. Therefore, if we can experience changes (as we most certainly can), we are forced also to admit the existence of that without which change would have no meaning.

Here is another argument of the same kind respecting causation, which I quote from Professor Green's introduction to Hume : 'A uniformity

---

[1] *Critique*, pp. 140, 141. Tr.

which can be thus (*i.e.*, by a single instance) established is, in the proper sense, necessary. Its existence is not contingent on its being felt by anyone or everyone. It does not come into being with the experiment that shows it. It is felt because it is real, not real because it is felt. It may be objected, indeed, that the principle of the "uniformity of nature," the principle that what is fact once is fact always, itself gradually results from the observation of facts which are feelings, and that thus the principle which enables us to dispense with the repetition of a sensible experience is itself due to such repetition. The answer is, that feelings which are conceived as facts are already conceived as constituents of a nature. The same presence of the thinking subject to, and distinction of itself from, the feelings which renders them knowable *facts*, renders them members of a world which is one throughout its changes. In other words, the presence of facts from which the uniformity of nature as an abstract rule is to be inferred, is already the consciousness of that uniformity *in concreto*.'[1] In this extract the argument is, that facts are unknowable, *i.e.*, are no facts for us, except as members of a uniform nature. We may be as certain, therefore, of the uniformity of nature as we are certain that we can know facts ; which is another way of saying that we need have no doubt about the matter at all.

[1] Pp. 273, 274.

These quotations are not long enough, perhaps, to do full justice to the argument of which they contain one statement; but they are long enough to show of what sort the argument in either case is. And the essential force or point of those arguments, as against the sceptic, seems at first sight to lie in this: the sceptic, in questioning any principle, is shown to be making an illegitimate abstraction from the relations which constitute an object, an abstraction which is illegitimate, because it renders the object meaningless and unthinkable. He has to choose, therefore, between altogether giving up the reality of the object, or admitting a principle implied by one of the relations of which that reality can be shown to consist. He cannot, in all cases at least, do the first; he is bound, therefore, to do the second.

Now, before proceeding to examine the force of this reasoning, as it is employed in proving particular points, one difficulty must be discussed which attaches to it generally.

When a man is convinced by a transcendental argument, it must be, as I have explained, because he perceives that a certain relation or principle is necessary to constitute his admitted experience. This is to him a fact, the truth of which he is obliged to recognise. But another fact, which he may also find it hard to dispute, is that he himself, and, as it would appear, the majority of mankind, have habitually had this experience without ever consciously thinking it under this relation ; and this second fact is one which it does not seem easy to interpret in a manner which shall harmonise with the general theory. The transcendentalist would, no doubt, say at once that the relation in question had always been thought implicitly, even if it had not always come into clear consciousness ; and having enunciated this dictum he would trouble himself no further about a matter which belonged merely to the ' history of the individual.' But if an implicit thought means in this connection what it means everywhere else, it is simply a thought which is logically bound up in some other thought, and which for that reason may always be called into existence by it. Now, from this very definition, it is plain that so long as a thought is implicit it does not exist. It is a mere possibility, which may indeed at any moment become an actuality, and which, when once an actuality, may be indestructible ; but which, so long as it is a possibility, can be said to have existence only by a figure of speech.

If, therefore, this meaning of the word ' implicit ' be accepted, we find ourselves in a difficulty. *Either* an object can exist and be a reality to an intelligence which does not think of it under relations which, as I now see, are involved in it, *i.e.*, without which I cannot now think of it as an object ; *or else* I am in error, when I suppose myself and other people to have ignored these relations in past times. If the first of these alternatives is true, the whole transcendental system, as I understand it, vanishes in smoke; if the second, it comes into apparent conflict, not only with science, and with the avowed scientific opinions of many of its disciples, but with the later form of the transcendental philosophy itself. For by that system the development of thought is in stages; it is driven on by its own proper nature from one stage to another till the highest of them is reached, where alone it can find rest and satisfaction. But those who believe most firmly in this theory by no means intend to assert as a historical fact that every thinking being is intellectually restless until he has grasped the philosophy of the Absolute. What they must rather be held to mean is, that the inadequacy and self-contradiction of a universe thought under any of the lower categories can be demonstrated, and when demonstrated to me or any other thinking being, I or he may be obliged to seek repose by including the contradictory elements under some category which shall reconcile them in a higher unity; but, they must admit that, as a matter of fact, this demonstration has been vouchsafed to few. There are not many, for example, who, whatever their perplexities, can find intellectual satisfaction in such a formula as this: 'The universe is the process whereby spirit externalises itself, or manifests itself in an external world, that out of this externality, by a movement at once positive and negative, it may rise to the highest consciousness of self.'[1]　The great body of mankind certainly prefer a contradiction which they do not see, to a reconciliation which they do not understand; and what I desire is—not to be shown how, on transcendental grounds, such a position is untenable,—but how its existence, as a fact, is to be consistently accounted for.　The analogy of the ordinary logic is here misleading.　It is true, no doubt, that we may intelligently hold premises without perceiving all or any of the deductions which may be legitimately drawn from them, and that, in asserting the premises in such a case, we implicitly assert the conclusion; but this presents no difficulty, because it is not the recognition of the conclusion which makes sense of the premises.　In transcendental reasoning the case is exactly the other way.　The ground, and the whole ground, on which we are forced by that reasoning to recognise the reality of certain relations, is, that without those relations the object of which we have experience would be as nothing for us; it would have neither meaning nor significance; and what I wish to know is, how it happens that there exists any object at all for so many people who are wholly innocent of any knowledge of those relations by which it is said to be constituted.　If there is any value in this objection, it

----

[1] Caird's *Kant*, p. 427.

would apparently follow from it that movement or inference in this logic is an impossibility. So long as the transcendentalist refuses to move—so long as he merely declines to abstract the relations by which an object is already constituted,—he stands, perhaps, on firm ground; but directly he tries to oblige us to think a thing under new relations, his method becomes either ineffective or self-destructive. If, on the one hand, we *can* think the object *not* under these new relations, there is nothing in the method to compel us to do so ; for the method consists in showing that without this new relation the object would not exist for us as thinking beings. If, on the other hand, we *cannot* think it except under these new relations, then, either we were not thinking it before or the relations are not new ; and in either case there is no inferential movement of thought from the known to the unknown.

From these reflections it would appear that the transcendentalist must either give up the seeming fact on which his system depends, or explain away a seeming fact which is inconsistent with it. The first fact is, that a given relation is necessary to constitute a knowledge of an object ; the second fact is, that a great many intelligent beings, and the transcendentalist himself, during the earlier part of his life among the number, appear able to know it out of this relation.

Now, *one* solution of this difficulty has been

already disposed of; it has been shown, or rather stated (for the assertion requires no proof), that a thought which is merely implicit is really no thought at all, it is a creation of language, which can constitute nothing because it *is* nothing.   It may however, perhaps, be said that the thought is neither merely implicit nor wholly explicit, but exists in a kind of intermediate stage between nonentity and the fulness of clear consciousness; a stage in which it is strong enough, so to speak, to 'constitute an object,' but not strong enough to be known to the individual for whom it performs this important function.

This is apparently one of the views taken by the transcendentalist; for Kant says, with the approval of Professor Caird, that 'the consciousness (of a unity) may be but weak, so that we become aware of it only in the result produced, and not in the act of producing it: but that, nevertheless, the unity of consciousness must always be present, though it has not clearness sufficient to make it stand out.'[1] In other words, the unity of consciousness which is necessary for the existence of any experience may lie hidden, like a drop of some powerful chemical reagent, until its presence is made certain by the analysis of its results.

Such a theory as this requires us to hold that thought may, so to speak, diminish the amount of its being till it ceases to be known as thought,

[1] See Caird's *Kant*, p. 393.

thought not to behave as such; and no doubt the first half of this statement is correct. That a sensation can be weaker or stronger, can change its intensive quantity (to use the technical expression) is, of course, plain. It can also be thought of under more or fewer relations. And in both these ways it may be said to have varying degrees of being. The same may be said, *mutatis mutandis*, of thought. According as we fix our attention on the relation rather than on the things related, so we may, I suppose, say that our consciousness of the relation increases or diminishes; but the utmost diminution of which the consciousness is capable without annihilation, makes no alteration in its quality; and if the consciousness vanishes, the thought must vanish too, since, except on some crude materialistic hypothesis, they are the same thing. This quantitative or intensive diminution of being, then, will not explain the apparent fact that so many people do not feel the necessity of thinking things under their supposed necessary relations.

The second manner in which any object of thought can be imagined to vary its being depends on the number of relations by which it is qualified; and in this respect thought also, not less than sensation, may be said to increase or diminish. Relations may be compared and classed—that is, may be thought under relations not less than feelings; and as, no doubt, a relation which is not so compared and classed cannot be an object of thought, cannot be known as a relation, it may be supposed that here we have a definition of that intermediate stage which is required to smooth over our difficulties. Every man, it may be said, really thinks objects under the relations which seem to us, who have been enlightened by transcendentalism, to be necessary ; but he is not *aware* that he does so, because he has not taken the trouble to consider them from the points of view from which alone they can appear as relations to *him*. But if this be true, what becomes of the identity of the 'esse' and the 'intelligi' ?

If relations can exist otherwise than as they are thought, why should not sensations do the same ? Why should not the 'perpetual flux' of unrelated objects—the metaphysical spectre which the modern transcendentalist labours so hard to lay,—why, I say, should this not have a real existence ? *We*, indeed, cannot in our reflective moments think of it except under relations which give it a kind of unity ; but once allow that an object may exist, but in such a manner as to make it nothing for us as thinking beings, and this incapacity may be simply due to the fact that thought is powerless to grasp the reality of things.

The transcendentalist, then, would seem peculiarly bound to admit what no philosopher, perhaps, would be disposed to deny, that thought which is not known as thought cannot properly be said to exist at all. He is therefore reduced to one of two alternatives. Either he must maintain that it is an error of memory and observation to suppose that every intelligence does not at all times think objects under their necessary relations, or else he must hold that a necessary relation is, *not* a relation that is actually required to constitute an object for a thinking being, but is only one which, upon due reflection, a thinking being is unable to make abstraction of.

The first of these alternatives is somewhat too violent a contradiction of that experience which it is the business of transcendentalism to justify, to be seriously maintained by transcendentalists. Accordingly we find them admitting the fact that necessary relations are not always thought as qualifying the object they are supposed to constitute ; in other words, accepting the second of the alternatives mentioned above, but at the same time declining any responsibility concerning a circumstance which, according to them, has to do only with the *history of the individual.*

' The " I think," ' says Kant (I am quoting Professor Caird's translation), ' must be *capable* of accompanying all my ideas, for otherwise something would be presented to my mind which could not be thought ; and that is the same thing as to say that the idea would be either impossible, or, at least, it would be nothing for me.' Again, ' All ideas have a necessary reference to a possible empirical con-

sciousness . . . . but, again, all empirical consciousness has a necessary reference to a transcendental
consciousness. . . . The mere idea " I," in reference
to all other ideas (whose collective unity it makes
possible), is the transcendental consciousness. This
idea may be clear (empiric consciousness) or obscure.
This we do not need to consider at present, nor even
whether it actually exists at all ; but the possibility
of the logical form of all knowledge rests necessarily
on the reference of it and this apperception *as a
faculty.*' 'In other words,' says Professor Caird,
commenting on this passage, 'Kant is here examining what elements are involved in knowledge, and
therefore does not need to consider how far the clear
consciousness of them is developed in the individual,
*nor indeed whether the individual ever actually deve-
lopes* that consciousness at all. The individual (the
sensitive being who becomes the subject of knowledge) may be at different stages on the way to clear
self-consciousness. He may be sensitive with merely
the dawning of consciousness : *he may be conscious
of objects, but not distinctly self-conscious* ; or, he
may be clearly conscious of the identity of self in
relation to the objects. Thus we can imagine him
to have many perceptions, which he has not distinctly
combined with the idea of self ; or we may even
suppose him (like children in the earliest period of
their life) not to have risen to the idea of self at all,
to the separation of the *ego* from the act whereby

the object is determined.   But we cannot imagine him to have any ideas which are incapable of being combined with the idea of self, for such ideas would be ideas incapable of being thought, incapable of forming part of the intelligible contents of consciousness ; they would be for us a thinking being, " as good as nothing."   Though, therefore, we can think of an experience in which all the elements which the critical philosopher distinguishes are not consciously or separately present to the individual, we cannot think of an experience which does not imply them all.'[1]   From these extracts it would appear that both Kant and Kant's latest expositor are agreed in thinking that all that is required to constitute a perception—in other words, an experience—is *not* that the object of that perception should actually be thought in the relations which we are told are necessary to make it an object, but only that it should be *capable* of being so thought.   But with such an admission the whole transcendental argument appears to me to vanish away.   The rules which thought was supposed to impress upon Nature, according to which Nature must be, because without them she would be nothing to us as thinking beings,—these rules turn out, after all, to be only of subjective validity.   They are the casual necessities of our reflective moments : necessities which would have been unmeaning to us in our childhood, of which the mass

---

[1] *Phil. of Kant*, p. 396.

of mankind are never conscious, and from which we ourselves are absolved during a large portion of our lives. To argue from these necessities to the truth of things is merely to repeat the old fallacy about innate ideas in another form, for if thought does not make experience (and it appears that in any intelligible meaning of that expression it does not), then there is no reason for supposing that experience need conform to thought.

The net result of this discussion appears, then, to be that, according to transcendentalism, relations are involved in experience in at least two ways, the difference between which, though it is never recognised by that philosophy, is exceedingly important. According to the first way, an explicit consciousness of the relation in question is a necessary element in every possible experience ; without it the experience would be 'nothing to us as thinking beings,' and by it, therefore, the experience may very fairly be said 'to be constituted.' But the number of relations, necessary in this sense, cannot be large, even according to the transcendentalists themselves ; nor can the necessity ever be established by argument, since the mere fact that somebody who knows the meaning of the words he uses disputes it, proves that it does not exist. If a man does not find that a particular relation, about which there is a question, is involved in his experience, an argument founded on the circumstance that no experience is possible

which is not in fact constituted by an explicit consciousness of such a relation, is not likely to convince
him that it is there. The mere consideration that
proof is required makes proof impossible.

The second way in which a transcendentalist regards relations as involved in experience differs from
that just discussed in several important particulars ;
for whereas in *that* the explicit consciousness of the
relation was required to constitute the object, in *this*
all that is required is that the object must be *capable*
of being thought under the relation. It is plainly
incorrect to describe the relation in this last case as
‘ constituting the object ’; it cannot even be said
that the capability of being thought under the relation necessarily constitutes it ; for, according to the
transcendentalist, ‘ esse ’ is equivalent to ‘ intelligi ’—
that is, an object *is*, as it is apprehended by a
thinking being, and since a thinking being can, as is
admitted, apprehend it without in all cases perceiving the capability, this cannot be required to render
the object real.   As far then as this second class of relations is concerned, the transcendentalist's argument
seems involved in something like fatal inconsistency.
Because he finds himself, in bringing an object into
‘ clear consciousness,’ unable to make abstraction of
a certain relation, he elevates this incapacity into
a universal and necessary characteristic of objects ;
while at the same time admitting that other intelligences and his own intelligence at other times have

actually had objects presented to them without this characteristic.

Enough has perhaps been said about this general objection (if it be an objection) to the transcendental method, and it is now time to follow the philosophers who employ it, in their special endeavours to show that when the nature of experience is once brought to the 'clear consciousness' of the reader, he, at any rate, can be in no further doubt as to the necessity of regarding objects in space as persistent and independent, and all objects whatever as subject to the law of universal causation.

Kant's refutation of Idealism was only introduced into the second edition of the 'Critique,' and was the main occasion of Schopenhauer's assertion that Kant had changed his view between the first edition of that work and the second, respecting the external world. I understand, however, that this is not admitted by his later critics ; that they regard the 'Refutation' as satisfactory in itself, and as harmonising with the general course of its author's speculations ; and that the proof of realism contained in it is the one on which they would be disposed to rely. As such, therefore, I am forced to criticise it.

I say 'forced,' because it is somewhat unwillingly that I go to Kant direct for the statement of an argument, partly because there is never any security that his disciples will admit that his reasoning in any particular case is in consonance with the rest of his system ; partly because his obscurity is so great that his critics are as likely to be attacked for not understanding his arguments as for not having answered them, a proceeding by which what was intended to be a philosophic discussion is suddenly converted into a historical one. Yet the defects of his exposition are so great that no care will really avert this danger ; for he has contrived to state a theory—of great difficulty in itself, and of which his own grasp does not appear to have been at all times perfectly sure—in language which always seems to be struggling to express a meaning which it can never get quite clear, and which possesses in an astonishing degree the peculiarity of being technical without being precise.

As, however, I am not acquainted with any neo-Kantian statement of the transcendental argument on this subject, it is to Kant himself that I must appeal ; and, fortunately, the formal refutation of Idealism which he has advanced is so short (apart from the elucidatory notes) that I can quote it entire. It runs as follows :—[1]

THEOREM.

' The simple but empirically determined consciousness of my own existence proves the existence of external objects in space.'

---

[1] The translation here referred to is Mr. Meiklejohn's.

'I am conscious of my own existence as determined in time. All determinations in regard to time pre-suppose the existence of *something permanent* in perception. But this permanent something cannot be something in me, for the very reason that my existence in time is itself determined by this permanent something. It follows that the perception of this permanent existence is possible only through a *thing* without me, and not through the mere *representation* of a thing without me. Consequently, the determination of my existence in time is possible only through the existence of real things external to me. Now, consciousness in time is necessarily connected with the consciousness of the possibility of this determination in time. Hence it follows that consciousness in time is necessarily connected also with the existence of things without me, inasmuch as the existence of these things is the condition of determination in time. That is to say, the consciousness of my own existence is at the same time an immediate consciousness of the existence of other things without me.'[1]

This proof, it will be observed, is transcendental, *i.e.*, its method of procedure is to show that an experience which we certainly have [that, namely, of

---

[1] *Critique*, tr. p. 167.

the series of our mental states as they occur in time]
is impossible, unless the thing to be proved [which is
stated (though, as we shall see, inadequately stated)
to be the existence of external objects in space] be admitted. And the demonstration consists of two steps.
First, it is asserted that the experience of a succession of things in time is impossible except in relation
to something permanent, or in other words, that the
perception of change is inconceivable, unless we at
the same time perceive something which does *not*
change. And in the second place, Kant goes on
to say, that since that which changes in this case
is myself (my phenomenal self), since the 'things'
which succeed each other in time are my own
mental states, the unchanging object to which they
are referred must be *outside* myself; that is, must
be the external object whose existence was to be
proved. So that if we immediately perceive the
one, it can only be on condition that we immediately
perceive the other also.

Such is the formal answer which Kant has given
to Idealism ; but it is not in this way only that he
has treated the question, since in his proof of the
'principle of substance' [which precedes the 'refutation' in the 'Critique,'] he has brought forward
arguments which, if sound, would seem to render
any further 'refutation' superfluous. For, the 'First
Analogy of Experience' asserts this, 'That in all
changes of phenomena substance is permanent ; and

the quantum thereof in nature is neither increased nor diminished.'[1] And as by *substance* Kant means something which, if it is not (as I think it is) exactly equivalent to what is commonly called *matter*, is at any rate the genus of which matter is one species ; clearly this proposition is absolutely inconsistent with Idealism in the sense in which I use the term. If matter is to be thought of as permanent and indestructible, we are clearly under the necessity of thinking that there is in nature something besides the fleeting succession of our conscious states.

The proof of this Principle of Substance, which I give partly in Kant's words, partly in Professor Caird's, and partly in my own, runs somewhat in this way :—' All phenomena exist in time. Change is only conceivable in an unchanging time. But this time is not, and cannot be, itself an object of perception, but is rather a form given to the relations of perception which supposes that they are otherwise related. They must be otherwise related as determinations of a permanent substance. As all times are in one time, so all changes must be in one permanent object. The conception of the permanence of the object is implied in all determinations of its changes. Change involves that one mode of existence follows another mode of existence in an object recognised as the same. Therefore a thing which changes, changes only in its states or accidents, not

---

[1] *Critique*, p. 136.

in its substance. An experience of absolute annihilation or creation is impossible, for it would be an
experience of two events so absolutely separated
from each other that they could not even be referred
to one time.' The 'First Analogy,' therefore, is a
deduction from the possibility of experience, and
requires no empirical proof. When a philosopher
was asked, 'What is the weight of smoke?' he
answered, 'Subtract from the weight of the burnt
wood the weight of the remaining ashes, and you
will have the weight of the smoke.' Thus, he presumed it to be incontrovertible that even in fire the
matter (substance) does not perish, but only the form
of it undergoes a change.''

The reader will at once perceive that while there
is much that is common to the ' Refutation ' and the
' First Analogy,' there are some arguments and doctrines peculiar to each, a fact which makes the satisfactory discussion of the question rather difficult ;
because, while it is impossible to treat the two
arguments as identical, it is somewhat clumsy and
would lead to a good deal of repetition to consider
them altogether separately.

The most convenient course, perhaps, will be
first to consider the points which are to be found in
both, and then to proceed with the examination of
their mutual relationship and with what is special to
each of them.

' Cf. Kant, *Critique*, p. 136 ; Caird, p. 453.

The first difficulty, then, which occurs to me,
and which, perhaps, others may feel, refers to that
'transcendental necessity' which is the very pith
and marrow of the whole demonstration, both in the
'Refutation' and in the 'First Analogy.' Is it really
true that change is 'nothing to us as thinking beings'
except we conceive it in relation to a permanent and
unchanging substance ? For my part, however much
I try to bring the matter into 'clear consciousness,'
I feel myself bound by no such necessity. For
though change may perhaps be unthinkable, except
for what Professor Green calls a 'combining,' and,
therefore, to a certain extent a 'persisting consciousness,' and though it may have no meaning out of
relation to that which is 'not-change,' this 'not-
change' by no means implies permanent substance.
On the contrary, the smallest recognisable persistence *through* time would seem enough to make
change *in* time intelligible by contrast ; and I cannot
help thinking that the opposite opinion derives its
chief plausibility from the fact that in ordinary
language permanence is the antithesis to change ;
whence it is rashly assumed that they are correla-
tives which imply each other in the system of
nature. It has to be noted also, that Kant, in his
proof of the analogy, makes a remark (quoted and
approved by Professor Caird) which almost seems
to concede this very point, for he says, 'Only the
permanent is subject to change : the mutable suffers

no change, but rather *alternation*; that is, when certain determinations cease, others begin.'[1] Now there can be no objection, of course, from a philosophical point of view, to an author defining a word in any sense he pleases: what is not permissible is to make such a definition the basis of an argument to matters of fact; yet the above passage suggests the idea that Kant's proof of the permanence of substance is not altogether free from this vice. If (by definition) change can only occur in the permanent, the fact that there *is* change is no doubt a conclusive proof that there is a ' permanent.' But the question then arises, *is* there change in this sense? How do we know that there is anything more than alternation which (by definition) *can* take place in the mutable? All transcendental arguments convince by threats. ' Allow my conclusion,' they say, ' or I will prove to you that you must surrender one of your own cherished beliefs.' But in this case the threat is hardly calculated to frighten the most timid philosopher. There must be a permanent, say the transcendentalists, or there can be no change; but this surely is no very serious calamity, if we are allowed to keep alternation, which seems to me, I confess, a very good substitute, and one with which the ordinary man may very well content himself.

To those who agree with the preceding account of our intellectual necessities, who can either conceive

---

[1] *Critique*, p. 140.

change without permanence, or are content to get along with the help of 'alternation,' it will seem absolutely fatal to the whole Kantian argument, both in the 'First Analogy' and the 'Refutation.' To those who do not agree, it will only be a difficulty in so far as the existence of any mind unconscious of transcendental necessities is inconsistent with the transcendental theory,—a point I have already discussed. But let us pass over this, and grant, for the sake of argument, that change in general, or the succession of our mental states in particular, can only be perceived in relation to a permanent something; then I ask (and this is the next most obvious objection) why, in order to obtain this permanent something, should we go to external matter ? As the reader is aware, the 'pure *ego* of apperception' supplies, on the Kantian system, the unity in reference to which alone the unorganised multiplicity of perception becomes a possible experience ; and it seems hard to understand why that which supplies unity to multiplicity may not also supply permanence to succession. Kant has, indeed, anticipated this objection, and replied to it ; but as I understand the objection much better than I do the reply, I will content myself with giving the latter, without paraphrase, in Kant's own words : 'We find,' he says, ' that we possess nothing permanent that can correspond and be submitted to the conception of a substance as intuition, except *matter*. . . . . In the representation *I*, the consciousness of myself, is not an intuition, but a merely intellectual representation produced by the spontaneous activity of a thinking subject. It follows, that this *I* has not any predicate of intuition, which, in its character of permanence, could serve as correlate to the determination of time in the internal sense, in the same way as impenetrability is the correlate of matter as an empirical intuition.' [1]

Though I do not profess altogether to understand this reasoning, it is, at all events, clear from it, that ' the permanent ' whose existence is demonstrated must be an object of perception : a fact which is also evident from various passages in the proof of the ' First Analogy,' as, for instance, this : ' Time itself cannot be an object of perception. It follows that in objects of perception, that is in phenomena, there must be found a substratum,' &c. [2] It is difficult to see indeed how that which is a quantity, incapable of either increase or diminution, can be other than an object of perception : it cannot, at all events, be a concept ; and we may, I think, assume from the whole tenor of Kant's argument, as well as from his categorical assertions, that the substance of which he speaks is a phenomenal *thing*. But if it be perceived, and if it be a phenomenon, where is it to be found ? In the perpetual flux of nature, where objects do indeed persist for a time, but where (to all

<hr>

[1] *Critique*, p. 168.   [2] *Critique*, p. 137.

appearance) nothing is eternal, who has had experience of this unchanging existence? By a dialectical process, probably familiar to the reader, we may with much plausibility reduce what we perceive in an object to a collection of related attributes, not one of which is the object itself, but all of which are the changing attributes or accidents of the object. But if this process be legitimate, the 'substratum' of these accidents is either never perceived at all, or, at all events, is only known as a relation. In neither case can it be the permanent of which Kant speaks, since in the first case it is not an object of immediate perception; in the second it can hardly be regarded as an object at all. 'But (it may perhaps be replied), by a remarkable coincidence, science has established by a wide induction the very truth which Kant attempts to prove *à priori*. When men of science tell us that matter is indestructible, it is to be presumed that they attach some meaning to the phrase, and are referring neither to a metaphysical substance nor to an evanescent appearance. When Kant uses the same phrase, it may be supposed that he refers to the same object.' For my own part, I confess to a rooted distrust of these remarkable coincidences between the results of scientific experiment and *à priori* speculation; nor does a closer examination of this particular case tend to allay the feeling. It is true, no doubt, that science asserts matter to be indestructible; but what is the exact meaning of the

phrase, and what is its evidence ? Can we perceive
any thread of identity running through all the various
changes which (what we describe as) one substance
may undergo ? To a certain extent science assures
us that we can. There are two, though, so far as I
know, only two attributes of matter, namely, its relation to a moving force and its power of attracting
and being attracted by other matter, which never
alter ; or, to put it more strictly, if we take a certain
' area of observation ' (say a closed vessel) out of
which matter cannot pass and into which it cannot
enter, then, whatever changes occur within this, the
matter there, whether always the same or not, never
varies in respect of these two properties.

But it has to be observed, that though we can
directly perceive both velocity and weight, the fact
that there are unchanging relations between a given
portion of matter and a given force, or between two
portions of given matter, can only be established
by an elaborate process of inference involving a
large number of assumptions. It might, therefore,
be plausibly contended that though *they* are perceived, their *permanence* is not, so that they cannot
properly be said to form any permanent element in
perception. Passing over this possible objection,
however, and, granting for the sake of argument,
that we directly perceive the permanence of these
two properties of matter, it is still clear, that since
these are the only two properties of which we can

say as much, either they must constitute matter, or matter, in so far as it is permanent, cannot be an object of perception. The first alternation is inadmissible, because these properties are merely relations between certain portions of matter and something else. The second would seem to be inconsistent with the Kantian proof.

The reader will understand that I am not here contending that Kant's conclusion is inconsistent with science, or that the scientific inference is wrong, either in its method or its results. My point is rather this :—Though Kant does not, of course, conclude to the necessary permanence of matter merely from its permanence in perception, nevertheless its permanence in perception would seem to be involved in his proof. Now I assert that what we perceive, *in so far as it is perceived*, is either not matter or is not permanent ; and I maintain that an examination of that part of the ordinary scientific or empirical proof which bears on the question really confirms this view.

It may perhaps be thought (and some of Kant's expressions countenance the view) that he means to say no more than that we perceive the permanent substance by means of certain of its accidents. But this seems to raise new difficulties. First, how is the phenomenal substance thus mediately known, to be distinguished from the *noumenal* substance which, if it be known at all, is known precisely in the same way? Why should we suppose it to be in time or space? Why should we suppose it to be a quantity? And how, finally, can we say with any meaning, that such a substance is phenomenal at all? To put the matter in one sentence—when Kant says that 'all determination in regard to time presupposes the existence of something permanent in perception,' if his assertion is to be taken literally, it is in contradiction with experience, for there is nothing permanent in perception, unless we choose to describe the relations of matter to force and other gravitating matter in that way: if, on the other hand, he means that what we perceive *indicates* the existence of something permanent, he has first got to prove the fact, and has then got to show that the permanent whose reality is thus established is identical with the external world of science and common sense; and lastly, to point out how we can be said to be 'immediately conscious'[1] of that which we only know through, and by means of, its attributes.

Such, then, are the chief objections which, as I think, apply with equal force to the 'First Analogy' and the 'Refutation.' Before going on to explain any difficulties, which are special to either, let me point out a curious consequence which may be extracted from the two demonstrations considered together.

[1] *Critique*, p. 167.

Kant's argument in the ' Refutation ' consisted, it will be recollected, in showing that we could have no experience of our own changing mental states unless we perceived some permanent object outside us ; while in the ' First Analogy,' his argument involved the assertion that all changes are but the determinations of some permanent substance, which itself never changes.   According to the ' First Analogy,' therefore, our changing mental states, like all other changes, must be determinations, or, as they are usually called, accidents, of a permanent substance ; while, according to the ' Refutation,' this permanent substance must be an object of perception independent of us and outside us in space—in other words, matter.   Between them these two propositions would seem to furnish a complete transcendental proof that our conscious states must be thought as mere accidents of a material substance ; so that the crude materialism of certain modern physiologists, far from being the rash conclusion of an unphilosophic empiricism, is demonstrable *à priori* by approved critical methods !

The only further remark I have to make on the ' First Analogy ' is of the nature, perhaps, of a verbal criticism.   Kant speaks throughout of matter as if it were a definite quantity in nature, a quantity which could neither be increased nor diminished.   But this would seem to be inconsistent with his theory that a vacuum is impossible, because if matter is wherever space is, it must, one should think, be not less impossible to conceive the first as a totality than it is to conceive the second ; and the words 'increase' and 'diminution' must be altogether meaningless in their application to a quantity whose amount is necessarily indefinite. Kant's expression, therefore, is a somewhat loose one, and he must be held to mean simply that matter exists, and that no portion of it can be created or destroyed. I may add, that in his discussion of a vacuum he points out that matter may be a quantity in more than one way, but that neither in the 'First Analogy' nor the 'Refutation' does he explicitly tell us in which way it is incapable of diminution. It would be interesting to know this, in order that his results might be compared with the results at which, by very different methods, men of science have arrived.

My concluding criticism refers to the 'Refutation,' and I must ask the reader to turn back to it, and to compare the thing which Kant announces his intention of proving with the thing he professes to have proved. In the 'Theorem,' the thing to be demonstrated is the existence of external objects in space ; in the 'Proof,' the thing actually demonstrated is the existence of 'real things external to me' —that is, things which are not themselves something in me, though of course their representations are so, 'without me' being evidently equivalent to 'other than my conscious states, as determined in time.'

Now if these two expressions really meant the same thing, any further refutation of Idealism would be perfectly superfluous. No human being that understood the meaning of his own words would for a moment deny that there were objects in space, and therefore without him in the sense of being outside his body. The real question is this—Does being in space and outside the body imply that the extended and external object is outside the mind, and other than one of a series of conscious states? The realist asserts that it does, the idealist asserts that it does not ; and to assume, as Kant appears to do, that the one proposition is very much the same as the other is, in reality, to beg the whole question at issue. For unless Kant's intention is merely to demonstrate the existence of extended objects, which it is equally unnecessary and impossible to do, it must, I suppose, be to show that their existence is independent of their being perceived—neither beginning with it nor perishing with it ; and in order to do this he must prove, from his point of view, two things. The first of these is, that the consciousness of one's own existence in time is only possible on the supposition that something permanent exists outside, *i.e.*, other than, one's self ; the second is, that this permanent and independent thing is in any sense identical with extended matter. The evidence for the first of these positions I have already considered ; the evidence for the second is nowhere explicitly stated ; but I cannot help suspecting (though it seems scarcely credible) that Kant omitted to provide any, though a temporary lapse into the common though absurd assumption that ‘ outside ’ in one sense is equivalent to, or, at all events, necessarily implies, ‘ outside ’ in the other.[1] With the difficulty which most philosophers feel in understanding how that which is an immediate object of perception can be other than *in consciousness*, a difficulty which is certainly not lessened by the Kantian theory of space, Kant himself makes no attempt to deal. I turn now from the transcendental proof of an external world to the transcendental proof of the law of Causation.

In his proof of the law of Causation, contained in the ‘ Second Analogy of Experience,’ Kant, if I understand him rightly, adopts two lines of argument ; the one on which he appears to lay most stress being consistent neither with itself nor with the other. In discussing it I am unfortunately deprived of the assistance of Professor Caird, who, in the exercise of his discretion as an expositor of the Critical Philosophy, has chosen practically to ignore it. I will not venture to determine whether

---

[1] I do not of course suppose that Professor Caird and the Neo-Kantians are guilty of the confusion of thought which I here attribute to Kant. But (as I explained above) since they appear to be content with the argument in the form in which Kant left it ; since at all events they have not, so far as I know, thought fit to provide a corrected version of it, I am not only justified, but compelled, to treat it as if it were an authentic exposition of their views.

in so doing he has or has not somewhat transgressed
even the very wide limits imposed on him by the
plan of his work; but lest the reader should imagine
that the absence of the argument I am about to
state from the commentary, implies its non-existence
in the original, I will ask him to consult the
'Critique,' [1] and see whether it may not be attributed to Kant with as much plausibility as any in
the whole range of the 'Critique.'   It runs as
follows—I give it partly in my own words, partly in
Kant's, though the italics are always mine :—'Our
apprehension of the manifold of phenomena is
always successive.'   But sometimes we regard this
manifold of phenomena as constituting an object
(say a house), sometimes as a series of events (as
when a ship is seen to float down a river).   Subjec-
tively, in apprehension, these two series would seem
to be of the same kind ; objectively, as every one
knows, we widely distinguish them.   We no more
suppose that the upper story of the house, if we
begin looking at it at the top, is a phenomenon preceding in time the ground floor, than we suppose
the ship is at the same time at two different places
on the river.   Yet in consciousness we perceive the
ground floor *after* the upper story, exactly as we
perceive the ship lower down the river *after* we
perceive it higher up.   The problem then that
requires solution is this : How do we distinguish, as

[1] Page 142 *seq.*

in experience we certainly *do* distinguish, the first
series from the second ?   And Kant's answer is
that we can only distinguish them if we regard the
order of the first series as arbitrary, and that of the
second as subject to a rule.   ' In the former example
my perceptions in the apprehension of the house
might begin at the roof and end at the foundation,
or *vice versâ* ; or I might apprehend the manifold in
this empirical intuition by going from right to left
or from left to right.   Accordingly, in the series of
these perceptions, *there was no determined order*
which necessitated my beginning at a certain point
in order empirically to connect the manifold.'   In
the second case the order is objective : it in no way
depends on the mode in which we choose to represent it ; and this can only be if we suppose that it
occurs in conformity with a rule or law.   And this
becomes at once apparent, if for an instant we try
and imagine the contrary to be the case.   ' Let us
suppose that nothing precedes an event upon which
this event must follow in conformity with a rule.
All sequence of perception would then exist only in
apprehension, *that is to say, would be merely subjective*, and it could not thereby be objectively determined what thing ought to precede and what ought
to follow in perception.   In such a case we should
have *nothing but a play of representation*, which
would possess no application to any object.   That
is to say, it would not be possible through perception

to distinguish one phenomenon from another, as regards relation of time ; because the succession in the act of apprehension would always be of the same sort, and therefore there would be nothing in the phenomenon to determine the succession, and to render a certain sequence objectively necessary. And, in this case, I cannot say that two states in a phenomenon follow one upon the other, *but only that one apprehension follows upon another.* But this is merely subjective, and does not determine an object, and consequently cannot be held to be a cognition of an object—not even in the phenomenal world. Accordingly, when we know in experience that something happens, we always suppose that something precedes, whereupon it follows in conformity with a rule. For otherwise I could not say of the object that it follows ; because the *mere succession in my apprehension, if it be not determined by a rule in relation to something preceding,* does not authorise succession in the object. Only, therefore, in reference to a rule, according to which phenomena are determined in their sequence, that is, as they happen, by the preceding state, can I make my subjective synthesis of apprehension objective ; and it is only under this presupposition that even the experience of an event is possible.'

Starting then from the succession in apprehension, or the subjective succession of phenomena, Kant had to distinguish from it—*first*, the objective *coexistence* which constitutes a thing in space—a house, a tree, and so forth ; and *second*, the objective *sequence* which constitutes a series of events.   As I pointed out in the section on the independent world, he does not, so far as I know, furnish any principle of objective coexistence, but in the law of causation he finds the principle of objective sequence.   Or, to put it in a transcendental form, he holds that the experience of (objective) events is only possible if we presuppose the law of causation, and as we certainly have such an experience, &c.

Now, regarded as a proof of the law of universal causation, the argument I have just stated is scarcely worth criticising.   In the first place, Professor Caird, after Schopenhauer, admits that the conclusion is inconsistent with one of the premises.   If it can be said to prove that sequence in the object is 'according to a rule,' it is only by showing in the first instance that sequence in the subject is arbitrary ; so that the causation proved is at all events not universal.   But, in the second place, it does not prove, or attempt to prove, that there is actually an objective sequence according to a necessary rule, but only that *if* there is an objective sequence, it must be according to a necessary rule, because otherwise it could not be distinguished from the subjective sequence. Now these are very different propositions ; and the second or conditional one might be admitted to its full extent, without admitting the truth of the first or unconditional one, which is for purposes of science the proposition for which proof is required.

The second proof which Kant gives of the principle of causality is so hidden away in the recesses of the first, that some doubt might perhaps be thrown on whether he intended formally to put it forward as a proof at all. The fact that it is in direct contradiction to the first proof, does not perhaps go far towards helping us to a decision on this point ; but in any case the matter is not of much importance, as I am more concerned with the meaning which the post-Kantians extract from his writings, than with that which he himself intended to put into them.

The first proof attempted to show that the experience of an objective sequence was only possible if it was distinguished from a subjective sequence by being according to a rule. The second proof attempts to show that *no* sequence can be experienced except on the same terms. It is plain, therefore, that the second proof aims at demonstrating a causation which is universal, and which cannot, therefore, be reconciled with the partial causation contemplated by the first. It only remains for us to examine whether it is more satisfactory. I give it entire in Professor Caird's words : [1]—

'The judgment of sequence cannot be made without the presupposition of the judgment of causality. For time is a mere form of the relation of

[1] *Phil. of Kant*, pp. 454-5.

K

things, and cannot be perceived by itself. Only when we have connected events with each other can we think of them as in time. And the connection must be such, that the different elements of the manifold of the events are determined in relation to each other, in the same way as the different moments in time are determined in relation to each other. But it is evident that the moments of time are so determined in relation to each other that we can only put them into one order—*i.e.*, that we can proceed from the previous to the subsequent moment, but not *vice versâ*. Now, if objects or events cannot be dated in relation to time, but only in relation to each other, it follows that they cannot be represented as in time at all, unless they have an irreversible order ; or, in other words, unless they are so related according to a universal rule, when one thing is posited something else must necessarily be posited in consequence. In every representation of events as in time, this pre-supposition is implied ; and the denial of causality necessarily involves the denial of all succession in time.'

It appears to be asserted in this proof that we cannot conceive succession, unless we suppose that there is a necessary order in phenomena to enable them, so to speak, to correspond with and fit into the necessary order in the moments of time. ' Events are determined in relation to each other in the same [*i.e.*, I suppose, *some corresponding*] way, as different moments are determined in relation to each other.' But in so far as I can attach any definite meaning to these words at all, they seem to distinguish two things which are really the same, and to confound two things which are really distinct. The 'order' of events and the 'order' of moments are not two kinds of order, but one kind; and if we assert that two events succeed each other, we are describing precisely the same relationship between them as when we assert that two moments succeed each other. When, on the other hand, we assert that one event is the cause of another, we assert not only this actual succession, but also, by implication, a similar succession whenever an event resembling the cause or first term in the relationship may happen to occur. But this relationship is so far independent of time, that though it *must* occur in *some* time, it *may* occur in *any* time, and it in no way corresponds with the relation between actual successive events or successive moments which can never be repeated, because the related terms can never recur. Event A and moment *a* are followed by event B and moment *b*. This happens once actually and, if you please, necessarily; but it never happens again. The events vanish into the past as certainly as the moments in which they occur, and they can as little be recalled. But all this has nothing to do with causation. What the principle of causation, strictly speaking, asserts is, not that if event A recurs it will be followed by event B, for event A cannot possibly recur ; but that if an event similar to A recurs, an event similar to B will certainly follow : and how this second hypothetical assertion is involved in the categorical assertion of a simple historical succession between actual concrete events and moments, altogether passes my understanding.

The transcendental view appears to be, that because there is a necessary order between successive moments, therefore there must be a necessary order between successive events ; and this desired necessity can only be found in the principle of causation. But if there was no causality at all, the order of events would still be just as much or just as little necessary as the order of moments. An event is what it is because it happens when it does. A moment is what it is because it occurs when it does. Neither the one nor the other could occur at any other time, simply because by so doing it would cease to be itself. It is true of course (and this is no doubt the cause of all the confusion) that we habitually talk of the *same* event as occurring at *different* times, while we make no such assertion respecting particular moments. But this is simply because the whole essence of a moment consists in the time at which it occurs, whereas it is commonly the case that this is the least interesting of all the relations which constitute an event, and the one of which it is therefore most often convenient to make abstraction. Nor is it to the purpose to say that events cannot be dated in relation to time, but only in relation to other events; because in every sense in which this can be asserted of particular events, it can likewise be asserted of particular moments. If, therefore, this fact necessitates causation in the one case (which, however, I deny), it must necessitate it also in the other—which is absurd.

Other objections besides these might no doubt be taken against particular points in the transcendental proof, but the best refutation of it is to be found in its own version of its general nature and object. That object is simply to show that a clear idea of succession is impossible, except to those who first regard phenomena as necessarily connected according to the principle of causation; which, again, is as much as to say that by far the larger part of mankind have no clear idea of succession at all. And when I say the larger part of mankind, it must be remembered that in that majority are included not only all those who do not believe in the universality of causation, but also almost all those who do; since I will make bold to say that the greater number of these, however much they turn their minds to the nature of succession in time, do not find involved therein the principle of cause and effect. This necessity, then, under which the transcendentalists labour, if it is to be of 'objective' application, and is to have any philosophic value at all, requires us to believe that mankind has been, and is, suffering under a very singular illusion respecting the clearness of its own ideas, on a point which is commonly thought to be so simple as to defy further analysis. This by itself is sufficiently hard to believe; and the difficulty does not diminish when we come to examine the matter more closely. For what does the supposed necessity oblige us to hold? That when we perceive two events in succession, the first is the cause of the second? Not at all. But that when we perceive two events in succession, there exists *somewhere* a cause for the second—a cause possibly (indeed, probably) of which we are, and shall remain for ever, ignorant! So that what the transcendental doctrine comes to is this, that we can have, and do have, an idea of succession which is not causal, but that we cannot have such idea, at least in 'clear consciousness,' which does not involve the idea of some *other* succession which is indeed causal, but one element of which is, or may be, quite unknown to us!

On the whole, then, I cannot agree with Herr Kuno Fischer that Kant's 'giant strength'[1] has been very happily employed in this attempt to place the doctrine of causation beyond the reach of sceptical attack; on the contrary, it seems to me that all the difficulties inherent in the transcendental method, and all the confusion and obscurity which are so often to be met with in Kant's use of that method, are

---

[1] Fischer's *Kant*, p. 118.

strikingly exhibited in his treatment of this central
and important principle. It is commonly asserted
that it was Hume's theory (that our expectation or
belief in the uniformity of Nature is the result of
habit) which suggested to Kant the necessity of
finding some more solid basis on which to rest our
systematic knowledge of phenomena. If so, it is
unfortunate that it should be precisely at this point
that the ingenious and important method of proof,
which it is his chief glory to have invented, most
obviously and completely breaks down.

I have only to point out, in conclusion, that had
the transcendental demonstration been as sound in all
its parts as Herr Kuno Fischer and Professor Caird
suppose it to be, the thing proved is not sufficient
by itself to serve as a basis for scientific induction.

All that Kant can be said, on the most favourable
view of his reasoning, to have established is that,
to use his own words, 'the phenomena in the past
determine all the phenomena in succeeding time';
or, as Professor Caird phrases it, 'the subsequent
state of the world is the effect of the previous state.'

But something more than a fixed relation between
the totality of phenomena at one instant and the
totality of phenomena at the next instant, is required
before we can, in the scientific sense of the expression,
assert that these are 'laws of nature.' A law of nature
refers to a fixed relation, not between the totality of
phenomena, but between extremely small portions of

that totality ; and it asserts a fixed connection, not between individual concrete phenomena, but between classes of phenomena.   Now by no known process of logic can we extract from the general proposition, that ' the subsequent state of the world is the effect of the previous state,' any evidence that such laws as these exist at all ; and what is more, this general proposition might be perfectly true, and yet the course of nature might be, to all intents and purposes, absolutely irregular, even to an intelligence which, very unlike our own, was able to grasp phenomena in their totality at any given moment.   For ' regularity ' is an expression absolutely inapplicable to series, in which there is no kind of repetition ; and we have no reason for supposing—from the point of view of science we have every reason for *not* supposing—that the world will ever return exactly to the same state in which it was at some previous moment. If, therefore, we have grounds for believing that the states of the universe at two successive instants are connected only as wholes, and not necessarily by means of independent causal links between their separate parts, then of such a universe we could say, perhaps, that its course through time was *determined*, but we could not say that it was *regular*, nor would it be possible for a mind, however gifted, to infer, by any known process of reasoning, its future from its past.

If I may judge from a phrase of Professor Caird's,

he holds a different opinion, for he appears to think that the existence of causal links between individual phenomena follows necessarily from the fact of a causal connection between the totality of phenomena at different times. 'To find,' he says,[1] 'the special threads of causality which connect the sequent states of objects is of course a matter of careful observation and experiment. *But in asserting sequence we have already by implication asserted that the threads are there.*' I do not know whether the implication here spoken of is transcendental. Its nature is developed neither by Kant nor by himself, and my own unassisted efforts to find it in the 'clear consciousness' of sequence have, as perhaps was natural, met with no success. But if it is not transcendental, certainly it is not empirical. I showed before, that, admitting the existence of these causal threads, experience alone could never show their precise nature; still less, if we do not admit their existence, can experience alone prove it. It is not, however, necessary to waste the reader's time in establishing this point. The transcendentalist would be ready to admit it without demonstration, since, if he allowed that experience was a sufficient ground of belief in this case, he would find it hard to deny its sufficiency in other cases; while, on the empiricist's view of the question I have sufficiently dwelt in the earlier chapters of this essay.

[1] P. 459.

CHAPTER VII.

THREE ARGUMENTS FROM POPULAR PHILOSOPHY.

IN this chapter I propose to examine the philosophic value of three arguments which may be called, respectively, the ‘Argument from general consent,’ the ‘Argument from success in practice,’ and the ‘Argument from “common sense.”’

These arguments are not, perhaps, as a general rule, put forward as final and conclusive grounds of belief by writers having much pretension to philosophic insight; but they fill so important a place among the reasons by which men are, as a matter of fact, convinced, they constitute such a large part of actual popular philosophy, that they require some notice in this essay.

It is not necessary to remind the reader of a truth which has been already stated, that in discussing them no attempt can legitimately be made to demonstrate their insufficiency to furnish a basis of philosophic certitude. Neither this attribute, nor its converse can, from the nature of things, be demonstrated of any argument whatever. It is as impossible to prove that a belief *is not* to be accepted as one of the ultimate data of knowledge, as to prove that it *is* to be so accepted. This is a point the decision of which must in all cases be left to each man's individual judgment; and the duty of the philosopher can go no further than to make the decision as easy as possible, and to see that it is really given on the main question at issue, and, in the first instance at least, on that alone. If the verdict be given in the affirmative, and the belief in question is pronounced true and also ultimate, then it will be necessary, in the second place, to enquire how much ground it covers;—*i.e.*, what conclusions we may draw from it, and what proportion these conclusions bear to the total number of beliefs we desire to establish.

In conformity with this plan, let us discuss in the first place that particular argument from authority which I have called the 'Argument from general consent.' It will be admitted, I suppose, at once, that any one who regards the general consent of mankind as a final ground of belief must hold, 1st, that some of his particular beliefs either *are*, or may be deduced from, propositions assented to by the generality of mankind; and, 2nd, that propositions assented to by the generality of mankind are true.

Now with regard to the first of these positions. I would ask any one who holds it, whether he is immediately convinced of the fact that mankind assent generally to any given proposition, or whether he arrives at that conviction by a process of reasoning? If, as is more than probable, he adopts the latter alternative, by so doing he admits, at all events, that he believes *some* propositions which are *not* proved by general consent—all those, namely, which are required to establish the fact that this general consent exists. These, it is to be presumed, are of the same general character as those which are required to establish any other historical fact, and consist in the first place of evidence, oral and documentary, and in the second place, of those general principles which, as the reader is already aware, are required before any general induction can be based on these or any other particulars. Before, therefore, any use can be made of the fact (if fact it be) that 'propositions assented to by the generality of mankind are true,' we must both believe a large number of statements because they are assented to, not by the generality, but by a very small fraction of mankind, and also accept a large number of the very propositions for which we most desire to obtain proof, and in favour of which it is thought that the 'argument from general consent' may legitimately be invoked.

So much for what, in formal logic, is called the 'minor premiss' of the argument under discussion. Let us now turn to the 'major premiss,' which, as has already been stated, would run in this way :—

What mankind have generally assented to, is true.

Is this an ultimate proposition—one which we accept as neither susceptible of proof, nor as requiring proof? If any reader is in doubt as to the true reply which should be given to this enquiry, the answer which he feels disposed to make to the following question may, perhaps, help him to a decision. Does he regard the argument from general consent as an example, and a specially perfect example, of the ordinary argument from testimony? If he does, and I think he probably will, then the proposition we are discussing *is not* ultimate. We are commonly told, and when properly understood the assertion is perfectly correct, that we accept the greater number of our beliefs on the faith of testimony. But by this is not meant, or ought not to be meant, that the real ground of accepting an assertion is the fact that it is asserted. The real ground is, or should be, the belief that our informant or informants probably know the truth and are probably willing to communicate it. And this belief itself is one which all would allow required evidence, and could not therefore be considered ultimate.

Now I imagine that most people will, on reflection, admit that this is true, not only when we are dealing with the opinion of this or that individual, or body of individuals, but also when we are dealing with the united testimony of mankind. In other

words, they will admit, 1st, that the 'argument from
general consent' is merely an instance of the ordinary arguments from testimony, and, 2nd, that the
ordinary arguments from testimony depend on something beyond the fact that certain opinions have
been stated, and require us also to be assured, that
the persons stating them were truthful and well
informed.

This amounts, of course, to an admission that
the proposition we are discussing is not an ultimate
one.   Strictly speaking, therefore, we might consider
the discussion at an end.   But before leaving the
subject, it may be worth enquiring whether it is
nearly ultimate—*i.e.*, whether, without tracing the
thread of inference much further back, we can readily
find some satisfactory axiom on which to rest it.
Have we then any reason to believe that mankind,
as a whole, or any section of them, are well informed
(I will not dispute their truthfulness) respecting the
larger postulates of science ?   With regard to mankind as a whole, I can only imagine two reasons
being given for putting confidence in their opinion
on such a subject.   The first is, that a belief generally held for ages must in all probability be in harmony with the experience of those who hold it—
must 'succeed,' that is, 'in practice'; the other is,
that the universality of an opinion is a proof that
it results from the 'normal working of the human
mind'; in other words, is established by common

sense, according to one meaning of that ambiguous expression. As these arguments, however, form part of the main subject-matter of this chapter, and will be separately discussed in their proper place, I may for the present ignore them. It remains, therefore, only to consider whether a special reason exists for reposing confidence in the opinion of some particular section of mankind on these subjects; in other words, whether there is any body of men who hold a position towards philosophy at all corresponding to that which experts are supposed to hold towards science, or Churches and Popes towards theology.

The only persons, I suppose, who have any claim to an authority of this kind in philosophy, are philosophers; and if they had all agreed in their conclusions, and had forborne to make public the various lines of speculation by which they arrived at them, it might have been difficult, perhaps, precisely to estimate the value of their pretensions. As, however, they have not fulfilled the *second* of these conditions, we are compelled to judge each man by his arguments, and are so altogether carried out of the region of authority; and as they have not fulfilled the *first*, we should, if reduced to believing only what they agreed to recommend, be left without a philosophic creed at all. As is remarked[1] with great force and point by Sir James Stephen,

[1] *Nineteenth Century*, April, 1877, p. 290.

' the bare names of Spinoza, Leibnitz, Kant, Hegel, Descartes, Pascal, Bossuet, Voltaire, Comte, Hobbes, Locke, Berkeley, Hume, Paley, Mill, are quite enough to show how much the deepest thought, the most brilliant talents, the most pious feeling, the shrewdest practical sagacity, the most earnest and scrupulous conscientiousness have contributed to a practical agreement on this subject.' Sir James Stephen is here talking, I ought to mention, of the foundations of theology ; but the remark, with one slight omission, is at least as appropriate to the foundation of science, with which alone I am here concerned.

To sum up. The minor premiss of the argument from general consent (and the same is true of all arguments from authority) cannot be proved without assuming many, if not all, of those scientific postulates, which it is the business of that argument to prove. The major premiss, on the other hand, of the argument cannot, any more than the major premiss of any other argument from authority, be regarded as an ultimate belief ; and (the case of experts being excluded) if we ask what proof can be given of it, we are reduced either to the 'argument from success in practice,' or to the 'argument from common sense.'

I turn, therefore, to the first of these—about which a very few words will suffice.

The ' Argument from success in practice ' is nothing more than an appeal from the scepticism of theory to the faith which is born of experience. 'You assert,' it says, 'that no logical proof of ordinary opinions can be given, and that neither common sense nor universal consent can supply a basis of philosophical certitude. Grant that this is so ; it by no means necessarily follows that men ought to give up on a point of theory, or through some over-subtlety of speculation, beliefs which work admirably in practice. However ingenious may be your doubts, after all experience proves that they have no substantial foundation ; nor is it any use to say that the uniformity of nature, or any other great principle, is not proved to be true, when every hour of our lives shows that at all events it is true enough for all practical purposes.'

That men ought not to give up on speculative grounds the belief in 'the uniformity of nature, or any other great principle,' I hold, as the reader will see if his patience lasts till the end of the volume, with as much persistence as any man. But I must altogether take exception to the statement which is the central point of the argument just stated, namely, that the fact that these principles work in practice is any ground for believing them to be even approximately true. This is in reality an example of the illegitimate extension of a perfectly legitimate argument. *Given* certain laws of nature—*given* that there is a fixed plan according to which phenomena occur, and which we are capable of discovering, it is undoubtedly true that the fact that a certain theory 'works in practice,' *i.e.*, agrees, so far as our experience goes, with the real order of things, is a ground for putting confidence in it for the future ; how much confidence it is the business of the Inductive Logician to tell us.   But the earlier chapters of this essay have been written in vain if the reader requires to be told that experience is altogether incapable of establishing the truth—even the probable truth—of these initial assumptions.   It cannot prove the wisdom of a provisional belief in them, simply because it can prove nothing about them at all.   Its oracles are not so much ambiguous in their import, as altogether dumb ; and certainly give no reasonable encouragement to the compromise (which, however, I myself believe in) between theoretical scepticism and practical faith.

It is obvious indeed that to found such a compromise on the teaching of experience is a proceeding which, if the reasoning of the preceding chapters be sound, involves a logical contradiction. Experience is one of the chief idols which scepticism attacks ; to admit, therefore, the accuracy of the sceptical argument, but to add that experience demonstrates that in practice it may be neglected, is to say in the same breath that the sceptical reasoning *is*, and that it *is not*, sound.   If scepticism proves anything, it proves that experience proves nothing.

Similar considerations show that no process of

verification can produce or add to philosophic certitude. Against the practical use and necessity of verification I have not a word to say. It must always remain one of the most important instruments for determining the laws of nature, granting that by any known method the determination of the laws of nature is possible. But it is a mistake to suppose that there is any philosophic distinction between founding a belief on experience and founding a belief on experience *plus* verification. Into this mistake, I cannot help thinking that Mr. G. H. Lewes has fallen in his ' Problems of Life and Mind.' He seems to imagine that because knowledge of what he calls the ' super-sensible,' which is not derived from experience, differs from knowledge of the ' sensible ' and the ' extra-sensible,' which *is* derived from experience, in being incapable of verification, that therefore it is less worthy of belief. Whether a knowledge of the super-sensible, *i.e.*, theology and metaphysics, really rests on a less substantial basis than science, as Mr. Lewes contends, I will not argue here; but at all events the difference does not depend on the fact that the theories of the one CAN, and of the other *cannot*, be verified, since verification is not in reality a separate or distinct kind of proof. It is merely the name given to an observation or experiment which, instead of suggesting a new theory, supports one already framed. It does not in any essential particular differ from other empirical grounds of belief.   Philosophically speaking, it must stand with them or fall with them, nor can it afford any independent evidence for a system of which it is itself an integral part.

I now come to the 'Argument from common sense,' which differs from the two arguments that have just been discussed in the fact that it constitutes, nominally at least, an essential part of an actual philosophic system, and has been explicitly advanced as furnishing a sufficiently solid basis for belief, not merely by the vulgar, but by thinkers of influence and reputation.   Unfortunately, however, though these thinkers have added, by the sanction of their authority, to the dignity and importance of the term 'common sense,' this has not been accompanied by any increased accuracy or clearness in its definition. In their use of the expression they have not always been in agreement with themselves, with each other, or with the unphilosophic majority : though, as it is only with the opinions of the latter that we are here concerned, this is not a subject which at this moment need detain us.

Now when, in ordinary discussion, a belief is defended on the ground that it is in accordance with common sense, what is frequently intended to be conveyed by the argument I imagine to be something of this sort :—' The belief in question may not be exactly defensible on rational grounds, we admit that we cannot satisfactorily support it by reasoning

—nevertheless practically all men *must* assent to it, and all men *do* assent to it, and there is nothing more to be said about the matter.' I have no complaint whatever to make against any one who takes up this position, provided it be understood exactly what the position is. It is not an *argument* in favour of a belief : it is a confession that no such argument can be found, and an assertion that we must do without one. It is not a philosophy, either of common sense or anything else ; it is rather a negation of all philosophy. And therefore it is that, directly any attempt is made to raise what is a mere dogmatic assertion to the dignity of a philosophical reason, it is found necessary to buttress it up by various supplementary principles, which, as they are not always clearly distinguished from the original ground on which assent was demanded, are apt to introduce the strangest confusion into every part of the subject. This necessity of adding support to common sense pure and simple, as I have just described it, shows itself in various ways in ordinary quasi-philosophical discussion. Ask any man why he believes the dictates of common sense, and he is very likely to say that he does so because everybody else does so (which is the ' argument from general consent '), or that he does so because he and mankind in general find them answer—which is the ' argument from success in practice.' Though if, on some other occasion, he is asked why he puts confidence in these two latter arguments, it must be admitted that he is very likely to say that he does so because they are recommended to him by 'his common sense.'

But there is another argument sometimes used to eke out the bare assertion that proof must be foregone, which is so important that it may be doubted whether it does not better deserve the title of *the* argument from common sense; more especially as it really is an argument (though not a very good one), which the other is not. It may be stated somewhat in this way :—' Human intelligence, like any other machine, may work rightly or wrongly. It may do its proper and normal work, or it may do something altogether different and abnormal. In the former case we shall obtain from it truth ; in the latter, error. In order, therefore, to get at the truth, we have only to observe what an intelligence working normally turns out, in other words what common sense naturally believes, and to put our faith in that.'

But then the question arises—What is an intelligence ' working normally ' ?

It is not enough to say that it is an intelligence working in such a way as to perceive the truth, for, when asked what was the truth, we could merely reply that it was that which an intelligence working normally perceived to be true, and when asked what an intelligence working normally was, that it was an intelligence which perceived the truth—a pair of statements which, taken by themselves, would not bring us much nearer to the discovery of a philosophy. Nor is it of any use to say that a normal intelligence is one which obeys natural laws ;—not only because, if science is to be believed, every intelligence, sane or insane, does that, but because we should then be in the singular position of maintaining that we know what are natural laws by means of an intelligence in whose judgment we had confidence because it was governed by natural law. Nor yet is it possible to say that the question of what is normal and therefore (indirectly) of what is true, can be decided by majorities however large : to do so would be to revert to the ' argument from general consent,' which has been already disposed of. If anything is to be made of this principle, it can only be by supplementing it in some form or other by the idea of *design.* We must either presuppose a Creator who constructs our intelligences in such a manner that on the whole what they incline to believe is true, or else we must adopt the modern substitute for a Creator, and suppose that there is some process by which right-thinking intelligences tend to multiply and wrong-thinking ones to die out. On either of these suppositions, it is undoubtedly the fact that there is a considerable probability that what all men practically agree in believing is worthy of belief : but then, not to speak of the difficulty already dwelt on of showing, without a *petitio principii,* what it is that all men agree in believing,—the question still remains, what reason have we for thinking that either of these suppositions is true?   Nobody has as yet, so far as I know, maintained that the theory of natural selection is self-evident; and though the same cannot absolutely be said of Theism, yet the common opinion seems to be that it is desirable to have, if possible, some kind of proof for the existence of a God.   In any case, as mankind in general are not more disposed to believe the fundamental principle of Theology than they are to believe the fundamental principles of Science, it is absurd without further evidence to adduce the first in support of the second.

Design, therefore, whether Theistic or atheistic, whether depending on an intelligent Creator or the blind operation of natural selection, requires proof.   And what kind of proof is possible?   I have never heard of any, nor can I imagine any, which does not depend on those very principles for which proof is required; and in support of which the hypothesis of a normal intelligence contrived by design was adduced.   The circle, therefore, in which the argument turns is evident.   We are required to believe in certain propositions because they are believed in by a normal intelligence: we are required to believe in the existence and testimony of a normal intelligence because intelligence is the product of design or of something equivalent to design : and we are required to believe in design because of certain facts which can only be established if the propositions we originally set out to prove are true !

Of the two meanings then, which, so far as I can judge, may be attributed to the 'argument from common sense' as it is ordinarily used, the first is not so much an answer to scepticism as an admission that no answer is forthcoming ; while the second ceases to be effective as soon as the various propositions which compose it are brought into clear relief,—it is plausible only so long as it is confused.

CHAPTER VIII.

THE AUTHORITY OF CONSCIOUSNESS AND OF ORIGINAL BELIEFS.

THE reader may, perhaps, be surprised that hitherto while discussing the argument from common sense, I have not had occasion to do more than allude to the philosophic version of that argument, large as is the space which it occupies in the field of English speculation. This omission, which will be immediately remedied, has been dictated by several reasons ; among which is the circumstance that the philosophy of common sense is, according to the statement of its most eminent modern exponent, in reality not founded upon common sense at all, but upon consciousness : common sense being merely a name given to the attitude of mind which receives the verdicts of consciousness, or what are thought to be such, in unhesitating faith.[1] It is needless to say, that this is an attitude of mind to which many

---

[1] This refers to Sir William Hamilton's opinions as expressed in the ' Dissertation on Reid.' In the ' Lectures,' see Chap. xxxviii., he gives (after his fashion), a different account of the matter. But whatever version of his opinion be taken, it must, I believe, if clearly expressed, be substantially identical either with the theory criticised at the beginning of this chapter—*i.e.*, the theory of the ' Dissertation,' or that dealt with at the end, which I attribute to Mr. Mill.

philosophers lay claim whose philosophy has nothing to do with common sense ; and the reader therefore may naturally expect that the ensuing controversy will mainly turn, not on whether we ought to trust consciousness, but on what the consciousness is which we ought to trust. This statement, however, though perhaps it fairly enough describes the character of Mr. Mill's polemic against Hamilton, does not precisely indicate the point of view from which the question is approached in the sequel.

' Demonstration,' says Sir William Hamilton, ' if proof be possible, behoves to repose at last on propositions which, carrying their own evidence, necessitate their own admission.'[1] Nothing can be truer. This is the fundamental doctrine on which this essay rests, and which has been repeated in the course of it even to weariness. But surely it is a strange assertion with which to introduce a discussion on the grounds we have for believing those propositions 'which carry their own evidence.' If they carry their own evidence, if they ' necessitate their own admission,' what can be the use of introducing a *deus ex machinâ* in the shape of consciousness in order to recommend them ? The reason is not far to seek. There are, indeed, if knowledge is possible, beliefs which lie at the root of all knowledge, which 'carry their own evidence ' and ' necessitate their own admission '; but there are others which no doubt every

<hr>

[1] *Dissertation on Reid*, p. 742.

one would wish to have proved, but for which unfortunately no proof is readily forthcoming. These two classes agree in nothing but the single fact, that for neither of them can any reason be given; while they differ in the somewhat important peculiarity that whereas the self-evident do not *require* proof, the beliefs of common sense (as we might call the second class) cannot *obtain* it. The device, which, in this difficulty, occurred to Sir William Hamilton, was partially to amalgamate the two sorts of belief by inventing an authority which he called by the time-honoured name of consciousness, which should testify to both of them,[1] not indeed, as he admits, in precisely the same way, or to precisely the same degree, still sufficiently in the second case, as well as in the first, to require our assent.

To my thinking, this idea of a faculty within the mind, whether called conscience, consciousness, or common sense, inducing the mind by the mere weight of its authority to accept certain propositions, is one of the most singular fictions which has ever appeared, even in metaphysics. It is a fiction, moreover, which is particularly unfortunate from the fact, that, in all cases where it is not superfluous, it is misleading. In the case of propositions which have other evidence, it is clearly superfluous; in the case of propositions having no other evidence but which are certain in themselves, it is also superfluous;

[1] P. 744.

while in the case of propositions which have neither
external evidence nor internal certainty, it is misleading, since it can, as I shall presently show, only
simulate the appearance of an independent and
original ground of belief.

I may be told, indeed, that the consciousness
which Sir William Hamilton and many other philosophers set up as the final arbiter of truth is no
separate faculty within the mind, but is co-extensive
with the mind itself. If this were so, their theory
might be much more tenable *psychologically*, but it
would be much less tenable *philosophically*, than
it was before. They would be guiltless of founding
their philosophy on an imaginary faculty ; but they
would, on the other hand, be deprived of any
single and supreme authority on which to found
it at all. It may be readily admitted that, without doing violence to established usage, consciousness
might be used as a general name for mental phenomena, or our apprehension of them ;—but in that
case it ought not to be regarded, any more than
other general names, as denoting anything separate
and distinct from the several particulars it describes.
Though, doubtless, the ‘ I ’ in relation to which all
mental phenomena are apprehended is a unity, yet
every such phenomenon is distinct from every other,
and consciousness, if it be used as a general term for
describing these phenomena, is a unity only in the
sense of being one name which belongs to a great

many things, and in this sense it is evident that it cannot be regarded as a single authority.

This is equally true if consciousness is taken to be, as it might perhaps be maintained that Sir William Hamilton in this connection intends it to be, a general name for our acts of intuitive judgment. This use of the word certainly excludes the notion of consciousness being set up as a kind of separate faculty, but then it also excludes the idea of consciousness testifying to anything.   Either there is *no* criterion for the truth of intuitive judgments, in which case consciousness cannot be that criterion ; or there *is* a criterion, in which case it must be something more than a general name by which those judgments are described.   In the first case,[1] much of Sir William Hamilton's language must be regarded as metaphorical, and some of it as erroneous ; in the second case, it would seem that he stands committed to a doctrine (which, I believe, he really held), according to which consciousness is regarded as a kind of judge whose veracity and whose competence are equally above suspicion.

Now, it is evident that a theory of this sort, by which consciousness is raised to a position in philosophy similar to that which conscience occupies in popular morality—*this* telling us what we ought to *do*, just as *that* tells us what we ought to *believe*—cannot be proclaimed without immediately provok-

---

[1] Cf. *Lectures*, p. 5.

ing three questions : First, Does such an authority exist ? Second, Why ought we to believe it ? Third, What does it tell us to believe ? I waive the first of these questions, though it raises points of great interest about which much might be said, and I pass on to the second, Why ought we to believe it ? Sir William Hamilton is in no way embarrassed for an answer, indeed, in the ' Dissertation ' he gives no less than five, of which the following is a list :

1. Consciousness ought to be presumed to be true till it is proved to be false.[1]

2. Some of the data of consciousness cannot be doubted, because the doubt would annihilate itself.[2]

3. The data of consciousness have the negative proof of consistency, *i.e.*, so far as at present appears they have never been proved inconsistent with each other.[3]

4. If they are untrue, then we must have been deliberately deceived by a perfidious Creator.[4]

5. To doubt consciousness involves a contradiction.[5]

With regard to the first of these proofs, it is only necessary to say that some more solid foundation for a creed is required than that the rules of debate, according to Sir William Hamilton's interpretation of them, throw the burden of proof on the objector.

The second proof is not strictly speaking a proof

[1] Pp. 743, 745.   [2] P. 744.   [3] P. 745.
[4] Pp. 743, 745.   [5] P. 754.

that the authority of consciousness is to be trusted ;
it is rather, in so far as it is sound, an assertion that
in some cases that authority is not required ;—that
certain of its utterances are intrinsically certain.

The third proof, like the first, is of too negative
a character to make it worth while discussing it at
any length : at the best, it only removes a hypothetical objection.

The fourth proof has been, I imagine, sufficiently
dealt with in the remarks made above in the course of
the discussion on the ordinary view of the argument
from common sense.[1]   Some additional observations
will be found in Mill's ' Examination,' p. 164.

The fifth argument has the peculiarity of not
only being intrinsically unsound, but of being so on
the evidence of Sir William Hamilton himself, given
a few pages previously.   On p. 754 he asserts that
to doubt the truth of consciousness when it testifies
to what he elsewhere calls a fact ' beyond its own
ideal existence,' is tantamount to ' believing that the
last ground of all belief is not to be believed, *which
is self-contradictory.*'   While, on p. 744, he assures
us truly enough that ' doubt does not in this case
. . . refute itself.   *It is not suicidal by self-contradiction.*'   If self-contradiction is suicidal, the vitality
of Sir William Hamilton's opinions on this particular point can hardly be such as to make any
lengthened discussion of them necessary.[2]

[1] See ante, p. 151.   [2] Vide Mill's *Examination of Hamilton*, p. 158.

These proofs, it will be recollected, are proofs at the second remove of judgments which, though they were originally pronounced to 'carry their own evidence' and to 'necessitate their own admission,' are many of them, in reality, open to doubt. We are first called upon to believe these truths on the authority of consciousness : and we are now called upon to believe the authority of consciousness on the strength of the five somewhat inadequate reasons.

But now the question arises, By what means are we to discover the judgments to which consciousness certifies ?   Instead, however, of answering this question, Sir William Hamilton answers quite another one, namely, What are the marks by which we may discover those judgments which are original ? Whence, it would appear, that he considers that all deliverances of consciousness are original judgments, and that all original judgments are deliverances of consciousness. Before examining what grounds he may have for such an opinion, I must say one word on the meaning of the word 'original,' round which much confusion has arisen in connection with this subject in the writings of more than one author.

The word 'original,' when applied to a belief or judgment, may be legitimately used in two senses, which are perfectly distinct, though they are not always distinguished, It may mean *either* that which stands first in order of logic, that which is a premiss, but not a conclusion, *or* that which stands first in order of time, that which (to put it more strictly), in the chain of phenomena governed by psychological laws, may be a cause, but is not a product. When it is said that all proof must finally rest on original propositions which are not themselves proved, the term is used in its first meaning : when it is said that 'necessity is a criterion which will enable us to distinguish an original datum of intelligence from a result of generalisation and custom,'[1] it is used in its second meaning. Mr. Mill, as will appear directly, habitually uses it in the second sense, and seemed to think that Hamilton did the same. In this, I think, he was mistaken. Hamilton used it, I believe, in both senses (though without distinguishing between them), and, on the whole, more frequently in the first sense than in the second.

On what grounds then (to return to our argument) does Sir William Hamilton identify our original judgments (according to either definition of the word 'original') with the deliverances of consciousness ? He gives no reason himself ; and as I know nothing but what can be gathered from his writings respecting the nature of that internal authority, not even the fact of its existence, I am unable to supply any. But this omission, it is evident, destroys the value of the whole argument from common sense. Grant that consciousness is shown to be trustworthy by the five arguments, and that original judgments

---

[1] Cf. Hamilton's *Lectures*, pp. 268, 270.

may be recognised by the four marks[1] enumerated
by Sir William Hamilton, how are we advanced,
unless we know that the original judgments are
identical with those which are certified by consciousness ? Perhaps I shall be told that their identity
follows from the definition of the terms employed—
that original judgments and deliverances of consciousness must *be* the same thing, because the two
expressions *mean* the same thing ; or to put it tech-
nically, that their *de*-notation cannot be different since
their *con*-notation is identical. If this really be so,
it is plain that Sir William Hamilton used one or
other of the terms 'consciousness' and 'original'
in an altogether different sense from that which I
have supposed. If we are to identify *in meaning*
'deliverance of consciousness' with what is properly
an original judgment, then consciousness cannot be
an authoritative faculty ; if, on the other hand, we
are to identify 'original judgment' with judgment
delivered by authority, then 'original judgment'
must signify something different from either *first in
logic*, or *first in causation.*

On the first of these suppositions, by which
consciousness is dethroned from its dignity, and
serves merely to furnish a general name for certain
of our convictions (those namely which are original),
I wish to know what is meant by such an assertion
as this—that consciousness assures us of, or gives

----

[1] *Dissertation*, p. 754.

testimony to, its own existence, and also to something beyond its own existence?[1]   If this is not language gratuitously metaphorical, it clearly implies that consciousness is an authority which can give us two kinds of information; information, namely, about itself, which Hamilton says we cannot doubt, and information about something else, which he tells us we can doubt.   What, again, is meant by telling us that 'the credibility of consciousness must be determined by the same maxims as the credibility of any other witness'[2] if consciousness be a mere fictitious unity?   And, finally, what plausibility remains in the reasons by which Hamilton tries to persuade us that consciousness is veracious?   If consciousness be an authority implanted in us for our guidance, there may be some reason (on the Theistic hypothesis of the universe) for supposing that it is inconsistent with the Divine veracity that it should be otherwise than trustworthy.   But what shadow of reason can there be for making the Deity specially responsible for certain beliefs solely because they do not happen to be produced by known psychological laws, or because no other reason for accepting them happens to be forthcoming?   And why are such laws to be presumed true till they are proved to be false, like the utterances of a respectable witness who has never been detected in an untruth?   These reasons are bad if the common

<hr>

[1] Cf. *Dissertation*, p. 745.   [2] P. 749.

sense philosophy is founded upon the existence of a single subjective authority ; but if it is not so founded, they cease, I think, even to be specious.

The difficulties on the opposite view of Hamilton's meaning are perhaps not less serious.   He never scruples to talk of fundamental beliefs,[1] primary beliefs,[2] original bases of knowledge,[3] original (as opposed to derivation) convictions,[4] &c., &c., when an argument founded solely upon the authority of consciousness would require him to talk of 'the deliverance of consciousness.'   And it is hardly conceivable that he should so far ignore the proper use of language as to employ all these terms, every one of which naturally implies originality in one of its two legitimate meanings, as *merely* signifying that which emanates from consciousness regarded as a subjective authority.

I believe, then, that in his exposition of the common sense philosophy there is an ambiguity ; but I further hold that this ambiguity is essential to the plausibility of that celebrated system, otherwise I should not have so long detained the reader over the matter.   The problem that Sir William Hamilton desired to solve was a perfectly legitimate one.   He found certain beliefs, those respecting the existence of our actual conscious state, which no sceptic had questioned.   He found others whose

[1] P. 743.

[2] P. 742.

[3] P. 743.

[4] P. 754.

truth it was scarcely less desirable to raise beyond suspicion, which scepticism had made, at least theoretically doubtful. What was to be done ? It seemed as impossible to find anything like a reason for these convictions as it was to give them up because no reason was forthcoming. The Kantian device for getting over the difficulty never seems to have been understood by him ; merely to say that the beliefs were innate was out of fashion since Locke ; nothing therefore was left but the scheme which I have just been considering. Ask a common sense philosopher of the Hamiltonian school *what* he believes, and he tells you that he believes all the original convictions of mankind ; ask him *why* he believes them, and he tells you that it is because they are deliverances of consciousness. It is because some of the original convictions of mankind are not, considered by themselves, beyond the reach of scepticism, that the authority of consciousness is invoked in their behalf ; it is because no mere reflection on the nature of that imaginary faculty can make known what are its deliverances, that it is necessary to take for granted that they are identical with the original convictions of mankind. Some of the confusion and ambiguity incident to Hamilton's exposition of the theory are therefore really necessary to its plausibility. If you improve his statement, you destroy his system— always supposing that his system is as I have represented it.   On this point, however, I admit I may have been mistaken.   Mr. Mill's version of it, which is very different, may be, after all, the correct one; and to this, which, strange to say, he not only attributed to Reid, to Hamilton, and to the philosophic world at large, but also fully accepted himself, I now address myself.

To many the last sentence of the preceding paragraph will seem a paradox.   That Mr. Mill, who has criticised the Hamiltonian theories at length, and who in the chapter devoted to the 'Common Sense Philosophy,' has declared that he and Hamilton differed on the most important question about which philosophers were divided, that he should really hold the philosophic opinions which he attributes to his opponent, may easily excite surprise.   It is, nevertheless, true.   He agreed with what he considered the philosophy of Hamilton to be; and where he differed from him was not on a point of philosophy, but on a question whose interest, which I admit to be great, is almost purely psychological.

His theory was this.   The premises[1] of all knowledge consist of immediate and intuitive beliefs. Some of these immediate and intuitive beliefs are those we have concerning our own actual subjective

---

[1] *Examination of Hamilton*, p. 151.

states :[1] but there are, or may be, others not less worthy of credit,[2] which are described as 'facts[3] which have been in consciousness from the beginning,' 'the original elements of mind,'[4] 'our original beliefs.'[5]   That these judgments, if they exist, are to be trusted he did not doubt himself, and he seemed to think that no other philosopher could have doubted.   The real difficulty arises, according to him, when the question comes to be discussed as to what these original beliefs are : and it was on this point that he thought the philosophic world was divided into two great parties, according as they pursued one or other of two methods, which he names respectively the *psychological* and the *introspective*.   The former of these consists in rejecting from among the list of apparently original beliefs all those to which the operation of the law of the association of ideas or (I presume) any other psychological law, would give an appearance of immediateness or necessity :   the latter, in accepting these attributes as conclusive proof that the convictions to which they belonged were part of the original furniture of the mind.

If the philosophic world really were divided mainly on this point, the small progress that philosophy has made would cease to be surprising.   For, in reality, the question is one chiefly of psychological

[1] P. 151.   [2] P. 172.   [3] P. 157.
[4] P. 173.   [5] P. 178.

interest, and has little direct bearing on philosophy properly understood.   As a matter of mere historic fact, I should be unwilling to admit that the marks by which original judgments are to be discerned have been universally considered the chief battle-ground of philosophy, though this is not the occasion on which to discuss the question.   I am rather concerned with discovering whether Mr. Mill's view of the foundation of knowledge, taken even in connection with the psychological method, can furnish any solid philosophical results.

But before doing so, or rather in order to do so effectively, it is necessary to determine in what sense he uses the word *consciousness*.   As we have seen, the ultimate beliefs which may or rather must be accepted with confidence are, according to him, of two kinds : the beliefs we have respecting our own actual mental states, and the beliefs, if any, which are part of the original furniture of the mind.   He frequently asserts that we hold both these kinds of belief on the authority of consciousness.   Are we then to attribute to him the theory which I have attributed to Sir William Hamilton—the theory, I mean, that consciousness is an internal witness which must be distinguished like other witnesses from the statements to which it certifies ?   I think not.   He used the language in this respect of the common sense philosophy, language sanctioned by general philosophic tradition ; but as the fiction suggested by it is not in any way necessary to his system, it will be more convenient to assume that he did not believe in it. The reason why an authoritative consciousness is a necessary part of the common sense philosophy is, as I have explained above, because the aim of that philosophy was to obtain proof for certain judgments about which scepticism is possible. Mr. Mill was of opinion that all original beliefs, if such exist, stand on the same level of certainty as our beliefs respecting our actual states of mind : and about these he was of opinion that scepticism was impossible. Now it is evidently superfluous to say that we believe that we feel cold because consciousness tells us that we feel cold. Even if these two statements asserted different things instead of, as they really do, the same thing, it is obvious that what in point of form appears here as the premiss can add nothing to the certainty of what in point of form appears here as the conclusion : and thus to adduce the testimony of consciousness in favour of anything which is as certain as our immediate feelings must always be superfluous. Moreover, it is not, according to Mr. Mill, *consciousness* whose authority is thus indisputable, whatever occasional phrases may imply to the contrary, but only consciousness 'in its pristine purity,' [1] 'before its original revelations have been overlaid :' consciousness in its developed, and therefore corrupted condition, being

[1] P. 171.

capable apparently of any amount of deception. So
that if we are to credit him with the 'independent
authority' theory of consciousness, besides all the
other difficulties in the way of that theory which
have been, or might be, enumerated, he would have
to overcome the presumption which Sir William
Hamilton says [1] must lie against any witness detected in error ;—*falsus in uno, falsus in omnibus.* If,
in addition to all these objections, it is recollected that
the theistic or teleological assumption, which really
lies at the root of the common sense philosophy, was
wholly foreign to Mr. Mill's modes of thought, it
will be admitted, I think, that I am not illegitimately
improving the substance of his teaching if I venture
always to describe as 'original beliefs' or 'judgments,' what he occasionally calls the 'revelations
of consciousness,' *or* the 'genuine' or 'original deliverances of consciousness.'

The nature of his theory being thus determined,
let us next turn to the question of its value.

'Could we try the experiment' of the first consciousness in any infant,' says Mr. Mill,[2] 'its first
reception of the impression we call external, whatever was present in that first consciousness would be
the genuine testimony of consciousness" (*i.e.*, would,
as I should say, be an *original judgment*), 'and
would be as much entitled to credit, indeed there
would be as little possibility of discrediting it, as our

<hr>

[1] *Dissertation on Reid*, p. 746.   [2] P. 179.

sensations themselves. But we have no means of now ascertaining by direct evidence whether we were conscious of outward and external objects when we first opened our eyes to the light. That a belief or knowledge of such objects is in our consciousness now whenever we use our eyes or muscles, is no reason for concluding that it was there from the beginning, until we have settled the question whether it was brought in since. If any mode can be pointed out in which within the compass of possibility it might have been brought in, the hypothesis must be examined and disproved before we are entitled to conclude that the conviction is an original deliverance of consciousness. The proof that any of the alleged Universal Beliefs, or Principles of Common Sense, are affirmations of consciousness, supposes two things : that the beliefs exist, and that there are no means by which they could have been acquired.'

From this very remarkable extract, which contains explicitly or implicitly the whole psychological theory of ultimate beliefs I have just endeavoured to explain, it is clear, as I before stated, that a belief may be either of the highest conceivable certainty, or of no certainty at all, according as it *has* or *has not* been in consciousness from the beginning : *i.e.*, according to whether pyschological laws *have not* or *have* been concerned in its production. The grounds, however, on which this very singular doctrine is based are not so plain. Why are our earliest beliefs elevated to this exceptional dignity? Why are we to regard infants as (at least potentially) occupying the place in matters of reason which Councils and Popes have claimed in matters of faith? And if infants are to be credited with this unerring insight into the mysteries which have puzzled philosophers, are we to deny the same gift to the lower animals? And if we are, why are we?

These are some of the first questions which the pyschological theory suggests; but they are by no means the only ones. Beliefs which have been the product of pyschological laws—association of ideas, and so forth—are, it appears, on a much lower level of certainty than those which have not been so produced. But why has the action of those pyschological laws so much more pernicious an effect upon their products than the operation of any other laws? Mr. Mill and the thinkers of his school would be the last persons to deny that the most original of all beliefs, those which have been in consciousness since conciousness was, are still produced by *some* laws. Why are these laws so much more fortunate in their operation than those which, by a conventional classification, are regarded as specially mental, that we may regard their results as having attained 'the certainty which we call perfect.'[1] I cannot tell, and neither Mr. Mill nor the great body of philosophers

[1] P. 152.

which according to him shares his opinion on this point, appear willing or able to do so.

Now let us turn for a moment from the consideration of how we know that beliefs which are original are specially certain, to the question of how we come to know in the first instance that they are original. In their mode of dealing with this problem lay, in Mr. Mill's opinion, the special glory of the school to which he belonged. It consisted, he thought, in adapting to pyschology 'the known and approved methods of physical science,'[1] and more particularly in bringing to light the original elements of consciousness 'as residual phenomena, by a previous study of the modes of generation of the mental facts which are not original.'[2] Against this 'pyschological method,' when confined to pyschology, I have not a word to say. I am perfectly ready to admit that it has all the merits which may appertain to the 'known and approved methods of physical science'; but what I wish to point out is, that though it may give us a pyschology, it can never give us a philosophy. In the first place, the known and approved methods of physical science unfortunately take for granted most of the judgments which it is the pressing business of philosophy to establish, and which therefore, it is evident, cannot be proved by that method without arguing in a circle. In the second place, even if these scientific assumptions were established by some

[1] P. 173.   [2] Ibid.

other means, still no belief shown by this method to be original can be ultimate *for us*, simply because the fact is one that *has* to be shown. Grant that it is original, and then, may be, ' there would be as little possibility of discrediting it as our sensations themselves '; but as we can never know that it was original without a previous argument, the fact, if fact it be, does not help us much nearer to the foundations of a creed. To Mr. Mill's hypothetical baby no doubt its first impressions may supply a solid ground of belief. But to us who have to arrive at a knowledge of what these are by the laborious use of the ' approved methods of physical science,' this circumstance is, philosophically speaking, of small value, and can afford us but little consolation.

There seem, therefore, to be three fatal objections to a philosophy founded upon the authority of original beliefs. In the first place, there is no ground for supposing that original beliefs are particularly fitted to serve as the foundation of a creed; in the second place, there is no ground for supposing that acquired beliefs are particularly unsuited for such a purpose; and, in the third place, it is impossible to determine what beliefs are original and what are acquired without assuming the truth of many propositions whose only evidence can on this theory be that they *are* original.

I shall, perhaps, be told that though Mr. Mill attaches in theory this absolute certitude to our original beliefs, yet that in practice he supposed himself to require as a foundation for his inferred beliefs no immediate knowledge but that which the mind has of its own states.   I admit the fact, but I deny that it is any defence.   It relieves him, no doubt, from the charge of practically committing the logical error pointed out in my third objection, but at the cost of falling into one of greater magnitude still.   He cannot be accused of founding his creed on judgments proved by the psychological method to be original, and therefore true, simply because the psychological method, in his opinion, showed that no judgments *are* original.   His philosophy of ultimate beliefs, therefore, was not only unsound, but if sound it would have been useless.   My complaint against him, however, does not end there.   That the philosophy which he speculatively maintained should be incapable of solving the problems which most press for solution is bad, but it is worse that the philosophy to which he adhered in practice should ignore the very existence of these problems.   And here I think Sir William Hamilton is greatly his superior.   The Common Sense Philosophy, whatever be its shortcomings, and they are many, was at all events constructed with a view to our actual necessities.   It recognised, in a more or less confused manner, the fact that most of the judgments whose truth we habitually assume are not beyond the reach of scepticism ; that some sort of proof for them is

therefore required, and that none of the usual proofs
from experience are sound. The hypothesis of a
consciousness whose veracity is in some way involved in that of the Deity, and which shall give its
testimony in their favour, is not one perhaps very
well calculated to stand hostile criticism, but at any
rate, if true, it would go some way towards solving
the difficulty. To the psychological school, on the
other hand, it hardly seems to have occurred that
there was a difficulty to be solved. Their psychology so overshadows their philosophy that when
they have once discovered to their satisfaction how
a thing came to be believed, they seem comparatively
indifferent as to the more important questions of how
far, and why, it ought to be believed. If only they
can apply the 'approved methods of physical science'
to the discovery of the genesis of mental phenomena,
they take a very optimistic view of the difficulties
which attach to the proof of the principles on which
the legitimate application of the 'approved methods'
must finally depend. One example of their easy
acceptance of insufficient proof I have already discussed when I was dealing with the law of Universal
Causation. A still more remarkable case of ignoring
difficulties remains to be treated of in the criticism
which follows on the psychological theory of the
external world.

CHAPTER IX.

PSYCHOLOGICAL IDEALISM.

BERKELEIAN Idealism is of all speculative theories concerning the external world the one which, perhaps, most quickly and easily commends itself to the philosophic enquirer. The greater number of persons who dabble in such subjects have been idealists at one period of their lives if they have not remained so ; and many more, who would not call themselves idealists, are nevertheless of opinion that though the existence of matter is a thing to be believed in, it is not a thing which it is possible to prove. The causes of this popularity are, no doubt, in part, the extreme simplicity of the reasoning on which the theory rests, in part its extreme plausibility, in part, perhaps, the nature of the result which is commonly thought to be speculatively interesting without being practically inconvenient. For it has to be observed, that the true idealist is not necessarily of opinion that his system, properly understood, in any way contradicts common sense. It destroys, no doubt, a belief in substance ; but then substance is a meta-physical phantom conjured up by a vain philosophy :

the Matter of ordinary life it supposes itself to leave untouched. 'That the things I see with my eyes and touch with my hands do exist, really exist, I make not the least question. The only thing whose existence we deny is that which philosophers call Matter, or corporeal substance. And in doing of this there is no damage done to the rest of mankind, who, I daresay, will never miss it.'[1] 'I affirm, with confidence,' says Mr. Mill, 'that this conception (*i.e.*, the idealistic one) of matter includes the whole meaning attached to it by the common world, apart from philosophical and sometimes from theological, theories.'[2]

But though idealist philosophers have said this, the world has never believed them. Plain men have continued to think that something more is in question than a metaphysical invention, about which they neither know nor care anything ; and that in losing substance they would lose something essential to their idea of the scheme of the universe.

This is an opinion which I also share ; and it is to Idealism considered from this point of view, and this point of view alone, that I wish to direct the reader's attention in this chapter. There are, therefore, at least, two important controversies connected with this theory which I shall not discuss. I shall not discuss either the real nature of the object of

---

[1] Berkeley, *Principles of Human Knowledge*, Part i. § 35.
[2] *Examination of Hamilton*, p. 227.

perception, which is what especially occupied Berkeley, nor the psychological account of the origin of
our belief in matter, which is what especially
interested Mr. Mill. I am prepared, for the sake of
argument, to assume, with the former, that we know
and can know directly only our own ideas and sensations,[1] and with the latter that any belief in the
existence of an external reality which is neither a
sensation nor a possibility of sensation, is the product
of the laws of the association of ideas. There is also
a third subject which I shall absolve myself from
dealing with—I mean the constructive side of Berkeley's philosophy. As is well known, he replaced
the material world by the Divine Mind; and found
in this the permanent substance which ordinary men
sought for in matter. But though this theory is as
good as many which have succeeded it, yet it does
not fulfil the conditions which limit the discussions
in this essay : it has had no appreciable influence on
the current of modern English speculation. I shall,
therefore, put this on one side, and shall confine my
criticisms to the Idealistic Theory, on what may be
called its negative or destructive side.

The thesis I wish to maintain is a very simple
one, and it is this :—Received science cannot be true
if the idealistic account of the universe be accurate :
nor is the discrepancy between the two merely
verbal ; it is fundamental and essential, and can be

---

[1] Berkeley usually describes them both as 'ideas.'

bridged over by no mere artifices of terminology. That there is a verbal discrepancy requires, I imagine, no proof.   Natural science (of which alone I am here speaking) assumes the independent existence of matter in all its utterances.   A theory which denies this independent existence is undoubtedly therefore in *primâ facie* contradiction with Natural science ; and the question we have to determine is, whether under this superficial contradiction there is or is not a real and substantial harmony.   Now we must beware of confounding with this question another with which it is liable to be mixed up—namely, whether Idealism is or is not consistent with our ordinary experience. If we admit the legitimacy of the ideal psychology— if we admit that objects as perceived may be resolved into ideas or sensations, there is no doubt that this last question must be answered in the affirmative. That is, we may suppose Idealism to be true without being obliged to suppose that we should either see, hear, or feel under any circumstances what we should not see, hear, or feel if independent matter existed.

Supposing, therefore, that Science consisted in nothing more than a series of propositions asserting what, under given conditions, our experience would be, there might be no fundamental discord between it and Idealism.   If, for example, as Berkeley declares,[1] 'the question whether the earth moves or no, amounts in reality to no more than this to wit,

---

[1] *Principles of Human Knowledge,* § 58.

"whether we have reason to conclude from what has been observed by astronomers, that if we were placed in such and such a position and distance both from the earth and sun we should perceive the former to move,"[1] &c., no doubt astronomy and the theory under discussion might easily be harmonised. But in truth Science does much more than this. It tells us not only what we should perceive if we were rightly circumstanced to perceive it, but also how it comes about that we should perceive that particular thing and no other, and what it is that would happen or has happened whether we or anybody else were there to perceive it or not. It tells us that perceiving organisms were evolved from a world which was itself neither perceiving nor perceived, and that processes take place within that world which, like the elements of which it is composed, are too subtle to be apprehended by sense, or even, in some cases, to be represented in imagination. In short, it asserts the existence of a vast machinery, composed of that 'inert, senseless, extended, solid, figured, moveable substance existing without the mind,' which Berkeley declares[1] to be a contradiction in terms, and which causes, among an infinite number of other effects, our perception of itself.

If this be not in direct irreconcilable contradiction with a theory which asserts the existence of no causes besides spirits and no effects besides ideas,

[1] *Principles of Human Knowledge*, § 67.

then such a thing as contradiction does not exist in the world. But if (which I hardly think) any reader is still unconvinced on this point, let him try to state the doctrine of Evolution in ideal language—without of course postulating the Deity, whom Berkeley would have introduced to save the situation. The attempt will, I think, leave no doubt on his mind that Mr. Spencer is right when he declares that ' if Idealism be true, Evolution ' (for *Evolution* we may read *Science*) ' is a dream.'

Perhaps it will be objected that in these remarks I have only dealt with Psychological Idealism in the form in which Berkeley left it ; and that I have not done justice to it even in this shape, since I have omitted to consider all the constructive part which, though it has received little attention subsequently, its originator considered essential to his scheme. I am quite prepared to admit that there is some force in these criticisms, and also that Berkeley's version of the system is the less likely to be in harmony with Science, from the fact that he seems to have regarded the scientific hypothesis of his own day—the ' corpuscular philosophy ' and ' the mechanical principles which have been applied to accounting for phenomena,'—with a very lukewarm approval.[1] Let us turn then to Mr. Mill, who is above all things the philosopher of men of science, and observe whether his statement of the

<hr>

[1] *Principles of Human Knowledge*, § 50.

case is more agreeable to ordinary science than that
of his theological predecessor. At first sight there
seems a promise of reconciliation in his language, for
verbally at least, he recognises the existence of a
permanent something which may serve as a substitute for matter. The external world which is
dealt with by natural science consisted, according to
Berkeley, in ideas. According to Mr. Mill it consists of sensations and permanent possibilities of sensation.[1] An object when it is perceived may be
resolved into sensations *plus* permanent possibilities
of sensation ; an object when it is *not* perceived may
be resolved into permanent possibilities of sensation
alone.

What sensations mean is tolerably plain, whether
the partial resolution of a perceived object into them
be legitimate or not. But what are possibilities of
sensation ? And in what sense can they be permanent ? Mr. Mill habitually speaks of them as if
they could exist in the same sense in which positive
entities exist. But this surely is an entire delusion.
A possibility *is* nothing till it becomes an actuality.
It *will* be something, or it *may* be something at some
future time, but, until then, it is nothing. You may
verbally indeed give a kind of present being to a
future sensation by saying that the possibility of it
exists now. But there is no reality in nature corresponding to this phrase. A sensation must either be

---

[1] *Examination of Hamilton*, p. 248.

or not be; and if it is only a possibility, it certainly
is *not*. A universe therefore which consists of such
possibilities is a universe which for the present does
not exist at all; it is a verbal fiction, and cannot
form the subject-matter of any science deserving the
name.

Mr. O'Hanlon, whose criticism on Mill, unfortunately, I only know from the note in Mill's ' Examination,' from which the following extract is taken,
states the difficulty in these terms : ' Your permanent possibilities of sensation are, so long as they
are not felt, nothing actual. Yet you speak of change
taking place in them, and that independently of
our consciousness ' ;[1] and it is evident, though this
Mr. O'Hanlon does not add, that unless change
in something outside consciousness be possible,
science, as we know it, cannot exist. How does
Mr. Mill meet this objection? He refers ' his
young antagonist' generally to what is said on the
subject in the text; from which, as far as I am
able to judge, the following quotation may be most
conveniently selected as containing the essence of
what Mr. Mill would have us understand to be
his answer. ' If body altogether is only conceived
as a power of exciting sensations, the action of one
body upon another is simply the modification by one
such power of the sensations excited by another ; or,
to use a different expression, the joint action of two

---

[1] *Examination of Hamilton*, p. **251**, *note*.

powers of exciting sensations.   It is easy for anyone
competent to such enquiries who will make the
attempt, to understand how one group of possibilities of sensation can be conceived as destroying
or modifying another such group.'   Undoubtedly it
is easy to understand this, if by possibility of sensation is meant (as the first sentence in the above
extract would seem to show) *power of exciting sensation*.   But if Mr. Mill meant this, he was not an
idealist, but a realist.   He must have held that
besides sensations there were permanent powers of
producing sensations—inaccurately described as permanent possibilities of sensation—which are to be
distinguished, if they are to be distinguished at all,
by very subtle differences from the 'substances' of
certain metaphysicians.   As, however, there can be
no doubt that Mr. Mill considered himself an idealist,
we must suppose that he adopted this realistic theory
only under the pressure of an immediate objection ;
and that in his ordinary moments he conceived that
the 'permanence' of a possibility might satisfy the
requirements of Science since it was a permanence,
and the requirements of Idealism since it was only
the permanence of a possibility.   Let us look a little
more into this matter.

If we say that a barrel of gunpowder constitutes
the permanent possibility of an explosion, what do
we mean ?   We mean that in a barrel of gunpowder
we find a large number of the conditions of an explo-

sion in a permanent form, and that the other conditions necessary to that effect may at any moment be supplied. It is perfectly accurate to talk of a permanent possibility of sensation in the same sense ; as equivalent, that is, to a set of permanent causes of sensation by which, when they are properly supplemented by causes which are not permanent, but only occasional, a sensation will actually be produced. But though Science may be consistent with a belief in a world composed of such possibilities, the teaching of Idealism certainly is not.

Again, the permanence attributed to the possibilities of sensation might be a permanence—not of the conditions by which sensations are produced but— of the laws which regulate their production. If we conceive a being whose states of mind at successive moments should occur strictly in accordance with law, but *with law acting only between his states of mind,* we might, perhaps, say (though the expression would not be a happy one) that a given law constitutes a 'permanent possibility' of his having a particular sensation. But a theory, which should admit the existence of nothing permanent except in this sense, though it would be entirely consistent with Idealism, would unfortunately be altogether at variance with Science.

'For any statement,' says Mr. Mill,[1] 'which can be made concerning material phenomena in terms of the Realistic theory, there is an equivalent meaning

____

[1] *Examination of Hamilton,* p. 246.

in terms of sensation and possibilities of sensation.' Let us see how this is.   Here is a proposition which may prove convenient for purposes of illustration :— ' The candle at which I am looking produces in me certain sensations of light, colour, and shape.'[1] Stated in terms of the Psychological Theory this proposition would run :—' The group of sensation and of permanent possibilities of sensation known as a candle produce in me certain sensations of light, &c.'   Now the candle, which is here asserted to be a cause, is, like other perceived objects, constituted (on the Psychological hypothesis) by two elements—viz. sensations and possibilities of sensation.   Are both of these necessary to produce the effect? Certainly not. One of them *is* the effect.   The sensations which the candle produces are part of the candle.   What produces the sensations must, therefore, be the other part of the cause—namely, the possibilities of sensation.   But the possibilities of sensation are, *ipso facto*, not in my consciousness, and (to avoid side issues) we may suppose them not to be in anybody else's either. So that, though starting from a proposition professedly idealistic in its terms, we are forced to conclude that the cause of my sensation of colour, &c., is something out of, and independent of consciousness !

This may be true, but, again, I must point out that it is not Idealism.   On the contrary, it is a kind

---

[1] Of course I am not responsible for the psychology which renders such an expression as ' sensation of shape ' permissible.

of Transfigured Realism (as Mr. Spencer would say), of a particularly absurd type. For we might imagine a being so endowed that he could perceive at one moment every quality of the candle, which would in that case, it is evident, consist entirely of sensations ; the possibilities of sensation being all converted into actualities. He might also perceive all the physiological changes which are the necessary antecedents of these sensations, and which would thereby in the same way become sensations themselves. Now it would clearly be erroneous to say of such a being that the immediate causes of the sensations which constitute his perception of the candle were permanent possibilities of sensation (since by hypothesis the possibilities are all converted into actualities) ; and it would clearly be absurd to say that these sensations were self caused ; and it would be altogether impossible to say that they were not caused at all. What fourth reply could be given on any theory which was both idealistic and scientific I am unable to imagine. So that we come to this final result : that if we take a plain scientific proposition asserting the action of external bodies, or what are commonly thought to be such, on mind, we can, in the first place, only express it in terms of possibilities of sensation by attributing to these a realistic signification ; and in the second place if, as we have a perfect right to do, we conceive such possibilities of sensation all converted into actualities, we cannot express the proposition in terms of the psychological theory at all.

'But,' the reader may, perhaps, be inclined to say, 'these difficulties are just what might have been expected. The various renderings of the original proposition are all absurd, because that proposition was an absurd one to start with.' Extremely absurd I admit, if Idealism be true; but not at all absurd, if Science be so. And that is just the point. Science cannot get on for an hour unless it be allowed to employ propositions of this kind, which assert the action of some x upon the mind. Idealism, in the hands of a true follower of Berkeley, would either deny the existence of the x, or would identify it with the Divine Spirit; and in both cases would make received Science impossible. Natural Realism again would identify the x both with the immediate object of perception and with independent and extended matter, and, like all other realistic systems, would present, at any rate, an appearance of harmony with Scientific doctrine. But when we ask the Psychological school how they deal with the x, we can extract from their teaching nothing but confusion. They give us to understand that they are idealists, that in their opinion the world consists of nothing besides sensations and possibilities of sensation; and we readily accept this as the true idealistic identification of the *real* with the *felt*. But on asking how this identification is consistent with a science which nominally at least postulates a world independent of mind, we find that they are forced to convert their

possibilities into objects which exist without being
perceived, which can act as causes, which can suffer
change, and which are therefore as little ideal as the
most vehement realist need desire.

'But how,' it may be asked, ' if there is this radical
discrepancy between Idealism and Science, happens
it that so many philosophers have accepted the first,
and yet have never cast speculative doubts upon the
second ?   How do you account for the fact that
neither Berkeley nor Mill (to go no further) ever
detected a difficulty which, if it exists at all, is
sufficiently obvious ? ' One reason of this oversight I
take to be that Idealists have occupied themselves
more with showing that their particular system was
consistent with ordinary experience than that it was
consistent with the more remote conclusions of
Science.   The sort of objection which they chiefly
anticipated, and with reason, was that of the persons
who thought that a disbelief in matter ought to
take the form of running up against posts or tumbling
into the water ; and so much of this objection depends on a gross misconception, that the grain of
truth which lies hid in it is easily overlooked.

I have already pointed out two further reasons
which, in the case of Berkeley, go far towards
accounting for his insensibility to a difficulty with
which he several times formally professes to deal.
The first is, that his scientific beliefs were certainly
lukewarm, and probably heterodox ; the second is,

that his theology supplied the basis of a possible, though not of any actual, science of phenomena, by providing a permanent thinking substance in place of the matter which he destroyed. In Mr. Mill's case neither of these reasons hold good. His scientific faith was fervent and orthodox ; while it is generally understood that his theological creed, whatever may have been its precise nature, did not at all events include a belief in an Infinite Mind who should be the immediate cause of all our sensations.

Mr. Mill, however, had sources of error peculiar to himself. As I stated in the last chapter, one of the disturbing elements in his philosophy, which no doubt largely affected his views on this particular subject, was the overpowering interest he took in the *genesis* of a belief to the exclusion of a thorough examination into its *truth*. Thus the main part of the space devoted (in his ' Examination of Hamilton ') to the Psychological theory of the external world is occupied, not with discussing the general philosophic ground and bearings of Idealism, but in showing how a belief in matter originally came into existence. But, besides this more general cause of error, there was another special to this question which Mr. Mill should not have fallen into, since it is one of a kind he was particularly fond of preaching against—I mean the error of supposing that because there exists in language a name, that therefore there must exist in Nature something corresponding to the name.   Because it is allowable to speak of a 'permanent possibility,' he permitted himself too easily to think that a world consisting of possibilities of sensation and these alone, could in any real sense be permanent, or, as I should prefer to say, persistent. That this is not so has been sufficiently shown, I hope, in the preceding pages.   It, therefore, only remains for those who accept Idealism as the one possible theory of the material world consistent with Psychological analysis, to choose between the results of Internal and those of External observation on the one hand, or on the other boldly to adopt a creed which is avowedly inconsistent with itself.

In the next two chapters I shall examine, so far as it is necessary for my purpose, the philosophy of a thinker, who though in a popular discourse he is frequently associated with Mr. Mill on the points with which I am concerned, resembles him but little in his teaching.

CHAPTER X.

THE TEST OF INCONCEIVABILITY.

MR. SPENCER's theory of the grounds of belief, like that of Sir William Hamilton, is intimately bound up with, and seems chiefly constructed with a view to the proof of, the reality of the external world.   For the moment, however, I shall deal with it separately, reserving till the next section any reflections which may be suggested by the use he has put it to in supporting the doctrine of what he calls, not inappropriately, ' Transfigured Realism.'

Sir William Hamilton, as we have seen, accepts his initial assumptions on the authority of Consciousness.   Mr. Mill again expresses his readiness to accept any belief which can be shown to have been ' in Consciousness from the beginning ' ; though until that (in his opinion apparently) improbable event occurs, is content to base his creed on the immediate knowledge the mind has of its own states ; and in practice, therefore, is truly an empiricist.   But Mr. Spencer, though anxious that it should be understood that he defends his doctrine in the interests of the experience hypothesis,[1] can hardly be described as

[1] *Principles of Psychology*, vol. ii. p. 407, note.

an empiricist in any but an esoteric signification of the word ; since even for facts given in experience he requires a warrant, which must be more certain than they are, because it is the test by which their certainty is recognised.

All propositions are to be accepted as unquestionable whose negative is inconceivable.[1] Such, in one sentence, is Mr. Spencer's doctrine ; but the sentence, though apparently simple, is capable of more than one interpretation, and points to more than one possible system of philosophy. ' Inconceivable,' to begin with, is commonly, though in my opinion very improperly, used in two quite distinct senses. It may mean either that which cannot be believed, or that which cannot be imagined. Mr. Spencer[2] protests against the idea that he uses it in the first or improper sense ; and, if I understand him rightly, he habitually uses it in the second and correct one. But as the point is somewhat important, I must be permitted to give one or two of the quotations on which this opinion is based.

' An inconceivable proposition is one of which the terms cannot by any effort be brought into consciousness in that relation which the proposition asserts between them.'[3] It is one of which ' the subject and predicate cannot be united in the same intuition.'[4] And as an example, ' the two sides (of

---

[1] *Principles of Psychology*, vol. ii. p. 392.   [2] Ibid. p. 407.
[3] P. 408.   [4] Ibid.

a triangle) cannot be represented in consciousness as becoming equal in their joint length to the third side, without the representation of a triangle being destroyed.' These quotations, which might easily be multiplied, would seem to make it perfectly clear that when Mr. Spencer says a thing cannot be conceived, he means that it cannot be imagined or re-presented in the mind ; indeed the world 'imagine' is one which he actually uses in this connection.[1] On the other hand, it must be admitted that he never [2] hesitates to use 'inconceivable' and 'unthink-able' as synonymes ; so that, if I interpret him rightly, 'unthinkable' and 'unimaginable' must with him be also synonymes, which is not in accordance with the best philosophical usage. Again, he quotes, in order to answer, the hackneyed instance of the inconceivability of the antipodes—as if he thought that the antipodes had once been inconceivable in his sense of the word. But it is certain, I appre-hend, that the antipodes were never unimaginable, though they were, or are said to have been, incre-dible. The difficulty can scarcely have been to represent men standing head downwards, though it might have been to believe that, when so standing, they would not fall off.[3]   Mr. Spencer's use of the

---

[1] *Fortnightly Review*, p. 544.

[2] *Principles of Psychology*, vol. ii. p. 409.

[3] Mr. Mill is not fortunate in his language on this point ; though I am inclined to think he held the right view. See *Exam. of Hamilton*, pp. 81, 86.

word 'inconceivable' is not then, in spite of all his explanations, perfectly unambiguous ; but neverthe-less we may say with certainty that the word with him refers to some mental incapacity which (he asserts) is not an incapacity of belief, and with a high degree of probability, that it is an incapacity of imagination or representation.

After this explanation, let us return to the doctrine under discussion, which states, it will be recollected, that all judgments the negative of which is inconceivable are to be accepted as true. Now, according to this theory, Is the inconceivability of its negative the ground on which any proposition ought to be accepted, or is it simply an attribute which in fact belongs to self-evident propositions and to no others ?   Is it a reason, or is it merely a mark ? It will be observed that the whole nature of Mr. Spencer's philosophy must entirely depend on which of these alternatives he selects   If he selects the second, then it would only remain to examine all the ultimate propositions on which his creed rests, and to observe whether it is true that the negative of each one of them is inconceivable.   But even if the result of this examination were to show (as I appre-hend it would show) that the negative of some of them might be conceived with the utmost facility, this would in no way tend to invalidate the grounds on which the remainder of his creed rests ; it would simply show that those grounds had been wrongly described.   If, on the other hand, he selects the first alternative, and means to assert that the inconceivability of their negative is the ultimate *reason* which is to be given for all his beliefs, then, if it can be shown that this is in reality no reason, the beliefs themselves must, so far as he is concerned, be regarded as *requiring* proof, but not as having *obtained it.*

There are, I think, some phrases used by Mr. Spencer, especially in the earlier version of his argument, which might lead one for a moment to suppose that he held to the second of these alternatives.   Nevertheless, I shall assume that the first represents his real opinion, because otherwise it is evident that his Universal Postulate or ultimate criterion of truth could never be brought forward as an argument at all.   If the inconceivability of the opposite is merely an attribute which is thought to attach itself to those ultimate beliefs which neither have nor require proof, the discovery of its absence in certain cases will affect no belief except the one which asserted its universal presence.   It can, therefore, never supply an ultimate ground of conviction, and sinks into a fact of secondary philosophic interest.

We must credit Mr. Spencer then with holding the first alternative, which, as the following quotations may serve to indicate, undoubtedly fits in naturally and easily with his habitual language.   ‘To

assert,' [1] he says, 'the inconceivableness of the negative (of a cognition), is at the same time to assert
the psychological necessity we are under of thinking
it, *and to give our logical justification for holding it.*'
Again,[2] 'How do we know that it is impossible for
the same thing to be and not to be? What is our
criterion of this impossibility? Can Sir William
Hamilton assign any other than this same inconceivability?'

Here, it will be observed, we have a general
statement of the theory, with a particular example
of its application; and from a consideration of these
and of other passages, too long to quote, it would
seem that Mr. Spencer regards our incapacity to
perform a certain mental act as the ultimate ground
on which all propositions, even those asserting truths
commonly thought to be necessary, are finally to be
accepted.

This mental act, I have already given reasons for
thinking, is one of imagination or representation;
but not to enter into unnecessary controversy, I will
describe it in Mr. Spencer's own words as consisting in 'tearing[3] asunder states of consciousness.' If
this operation cannot be performed—if the states of
consciousness persist in cohering, in spite of our
efforts to disunite them, then, according to Mr.
Spencer, we have not only the highest warrant which

---

[1] Page 407, the italics are my own.   [2] Page 425.
[3] *Fortnightly Review*, p. 544.

it is possible to attain for supposing that the attributes represented by these states of consciousness coexist in nature, but we have also the highest warrant which, constructed as we are, it is possible to imagine.[1]

If this be so, our prospects of discovering a satisfactory philosophy seem small.   In what possible way can a psychological fact—whether it consists in attempting to 'tear asunder states of consciousness,' or in anything else—afford a satisfactory warrant for some other fact, unless we first take for granted a very large number of propositions for which a warrant is very much needed?   Why should we assume this pre-established harmony between the 'subjective' and the 'objective' world?   Grant either some theological postulate, or some law of inherited aptitudes, and the harmony may cease to be surprising; but these are hypotheses which it is needless to say cannot themselves afford a warrant until they first obtain it.   Nor is this all.   Not only is the mental incapacity to 'tear asunder states of consciousness' no 'logical justification' for holding a belief, but, on Mr. Spencer's own principles, a belief in the incapacity would appear to require a 'logical justification' itself.   We are supposed by his theory to believe that 'it is impossible for the same thing to be and not to be,'[2] on the ground that we cannot conceive the opposite.   But how do we know that we

<hr>

[1] *Psychology*, p. 425.   [2] Ibid.

cannot conceive the opposite ?   Is this a belief which requires a warrant, or is it not ?   If it *is*, then the warrant must be that we cannot conceive that we can conceive the opposite ; and as this belief and all its successors will also require similar warrants, we are committed to an infinite regress.   If, on the other hand, it *is not* a belief which requires a warrant, then I desire to know why the belief that ' it is impossible for the same thing to be and not to be' requires one ? I am quite as certain that it *is* impossible, as I am that I cannot conceive it to be possible ; and if I am not expected to give a ' logical justification ' for the second of these beliefs, I see no reason why I should be expected to give one for the first.

On Mr. Spencer's own principle, indeed, the mental fact that we cannot conceive the opposite of a given proposition, in the only case in which, according to him, it can serve as a final ground of certainty, is not one of which we can have any immediate knowledge.   Only, it appears, when the proposition whose opposite is inconceivable happens also to be undecomposable,[1] can we say with assurance that it must be true.   So that before applying his postulate to the proof of some axiom (say ' that things which are equal to the same thing are equal to one another '[2]) we have to convince ourselves, *first*, that this is a proposition not capable of further decomposition ; and, *secondly*, that we are unable to con-

---

[1] *Psychology*, p. 410.   [2] Ibid. p. 411.

ceive its opposite. Surely the scepticism which is set at rest by such arguments as these must be of a very peculiar complexion ; for it must doubt that things which are equal to the same thing are equal to one another, and be certain of logical and psychological facts, not to my mind very easy to determine, and respecting which, by Mr. Spencer's own account, men have frequently been in error.

These objections, it will be observed, keep their weight whatever the nature of the psychological incapacity may be which Mr. Spencer describes as an 'inability to conceive the opposite' of a proposition. Though there is, as I before hinted, some obscurity hanging over this point, there can be little doubt that, at all events, the incapacity is, as has been hitherto assumed, one of imagination or representation. What seems more doubtful is whether Mr. Spencer does not suppose it to be this and at the same time something else from which it ought carefully to be distinguished. Much of his language suggests the idea that, in his opinion, necessities of imagination are not merely accompaniments of, or causes of, necessities of belief, but are actually the same thing, and that the representation of the attributes in one image is actually identical with the act of believing that two attributes are united in one object. He says, for instance,[1] 'An abortive effort to conceive the negation of a proposition, shows that

---

[1] *Psychology*, p. 425. Italics are my own. Cf. also p. 402.

the cognition expressed is one of which the predicate
invariably exists along with the subject [that is, I
suppose, shows that we cannot conceive them dis-
united] ; *and the discovery that the predicate invariably exists along with its object is the discovery that
this cognition is one we are compelled to accept.'*   And
again, in the very act of distinguishing between inconceivability and incredibility he seems to suggest
the idea that they differ in degree and not in kind.[1]
If the strange psychological doctrine thus adum-
brated is really Mr. Spencer's, he is no doubt
justified on his own principles in asserting that any
proposition of which the opposite is inconceivable
must be believed, because inconceivable with him
must mean not only that which is unimaginable, but
also, and at the same time, that which is absolutely
and in the extremest degree incredible.   In truth,
however, his philosophy gains nothing by a confusion
which (if it be his) is a serious blot on his psychology.   The statement that we are absolutely incapable of believing the opposite of a proposition may
carry with it the assurance that we *must* believe it,
for in reality the two expressions are equivalent ; but
I altogether fail to see how it can show us that we
ought to believe it.   I doubt myself, indeed, whether
it is possible to try to believe the opposite of an
axiom in the sense in which it is possible to try to
imagine the state of things opposite to that which it

---

[1] Page 408.

asserts. I doubt, for example, whether we can seriously try to believe that a thing can both be and not be, though some sort of attempt to imagine a space at the same time filled and not filled by an object might possibly be made. But however this may be, it is certain that the incapacity to believe one thing, though it may constitute a 'psychological necessity,'[1] cannot give a 'logical justification' for believing its contradictory; and that if it be once admitted that such a logical justification must be obtained for what are commonly thought to be self-evident propositions, we should require, as I pointed out before, not one, but an infinite series of justifications, before anything could be considered as proved at all. In short, whether inconceivable means un-imaginable, unrepresentable (if there is such a word), unthinkable, or in the highest degree unbelievable, its relation to the theory of ultimate premises of knowledge remains the same. Under no circum-stances can the recognition of the mental fact that the opposite of a certain proposition is inconceivable by me, be to me a satisfactory reason for believing it.

Mr. Spencer seems to be under the singular delusion 'that any one declining to recognise the Universal Postulate can consistently do this only so long as he maintains the attitude of pure and simple negation. The moment he asserts anything—the

[1] Page 407.

moment he even gives a reason for his denial, he may be stopped by demanding his warrant. Against every "because," and every "therefore" may be entered a demurrer, until he has said why this proposition is to be accepted rather than the counter-proposition. So that he cannot even take a step towards justifying his scepticism respecting the Universal Postulate without, in the very act, confessing his acceptance of it.'[1]

The confusion underlying these remarks has already been pointed out by implication; and if I may venture to give an opinion on such a question, it is the fundamental confusion which has vitiated all this portion of Mr. Spencer's speculation. He seems to suppose that the choice lies between founding a creed on the Universal Postulate, and founding it upon nothing at all : and in order to demonstrate the absurdity of the second alternative, he actually puts himself to the trouble of refuting a theory which he calls 'Pure Empiricism'—which 'tacitly assumes that there may be a Philosophy in which nothing is asserted but what is proved.'[2] Whether this singular system has any objective existence I do not know : if it has, Mr. Spencer may be allowed the credit of having effectually exposed its absurdity ; but I protest against the notion that we must choose between a philosophy of this type, and one ultimately based on the Universal Postulate ; nor can I the

least imagine the dialectical process by which Mr.
Spencer would compel the 'Metaphysicians' (who
come in for so many hard sayings at his hands) to
regard them as the only possible alternatives.

In one of the earlier chapters of his 'General
Analysis,' Mr. Spencer has found it convenient to
give us an amended version of one of Berkeley's
dialogues.[1] It will not, I hope, be thought disrespect-
ful if, also in the dialogue form, I give my idea of
the method in which Mr. Spencer and a 'Metaphysician' would discuss the necessity and validity
of the Universal Postulate. We must suppose this
imaginary individual to have so far forgotten himself
as to make some positive statement—say that a
thing must either be or not be. Instantly[2] Mr.
Spencer demands his warrant for the assertion, upon
which our Metaphysician would probably say—

Metaphysician.—I *have* no warrant for the assertion, and I wish for none. It expresses a belief for
which no proof is forthcoming, and for which none
is required.

Mr. Spencer.—Still you must say why this proposition is to be accepted rather than the counter-
proposition.[3]

Metaphysician.—Perhaps, if that is your opinion,
you will be good enough to give me your own version
of this reason.

Mr. Spencer.—Certainly. I believe that a thing

---

[1] Page 337.   [2] Page 427.   [3] Ibid.

must either be or not be, because this is a proposition of which I cannot conceive the negation.

Metaphysician.—Then in your opinion the fact that you cannot conceive the negation of a proposition is in all cases a sufficient logical justification for believing it?[1]

Mr. Spencer.—Well, not exactly. It is sufficient only in the case of those propositions ' which are not further decomposable.'[2]

Metaphysician.—Then I understand you to hold that all propositions which are not further decomposable, and whose negations are inconceivable, are true ; and that ' a thing must either be or not be ' is such a proposition.

Mr. Spencer.—That is my opinion.

Metaphysician.—Without disputing your major premiss—which, however, by no means commends itself to my mind—I am curious to know how you arrive at the conclusion that the proposition we are discussing (1) cannot be further decomposed, and has (2) a negation which is inconceivable ?

Mr. Spencer.—I arrive at the first conclusion[3] by a careful consideration of the proposition itself; I arrive at the second by a process of introspection.[4]

Metaphysician.—Speaking for myself, I do not feel more certainty respecting the accuracy with which these operations have been performed, than I

---

[1] Page 407.   [2] Page 410.   [3] Pages 394-399.
[4] *Fortnightly Review*, pp. 542-545.

did respecting the truth of the original assertion for which you informed me warrant was required; indeed, I do not feel nearly so much. Doubtless, however, as you are so particular on the subject of warrants, you have some warrant for your opinions on these points; could you inform me precisely what it is?

I shall not continue the imaginary dialogue, because it is hard to think of any reply which Mr. Spencer could make to this last demand which would not have about it a slight air of absurdity. If the reader desires to bring the conversation to a proper close, he will have no difficulty in filling in the blank for himself. I have said enough to make it clear why it is that Mr. Spencer's elaborate discussion on the Universal Postulate does not, in my opinion, constitute a valuable addition to Philosophic theory: and it only remains to examine how far his particular system of Realism, which is professedly founded on the Universal Postulate, is tenable if that be discredited. This I shall do in the next chapter.

CHAPTER XI.

MR. SPENCER'S PROOF OF REALISM.

I HAVE been in some doubt whether, having regard to the general plan of this essay, I ought or ought not to introduce into it any criticism on Mr. Spencer's Proof of Realism. My wish has been to consider merely those opinions which have gained some acceptance among English thinkers, and to criticise these in their most perfect shape ; but though, doubtless, Mr. Spencer's statement of his views is the best attainable, I am not aware that the portion of his speculations which he himself would describe as *metaphysical* fulfils the first of the above conditions, in having obtained any philosophic following.

But though Mr. Spencer's 'metaphysics' have not perhaps commanded much assent, his general theory of the universe, which logically depends on his metaphysics, is accepted in its main outline by so many thinkers in this country, and occupies so important a space in the field of general speculation, that a sort of reflected importance is shed over his defence of the foundations on which the imposing superstructure finally rests. It may, therefore, be convenient to state some of the reasons which exist for thinking that the defence is hardly as effective as Mr. Spencer seems to consider it.

Mr. Spencer sees clearly, more clearly perhaps than other philosophers with whom he is nearly allied, that the question of the external world is a fundamental one for Science, or, if not for Science, at all events for Evolution. 'Should the idealist be right,' he says, ' the doctrine of Evolution is a dream.' [1] As, previous to this utterance, Mr. Spencer had written (I think) five volumes of ' Philosophy,' which, if the doctrine of Evolution be a dream, can be little better than waste paper, it is clear that he is bound under heavy penalties to prove that the Idealist is wrong. Accordingly, he gives a defence of Realism which certainly does not err on the side of meagreness. It consists of some nineteen chapters, occupying nearly two hundred pages, divided,[2] as the reader acquainted with Mr. Spencer's favourite method of arrangement will be prepared to expect, into an Introduction, an Analytical Argument (subdivided into a proximate Analysis and an ultimate Analysis), and a Synthetical Argument ; and enriched with even a larger number than usual of those apologues with which Mr. Spencer so often finds it convenient to prepare the minds of his readers for the comprehension of his more abstruse speculations.

<hr>

[1] *Psychology*, vol. ii. p. 311.   [2] Ibid. 367.

It is evidently impossible within the limits of this essay to criticise so elaborate a discussion in all its details. The most convenient plan will perhaps be to say a few words on the substance of those chapters which seem to call for remark, taking them in their existing order. But before doing this, it will be well to determine certain preliminary points, which will greatly facilitate the progress of the argument.

In the first place, Mr. Spencer and the idealists are agreed in asserting that we do not directly perceive the permanent reality—if such a thing exists. 'What we are conscious of,' says Mr. Spencer,[1] 'as properties of matter, even down to weight and resistance, are but subjective affections produced by objective agencies which are unknown and unknowable.'

In the second place, the idealist denies that there is any proof that this permanent reality exists, while Mr. Spencer asserts that there is such proof; and that he is in possession of it.

And in the third place, I understand Mr. Spencer to maintain that the unknown and unknowable, unperceived and unperceivable reality, varies in some fixed relation with the known and perceived subjective affection which it produces.

The thing to be proved being thus to a certain extent made clear, let us proceed to the proof.

In doing so I shall take the liberty of omitting

---

[1] *Psychology*, vol. ii. p. 493.

any detailed reference to the first four chapters which Mr. Spencer describes as an Introduction. My justification for doing this is that, as the object of these chapters is merely to foreshadow[1] the succeeding arguments, I shall overlook nothing essential to his case by taking such a course. While my motive for doing it is in the first place to save space, and in the second place to avoid having to enter, not merely into Mr. Spencer's views, but into his views of other people's views. Three out of these four chapters consist in an attack on that miscellaneous body of thinkers whom Mr. Spencer is in the habit of holding up to general contempt under the collective name of 'Metaphysicians'; and though my private conviction is, that could they reply they would make very short work of some of his objections, still, as I am anxious to keep as clear as possible of historical discussion, and as I am in no way concerned to defend the philosophers in question, the better course will be to proceed at once to the main body of the argument, without indulging in any preliminary skirmishing.

Chapter V. is merely explanatory of the general arrangement of the discussion.

Chap. VI. contains 'The Argument from Priority,' thus summarised by Mr. Spencer:[2] 'In the history of the race, as well as in the history of every mind, Realism is the primary conception; only after it has

---

[1] *Psychology*, vol. ii. p. 367.   [2] Ibid. p. 374.

been reached and long held without question does
it become possible even to frame the Idealistic conception, while resting upon the Realistic one ; and
then, as ever after, the Idealistic conception, depending on the Realistic one, must vanish the instant the
Realistic one is taken away.' With regard to the
first of these positions, Mr. Spencer observes,[1] that
his calling in question its converse 'will excite surprise in the metaphysical reader,' which will 'rise
into astonishment if he distinctly denies it.' If the
metaphysical reader is either surprised or astonished,
it will, I apprehend, be more probably at Mr. Spencer's thinking that the assertion that 'some form of
Realism is the primary and natural belief of mankind' is relevant, than at his thinking it true. I
never heard of anybody who supposed that the
Boys, Hottentots, and Farm-labourers, from whom
Mr. Spencer draws his illustrations, were either
Idealists or inferred the existence of the independent world from the consciousness of their own
sensations. Nor is it easy to see how anybody
holding Mr. Spencer's views can think it of much
importance what they thought, since their Crude
Realism is nearly as far removed from Transfigured
Realism as it is from Idealism. 'But,' says Mr.
Spencer,[2] 'Realism must be posited, before a step
can be taken towards propounding Idealism.' And
in the succeeding paragraph he implies that the

---

[1] *Psychology*, vol. ii. p. 369.   [2] Ibid. p. 374.

proof of Idealism logically requires us to assume the existence of external (? independent) objects. For this statement however, which, if true, would undoubtedly confute the idealist as distinguished from the sceptic, I cannot find a shadow of proof, unless the following extract (for the length of which I must apologise) is to be regarded as such.

' Tell (a labourer or farmer) that the sound he hears from the bell of the village church exists in himself; and that in the absence of all creatures having ears there would be no sound. When his look of blank amazement has waned, try and make him understand this truth which is so clear to you. Explain that the vibrations of the bell are communicated to the air; that the air communicates them as waves or pulses; that these pulses successively strike the membrane of his ear, causing it to vibrate; and that what exists in the air as mechanical movements become in him the sensation of sound, which varies in pitch as these movements vary in their rapidity of succession. And now ask yourself, What are these things you are telling him about? When you speak to him of the bell, of the air, of the mechanical motions, do you mean so many of his ideas? If you do, you fall into the astounding absurdity of supposing that he already has the conception you are trying to give him. By the bell, the air, the vibrations, then, you mean just what he means— so many objective existences and actions; and by no possibility can you present to him this hypothesis, that what he knows as sound exists in him, and not outside him, without postulating, in common with him, these objective realities. *By no possibility can you show him that he knows only his own sensations, without supposing him to be already conscious of all these things and changes causing his sensations.*'

If we may judge from this extract, and especially from the last sentence of it, which I have put in italics, Mr. Spencer imagines that an Idealist sets to work to prove that we know only our own sensations, by showing that, according to modern physical theories, our sensations are produced *in us* by the motions of objects in space : by showing, for example, that sound is subjective, because its objective cause is vibrations, which are something altogether different from the sensations they produce.   If any Idealist really argued in this way, his procedure would certainly exhibit what Mr. Spencer calls [1] 'a scarcely imaginable blindness to the contradiction between premises and conclusion.'   But I never heard of such an individual, and if he exists, he certainly is not representative.   It is true that many Idealists—for example, Mr. J. S. Mill [2]—have held, in my opinion erroneously, that Idealism was consistent with the usual physical theories respecting the causes of sensation, but they never founded their Idealism on

---

[1] *Psychology*, vol. ii. p. 374.   [2] Cf. section of this Essay.

those theories, and whatever be their errors, are certainly not guilty of 'unimaginable blindness.'

'The Argument from Priority' may therefore be dismissed, because, of the two main positions of which it consists, one is not relevant, and the other is not true. It is not relevant to say, that the first and natural belief of mankind is realistic ; it is not true to say, that the proof of Idealism logically involves Realism.

Chap. VII.[1] contains 'The Argument from Simplicity,' which is shortly this :—Since the proof of Realism contains much fewer steps than the proof of Idealism, it is therefore much less likely to be erroneous. I shall reserve my remarks on this piece of reasoning till we reach Chapters XIII. and XIV., where it is more elaborately repeated ; and shall only say here that if, as Mr. Spencer seems to think,[2] the proofs whose lengths have to be compared include not only all that can be said in favour of one view, but also all that can be said against the other—-the nineteen chapters we are now considering must furnish a powerful objection against the truth of Realism.

Chap. VIII.[3] contains 'The Argument from Distinctness.' It may be stated thus : [4]—' The one proposition of Realism is presented in vivid terms, and each of the many propositions of Idealism or Scep-

---

[1] *Psychology*, vol. ii. p. 375.   [2] Ibid. p. 377.
[3] Ibid. p. 379.   [4] Ibid. p. 380.

ticism is represented in faint terms'; *ergo*, Realism is to be preferred. Without wasting the reader's time by disputing the major premiss of this argument, viz.—that the propositions whose terms are vividly represented are to be preferred to propositions whose terms are faintly represented—absurd as this is when crudely stated, and ill as it fits in with our author's doctrine, that propositions are to be accepted in proportion to the strength with which their terms *cohere*,[1] I shall content myself with attacking the minor premiss.

What, then, is 'the one proposition of Realism' which is represented in vivid terms? In glancing through Mr. Spencer's defence of Realism, we come across a large number of propositions of a highly abstract character, and all of them equally necessary to his system. He has opinions on the nature of the connection between subject and object —proof of the existence of the object—explanation of the nature of the object—none of which can be omitted without depriving his doctrine of some essential element. Are these the propositions, or any of them, which are represented in vivid terms ? The reader shall judge from one specimen. Here is an extract describing the Real, as it is put before us by Mr. Spencer's Realism :—' These several sets of experiences unite to form a conception of something beyond consciousness which is absolutely inde-

---

[1] *Psychology*, vol. ii. p. 450.

pendent of consciousness ; which possesses power, if not like that of consciousness, yet equivalent to it ; and which remains fixed in the midst of changing appearances. And this conception, uniting independence, permanence, and force, is the conception we have of matter.' If the reader thinks the ideas called up by this sentence are particularly vivid, he must, as Mr. Spencer remarks [1] on another occasion, have 'a mental structure of a very peculiar kind.'

The real truth is that, because all idealists and sceptics, in the exposition and defence of their opinions, have indulged in a great deal of abstract Psychology, Mr. Spencer concludes that such speculations are more required by their opinions than they are by the opinions of their opponents. The quantity of such speculation which he has himself found it necessary to give to the world in support of Realism should have made him cautious in his assertions on this point, which are, in fact, as I shall presently show, founded on a misconception respecting the sceptical position.

The chapters from IX. to XI. inclusive, which contain Mr. Spencer's account of our ultimate criterion of belief, have been sufficiently dealt with in the last chapter.

Chapter XII. contains an account of the proper mode of comparing conclusions in those cases where

---

[1] *Psychology*, vol. ii. p. 327.

both sides make appeal to the Universal Postulate, on which (as Mr. Spencer thinks) all belief and all reasoning are ultimately founded. His view is, that the 'conclusion which involves the postulate the fewest times' is the one to be accepted ; and though I shall for obvious reasons ignore that part of his remarks which assume the truth of the postulate itself, it will be well to say something respecting an argument which in its main outlines Mr. Spencer used before in Chapter VII.

This argument is essentially as follows :—Every piece of reasoning is, other things being equal, to be trusted, roughly speaking, in inverse proportion to its length. In other words, the longer it is the more likelihood is there of error having crept in at some point in its course. How far this argument, if sound, can be used in favour of Realism is a question which will be discussed immediately. At present I am concerned with the argument considered in itself. It may be admitted at once that the allegation contained in it is true. It is undoubtedly the fact that of any two computations the shorter is probably the more correct—*other things being the same.* But then, under what circumstances are other things the same ? To whom does it occur to know no other difference between two lines of reasoning but the difference between their lengths ? So far as I can see, to only two classes of people—to those who know no other difference merely because they know nothing about the matter, who are absolutely ignorant both of the history and of the character of the things compared ; and to those who know something about the subject, but can draw no conclusions from their knowledge, in whose eyes both lines of reasoning appear equally solid, and the authorities on both sides equally worthy of deference. This is not very different from saying that the only people who are likely to be convinced solely by the 'argument from sim- plicity,' are those who are either too ignorant or too stupid to make use of any other. These are not, I imagine, the only persons whom Mr. Spencer desires to persuade ; but it is clear that it is only in relation to them that the comparative lengths of two argu- ments can be regarded as [1] 'a rigorous test of the relative validities of their conflicting conclusion,' or as a 'method of ascertaining the comparative values of all cognitions.' [2] To all other people—to all, that is, who have some opinion respecting the intrinsic worth of the lines of reasoning compared—the relative length of those lines can at most be only *one* of the grounds on which their ultimate verdict is based ; and then the question arises, what is to be done when the longest argument appears to be in itself the soundest ? To judge by the confidence which Mr. Spencer appears to place in his 'test of relative validity,' his opinion would seem to be that,

---

[1] *Psychology*, vol. ii. p. 434.   [2] Ibid.

even in that case, the conclusion arrived at by the shortest route is to be accepted—a somewhat extravagant doctrine, according to which a long division sum, done by a charity school-boy, would be regarded as giving more trustworthy results than the calculations establishing the lunar theory. The better opinion seems to be that, though, other things being equal, the fewer steps an argument consists of the less likelihood is there of one of them being false ; yet that, since this risk may be indefinitely diminished by repeated examinations, it may be practically neglected in those cases where the balance of reason appears, on other grounds, to incline distinctly to one side or the other. And this opinion, I take it, is not only the most reasonable one in itself, but is that which is sanctioned by the ordinary practice of mankind.

Chapter XIII. contains the application of the general ' test of relative validity ' established in the preceding chapter to the particular controversy between Realism and Scepticism. As, however, we have found reason for thinking that the ' test ' is pretty nearly worthless, I might consider myself absolved from any obligation to consider how far, if valid, it would tell in favour of Mr. Spencer's particular opinions ; and should therefore pass this chapter over, were it not that it affords a convenient occasion for clearing up some of the misconceptions respecting the essential nature of the arguments to be compared, by which our author has been greatly misled.

I will begin, as he does, with the realistic argument. Here[1] is his own version of it :—'Let him (the reader) contemplate an object—this book, for instance. Resolutely refraining from theorising, let him say what he finds. *He finds that he is conscious of the book as existing apart from himself.* Does there enter into his consciousness any notion about sensation? Not so. .... Does he perceive that the thing he is conscious of is an image of the book? Not at all. .... So long as he refuses to translate the fact into any hypothesis, he feels simply conscious of the book, and not of an impression of the book—of an objective and not of a subjective thing. He feels that this recognition of the book as an external reality is a single indivisible act. .... And, lastly, he feels that, do what he will, he cannot reverse this act—*he cannot conceive that where he sees and feels the book there is nothing.* Hence, while he continues looking at the book, his belief in it as an external reality possesses the highest validity possible. It has the direct guarantee of the Universal Postulate ; and it assumes the Universal Postulate *only once.*'

This very singular passage is immediately followed by three pages of argument, intended to show

---

[1] *Psychology,* vol. ii. p. 437 (italics my own).

that we can and do have a knowledge of the *not-self*
without having at the same time a knowledge of the
self. How this is to be reconciled with the statement I have italicised above, which asserts that in
looking at a book we are conscious of it as existing
apart from ourselves ; how, in other words, it can be
possible to think of a thing as existing apart from
another thing, without at the same time thinking of
that other thing, I do not pretend to say. Possibly
the expression is a slip : in any case, I pass on to
objections of more importance.

I contend, then, in the first place, that the realistic
argument above stated, even if it proved all that Mr.
Spencer thinks it proves, is not sufficient to establish
the ordinary belief in an external world. I contend,
in the second place, that the psychological facts
on which the argument rests are, when properly
understood, not inconsistent with either Idealism or
Scepticism. And I contend, in the third place, that
if the argument is, as Mr. Spencer thinks it is, subversive of any theory of Idealism or Scepticism, it is
not less subversive of Mr. Spencer's own theory of
Transfigured Realism.

What is the thing supposed to be proved by this
argument ? Mr. Spencer states it in the clearest
terms. 'While (the reader) continues looking at the
book, his belief in it as an external (= independent)
reality possesses ' the highest validity possible.' This
is the conclusion which is so certain and so imme-

diate that scepticism is impotent to shake it. But surely it is evident that scepticism might admit it, and not be much the worse for the admission. If the only belief which, having 'the highest validity possible,' must be respected by the sceptic, is the belief in the objective existence of the second volume of Mr. Spencer's Psychology (or some other single object), and *that* only so long as the reader happens to be looking at it, it is plain that the field of legitimate doubt is not materially limited. So very modest a contribution to the Cosmos postulated by Science, is scarcely sufficient by itself to assure us that Evolution may not, after all, be 'a dream.' On this objection, however, which deals rather with the nature of the external world than with its independence, I do not dwell.

My second objection to Mr. Spencer's realistic argument is, that he assumes in it that the idealistic conclusion can be reached only by either ignoring or 'doctoring' (so to speak) the facts given in perception ; a misconception which I think has its root in the ambiguous use of the word *external*. In this connection external may mean external to (= independent of) the perceiving self, or it may mean external to (= outside of) the perceiving organism. It is using the term in the first of these senses, not in the second, that the sceptic and idealist doubt and deny respectively the existence of an external world ; but if we are rigidly to interpret Mr. Spencer's language, he seems to regard these two very different positions as equivalent.

A man looking at a book, he says, '*cannot conceive that where he sees and feels the book there is nothing.*' Nor is it necessary, in the interests of Idealism, that he should conceive it. Of course where he sees and feels the book there is something ; —there is the book. The idealist does not deny this on the one hand, nor does he assert on the other that, when he does *not* see and feel the book, it is *not* there, *in the sense of having vanished from that portion of space.* No idealist seriously maintains, I should imagine, that the universe consists of infinite space, empty except for those things which happen each moment to be perceived. But if they do not maintain this, what is the use of asserting, as against them, that we cannot conceive that where we see and feel a book there is nothing ?

My third objection to Mr. Spencer's realistic argument is, that the mode of refuting 'metaphysicians,' for which in this chapter and elsewhere he shows a marked partiality, is as effective against himself as it is against his opponents. Like the ' common sense ' school, he constantly assumes that the unbiassed deliverance of consciousness (as he would call it), the unsifted opinion of the vulgar (as I should rather describe it), carries with it some peculiar weight in the controversy. But, unlike the ' common sense ' school, the opinions which he really holds respecting the external world require us to do as much violence to our ordinary beliefs as any form of what he calls 'Anti-Realism.' Throughout the whole of the *Negative Justification of Realism* we are allowed to suppose that the errors of metaphysicians are aberrations from true and natural beliefs produced by artificial habits of analysis; and it is not till we come to the *Positive Justification of Realism* that we discover how different are the beliefs which are true from those which are natural; these last being ultimately described—contemptuously if truly—as constituting [1] 'a crude realism,' 'the [2] realism of common life,' 'the realism of the child and the rustic.'

A striking example of the facility with which Mr. Spencer adopts the reasoning of Crude Realism when it happens to suit his convenience, occurs in the chapter we are considering. His object for the moment is to contrast in a certain particular (which I have elsewhere shown to be immaterial) the arguments used by metaphysicians and the argument by which Realism is established. For the purpose of this comparison he selects, as a specimen of metaphysical reasoning, the argument of the hypothetical realist; as a specimen of realistic reasoning, the argument I quoted above. It would be easy in the interest of the 'metaphysician' to take exception to the first of these selections, which Mr. Spencer

---

[1] *Psychology*, vol. ii. p. 497.   [2] Ibid. p. 493.

justifies on the strange ground that Hypothetical Realism is 'the [1] comparatively unassuming parent' of all other Anti-Realistic doctrines ; but what I wish more particularly to insist on now is the impropriety of his attempting to refute an argument, with whose conclusion he substantially agrees, by means of one from whose conclusions he absolutely dissents. His opinion we know is that [2] 'what we are conscious of as properties of matter, even down to weight and resistance, are but subjective affections produced in us by objective agencies which are unknown and un-knowable.' This, I take it is also the opinion of the Hypothetical Realist : but it is by no means the opinion either of the ordinary man, or of the indi-vidual whom Mr. Spencer represents as arriving at a realistic conclusion by the simple process of looking at some single object—say the second volume of the 'Psychology'—with an unbiassed mind. This per-sonage (as we saw) [3] 'feels that the *sole* content of his consciousness is the book considered as an external (= independent) reality.' And the corre-sponding belief is one, we are further informed, which has 'the highest validity possible.' Now the ex-ternal reality is, according to Mr. Spencer, 'unknown and unknowable'—'a mode of being,' as we are elsewhere told, [4] represented to us by 'an indefinable consciousness.' Putting all these statements to-

[1] *Psychology*, p. 441.   [2] Ibid. p. 493.
[3] Ibid. p. 437.   [4] Ibid. p. 452.

Q 2

gether, we arrive at the conclusion that the individual looking at Mr. Spencer's book is unconscious of any of the properties of matter, and has, as the sole content of his consciousness, an indefinable consciousness standing for an unknown and unknowable mode of being beyond consciousness!

This is not a very satisfactory or instructive result; but it is one of a kind which can scarcely be avoided by any thinker who tries to use our ordinary and natural beliefs as weapons against the sceptic, at the very time when he is attempting to establish a theory against which all our ordinary and natural beliefs rebel. To my mind the effort to upset the results of critical analysis (whatever these may be) by an appeal to uncritical opinion is as reasonable in the case of the sceptical view of the external world as it would be in the case of the Copernican theory of the Solar System, and not nearly so reasonable as it would be in the case of the Freedom of Will. But however this may be, whether the method be good or bad, if it is applied to all it must be applied impartially. It will not do to reject Idealism because it is in opposition to natural convictions of mankind, unless you are prepared to say that you think the natural convictions of mankind are sound : and you cannot think that the natural convictions of mankind are sound unless you are prepared to endorse opinions which are not only unfitted to sustain criticism in themselves, but which would render Physical Science an absurdity. If our instinctive judgments are sufficient to prove that an independent object exists, they are sufficient to prove that it is coloured, extended, and with a particular weight, configuration, and texture. If physical science and introspective analysis are to be believed when they show that colour and the properties of matter are, as Mr. Spencer says, 'subjective affections,' they deprive the appeal to our instinctive judgments of all the weight it might otherwise possess.[1]

---

[1] An objection substantially the same as that given in the text has been urged by Mr. H. Sidgwick in the *Academy*, and Mr. Spencer has replied to it in an article afterwards re-published in the third volume of his Essays.[1] His reply, which he does not, I think, seem to be quite pleased with himself, need not detain us long. It turns essentially on a distinction between the Primordial Judgment, as he calls it,[2] of Crude Realism, which informs us that an object exists, and the *other* Judgments of Crude Realism which (as he cannot deny) tell us that it is coloured, and so forth. The first we are to believe in, whatever arguments may be brought against it, but not the second. Now on what is this distinction founded? He does not formally tell us, but he gives us to understand, by his examples, that it is founded on the fact, that the judgments of the second class *are*, while the 'Primordial' judgment of the first class *is not*, capable of an 'interpretation which equally well corresponds with direct intuition, while it avoids all the difficulties.'[3] I will content myself with stating one of the objections to which this doctrine seems open : which, if it remains unanswered, will, however, be sufficient.

Mr. Spencer admits that, according to the immediate deliverance of Crude Realism, the external reality has the properties of matter ; but we know that according to him 'the properties of matter, even down to weight and resistance, are but subjective affections.'[4] Crude Realism is, therefore, wrong ; but though wrong, it arrives at its

---

[1] *Psychology*, vol. ii. p. 282-286. [2] Ibid. p. 286.
[3] Ibid. p. 284. [4] Ibid. p. 493.

I have now said—not indeed all that might be said, but—all that need be said in answer to the negative justification of Realism. With Chapter XIV. begins the Positive Justification, which extends through four chapters, and completes Mr. Spencer's *case*.

This part of his argument need not, however, opinion by a single step. Mr. Spencer shows that it is wrong by a process of 'interpretation,' which is nothing else than an explanation of the usual physical theories of the origin of sensation,[1] and which is therefore an extremely long and complicated argument. How is this to be reconciled with that theory according to which results are trustworthy according as they are arrived at by the shortest trains of reasoning? What becomes of 'the test of relative validity'? The truth is, that Mr. Spencer's distinction between the 'Primordial' and the other Judgments of Crude Realism is perfectly arbitrary, as I think he will himself see, if he tries to show reason for restoring the following doctored quotation from the XIIIth Chapter of his 'General Analysis' to its original form. The words I have added, or substituted, are put in italics. The reader looking at a book 'finds that he is conscious of the book *as a coloured extended object* apart from himself. Does there enter into his consciousness any notion about sensation? No. . . . . Does he perceive that the thing he is conscious of is an image of the book? Not at all. . . . . So long as he refuses to translate facts into any hypothesis, he feels simply conscious of *a coloured and extended object*, and not of an impression of *a coloured and extended object*. . . . . He feels that this recognition of the book as an external *coloured and extended* reality is a single indivisible act. . . . . And, lastly, he feels that do what he will, he cannot reverse this act. . . . . Hence, while he continues looking at the book, his belief in it as a *coloured and extended* reality possesses the highest possible validity. It has the direct guarantee of the Universal Postulate ; and it assumes the Universal Postulate only once.'

This argument is not, as I have shown, a particularly good one ; but it is quite as good when devoted to proving that colour and extension (which are both, on Mr. Spencer's theory, subjective affections) are objective realities, as it is when used, as Mr. Spencer uses it, to prove that an object with (I presume) *no* knowable qualities, has an independent existence.

---

[1] See *Essays*, vol. iii. p. 286.

detain us long.   It consists in the main of a psychological theory of the manner in which we obtain our
ideas of Subject and Object ; and a single quotation
from the summary[1] will be sufficient to show its
general character. 'Simply by a process of observation we find, that our states of consciousness
segregate into two independent aggregates, each
held together by some principle of continuity within
it.   The principle of continuity forming into a whole
the faint states of consciousness, moulding and
modifying them by some unknown energy, is distinguished as the *Ego* ; while the *Non-ego* is the
principle of continuity holding together the independent aggregate of vivid states.   And we find
that while our states of consciousness cohere into
these antithetical aggregates, the experiences gained
by mutual exploration of the limbs, establish such
cohesion, that to the principle of continuity mani-
fested in the *non-ego* there inevitably clings a nascent
consciousness of force, akin to the force evolved by
the principle of continuity in the *ego*.'

There are difficulties in this conclusion, as, for
instance, the absence of any reason which should
make us identify ourselves with one of these principles of ' continuity ' rather than with the others ;
and there is also much material for criticism in the
process by which the conclusion is arrived at.[2]   But,

<hr>

[1] *Psychology*, vol. ii. p. 487.

[2] Cf. Articles by Professor Green, *Contemporary Review*, Dec.
1877, March 1878.

in truth, the whole of this Psychology, be it good or
be it bad, is irrelevant, and irrelevant on Mr. Spencer's
own principles.   It is true that he tells us[1] that the
'absolute validity' of Realism 'will be shown if we
find it to be a necessary product of thought proceeding according to laws that are universal,' by which
he means, I suppose, that our warrant for believing
in Realism is the fact that a belief in it is universally
produced by the natural operation of psychological
laws.   But this, which is merely an instance of the
persistent error which makes Philosophy dependent
on Psychology, does not, as I understand it, represent Mr. Spencer's more deliberate opinion.   The
real warrant on which he believes the 'mysterious'[2]
fact that 'we have a consciousness of something
which is out of consciousness,' is that he is obliged
to think it : and the three succeeding chapters
therefore of psychological analysis which are devoted—not to showing that he ought to think it,
but—to showing how it comes about that he is
obliged to think it—discuss a question which even
from his own point of view can have no philosophic
interest whatever.   With regard to the 'warrant'
itself, it is the same as that which was discussed at
some length in the last chapter, and no more need
be said about it here.   It is the 'inconceivability
of the negation' in a scarcely altered form.

There is only one more point that I feel in-

<hr>

[1] *Psychology*, vol. ii. p. 445.   [2] Ibid. p. 452.

clined to touch on before we reach the final stage of the discussion. It is a favourite practice with Mr. Spencer, whenever he happens to disbelieve a proposition, to inform those who *do* believe it that it 'cannot be realised in thought.' It would be interesting to know how far he can realise in thought the 'mysterious' fact of 'a consciousness of something which is yet out of consciousness?' To ordinary people it might be open to say that they believed it, though they could not realise it: but no such reply seems possible to Mr. Spencer. He is of opinion that we cannot really believe a proposition which we cannot think, and that we cannot think a proposition unless the subject and predicate are realised in thought.[1] Now 'a mode of being separate from myself produces changes in my conscious states,' is one proposition in which I understand him to believe. 'This mode of being, since it is unknown and unknowable, cannot be realised in thought,' is another. If he *can* believe the first proposition without its subject being realised in thought, his general theory of knowledge, and most of the positive positions contained in the *First Principles*[2] must be abandoned. If he *cannot* believe it except on those terms, then either he is wrong when he says he *does* believe it, or he is wrong when he supposes that it is incapable of being realised in thought. He would seem to be in the unfortunate

[1] Psychology, vol. ii. p. 445.   [2] Ibid. ch. ii.

position of having devised a theory of knowledge in the main for the purpose of establishing a realistic system, and of having devised a realistic system which is incompatible with his theory of knowledge.

That he is not unaware of the difficulties which surround a theory according to which we know the Unknowable, I admit ; for he struggles, not very successfully, to get over them in his *First Principles*,[1] by the help of such metaphorical expressions as 'nascent consciousness' and 'raw material of thought.' My complaint is that, holding these opinions, he considers it a sufficient answer to make to any belief of which he disapproves that its terms cannot be 'realised in thought,' or 'be joined together in consciousness'; though neither Theology nor Metaphysics contain, so far as I know, any proposition of which these things can more truly be said than the propositions respecting the external world, which Mr. Spencer assures us have the 'highest validity possible.'

We now come, in chapter the nineteenth and last, to a more precise account of what this external world really is. As the reader is already aware, Mr. Spencer holds, in the first place, that it is unknown and unknowable ; and, in the second place, notwithstanding some statements which seem to assume that it does not vary at all[2] that it varies in some determinate relation to the known

---

[1] Cf. especially, ch. iv.   [2] Cf. ch. ii. 483.

and knowable. The question, therefore, immediately suggests itself how we come to have what Mr. Mills somewhere calls this prodigious amount of knowledge respecting the Unknowable? Grant what Mr. Spencer asks—and admit that a belief in the reality of an independent Universe is valid—what grounds have we for supposing that it is precisely the kind of universe he postulates and no other? Why should it vary in a determinate relation to phenomena? Why, indeed, should it vary at all?

Perhaps Mr. Spencer will be inclined to say (though on what grounds I do not know) that, as the cause of varying effects, the object must itself vary. But from the preceding chapter[1] on the Developed Conception of the Object, we have learned that the object is the 'principle of continuity,' binding together the 'aggregate of our vivid states of consciousness.' A principle of continuity is, I should have thought, the unvarying element in the midst of incessant variations. If it varies itself, must it not require another principle of continuity 'to form it,' as Mr. Spencer says,[2] 'into a whole'? Furthermore, if the object varies, does the subject vary? Mr. Spencer represents the relation between the two by a diagram, which he seems to think affords a complete illustration of it. It consists of a cube (standing for the Object), a

---

[1] Cf. *e. g.* p. 487.   [2] *Psychology*, vol. ii. 487.

cylinder (standing for the Subject), and a reflection of the cube on the surface of the cylinder (representing our 'vivid state of consciousness'). In this case the cube varies, the reflection varies, but the cylinder does not vary. Are we to regard the parallel as in this particular accurate? If so, it would be interesting to know on what grounds Mr. Spencer asserts change in one of the unknown 'Principles of Continuity,' and denies it in the other.

Again, there seems some difficulty in understanding how that which is neither in Space nor Time can be a cause varying with the Phenomenal effects which are in Space and Time. Time as we know it, and Space as we know it, are (it is stated in the *First Principles*[1]) conceptions produced in us by some mode of the Unknowable. Since, therefore, we are not to imagine that the Unknowable is in Time, it does not seem easy to understand how we can imagine it as capable of change—change having no meaning whatever for us, except in relation to Time.

This criticism suggests the further reflection that Mr. Spencer's Unknowable is, after all, not identical with the subject-matter of physical science. Let us take, for illustration, some simple scientific proposition; *e.g.*, 'particles of matter vibrating seven hundred billions of times a second produce in us a

---

[1] Page 165.

sensation of violet,' and consider it in this connection. The particles of matter thus described as causes must, it is plain, be either in consciousness or out of it. And it is also plain that they are not in it, except in the shape of symbolical concepts belonging to what Mr. Spencer calls the 'faint aggregate of our conscious states'; in which condition they cannot either be permanent or produce changes in the vivid aggregate of the kind required. As causes of sensation, they must therefore exist out of consciousness; whence it is evident that they must either be modes of the unknowable, or else that something besides the unknowable must exist beyond consciousness. If Mr. Spencer accepts the first of these alternatives, I desire to know why he chooses to describe that which exists beyond consciousness as the unknowable, seeing that most of the knowledge which we possess professes to refer to it; if he accepts the second, I desire to know what proof he can supply of the existence of such a knowable beyond consciousness at all.

To put the same difficulty in another form. What Science requires to have proved is the existence of matter, which shall be independent of perception and sensation, shall produce perception and sensation, and shall at the same time possess mass, solidity, extension, and so forth. Is this matter Mr. Spencer's unknowable? We must answer, No. In the first place because, according to Science, it

is decidedly knowable; in the second place, because
Mr. Spencer tells us[1] that the matter which is
'extended and resistent' is related to the unknowable as effect to cause.   Is it, then, the knowable?
Again, we must answer, No; because, according
to Mr. Spencer, the 'objective agencies' which produce our 'subjective affections' are in themselves
'unknown and unknowable.'

Mr. Spencer's elaborate argument is, therefore,
altogether beside the mark.   In proving or, I should
rather say, in attempting to prove, the existence of
the unknowable, he has aimed at the wrong object.
The true state of the case is that the external world
required by Science is very much more like that
contemplated in the Crude Realism[2] (as he contemptuously calls it) of 'the child or the rustic' than
it is like that propounded by the Transfigural Realism affected by himself.   Even admitting, therefore, that the arguments establishing the latter are
as unanswerable as he supposes them to be, our
philosophic position would not be much improved.
If the scientific creed respecting the external world
be rejected, the unknowable will hardly save us
from scepticism; while, if the scientific creed be accepted, the unknowable is foredoomed to the same
existence of *otium cum dignitate*, which, according
to Jacobi, is enjoyed by Kant's 'thing in itself.'

If I rightly understand the line of thought taken

---

[1] *First Principles*, pp. 166, 167.   [2] *Psychology*, vol. ii. p. 452.

up in the *First Principles*,[1] Mr. Spencer would reply
to this by saying that matter as known to us, and as
dealt with by Science, may be regarded as permanent
and independent because it is the effect of the unknowable cause which is permanent and independent.
But, according to Mr. Spencer's doctrines, the only
effects of the unknowable of which we have immediate knowledge consist of ' subjective affections,'
which are neither permanent nor independent. These
are not the subject-matter of physical science. When
a Physicist asserts that vibrating molecules produce
the sensation of violet light, he means that certain
material particles which *are* not, which never *have
been*, and which never *will be* in (human) consciousness, and which would vibrate precisely as they are
doing now if (human) consciousness was destroyed,
produce certain conscious phenomena. What Mr.
Spencer must think that they ought to mean by the
assertion is, that a mode of the unknowable which is
symbolised (and, so far as I can see, quite arbitrarily
symbolised) by the member of the ' faint aggregate
of our conscious state ' known as the *concept of a
vibrating particle*, is the producing cause of a
' member of the vivid aggregate ' known as the *sensation of violet light*. No verbal contrivance can bridge
over the discrepancy between two statements, one
of which says that the cause of a phenomenon is a
vibrating material particle, and the other that it is

[1] *First Principles*, p. 158.

an entity possessing none of the attributes of matter, and which, since it is neither in space nor time, must be incapable of vibration. These are propositions which assert different things, and not merely the same thing in different language, so that Mr. Spencer, even if he had proved the truth of the second, would have done nothing towards establishing a realism such as is required by current scientific doctrines.

' The final remark to be made,' says Mr. Spencer,[1] ' is that Anti-Realistic beliefs have never been held at all. . . . . Berkeley was not an Idealist. . . . . Nor was Kant a Kantist.' Nor, I will venture to add, is Mr. Spencer a Transfigured-Realist. Without doubt the natural beliefs which in his ordinary moments hold a not less undisputed sway over the philosopher than they do over the 'child or the rustic,' will be as victorious against Mr. Spencer's doctrines as they are against those of any of the metaphysicians whom he accuses of losing themselves in the ' mazes of verbal propositions.'[2] On the whole, indeed, he is less fortunate than they. For it is his singular ill fortune to have failed with entire completeness in all the objects which a man may propose to himself in constructing a theory of the external world. Some may wish to justify the common sense of mankind, some to justify the teachings of Science, some to prove the being of a God, some to give free rein to speculation without any secondary object. It was reserved for

[1] *Psychology,* vol. ii. p. 500.   [2] Ibid.

Mr. Spencer to elaborate a theory which can pretend to justify the assumption neither of the man of science nor of the theologian, and which will satisfy the requirements neither of the ordinary man nor of the philosopher.

Looking back over the nineteen chapters we have been considering, and over the earlier half of the *First Principles*, it is impossible not to regret that the ambition to produce a ' System of Philosophy' should have forced our author into paths where his remarkable powers of mind show to comparatively small advantage. Could he have been content with giving to the world ' Suggestions towards a theory of the Universe on the basis of the ordinary scientific postulates,' his astonishing faculty for collecting from every department of knowledge the facts which seem to tell in his favour would have had free scope, while his somewhat blunted sensibility in the matter of difficulties and contradictions might have been of actual advantage. In trespassing on metaphysical ground, the virtues which he possesses as a thinker—his extraordinary range of information and his ingenuity in framing original and suggestive hypotheses—become comparatively useless, while the robust faith in his method and results by which he is animated, necessary as I admit it to be in order that he may be sustained through his protracted labours—is from a speculative point of view an almost unmixed evil.

R

PART III.

CHAPTER XII.

SCIENCE AS A LOGICAL SYSTEM.

THE reader will recollect that the only quality of objects for the existence of which in the first instance we required proof was their persistence. In point of fact no philosopher has set himself to prove this without at the same time attempting to prove much more, and as a necessary result, the foregoing examination of realistic systems has contained allusions, more or less frequent, to other and equally essential attributes of what is called 'the external world.' It is now time to desert the philosophers, and to say a few words about this 'external world,' as it is dealt with by Science—not for the purpose of determining how far Science is justified in assuming its reality, for this question has been already discussed, —but in order to obtain some idea of the general character of the existing scientific system regarded as a logical whole.

Granting, then, the reality of an external world, let us ask, in the first place, what is its real nature according to modern scientific teaching ?

Speaking generally, it consists, we are told, of atoms possessing mass, chemical affinity, and other qualities; and of a universally diffused medium, called ether, which, by means of certain very singular properties, transmits through space certain vibrations by which these atoms are affected.

Associated together by various laws in various groups, these atoms constitute the solid, liquid, and gaseous bodies scattered through space; from among the infinite number of which there is to each man assigned one of especial importance to himself;—I mean his own organism. The very interesting class of objects to which these belong, do not differ from the rest of the material universe in the nature of their ultimate composition. In many other most important respects no doubt they do differ. But the peculiarity about them with which at this moment we are specially concerned is the fact, that they are the immediate channels of communication between the world I have just described, and the thinking beings who by their means are made acquainted directly with the appearance of that world, and indirectly with its true nature and constitution.

Before going further in the consideration of the general system of Science, it may be as well to remind the reader how unlike the world just described is to the world which we actually perceive, or can represent by an effort of the imagination. I do not of course mean to say that the world of perception and the world of science are numerically distinct. This is evidently not so. When astronomers talk of the moon, they mean the moon we see ; when chemists talk of elementary substances, they mean things we can touch and handle. But when they go on to tell us about the intimate structure of these bodies they are soon compelled to use words which have only a symbolic meaning, and to refer to objects which (it may be) can be *thought*, but which certainly cannot in their real nature be either perceived or imagined.

That knowledge or what passes for knowledge soon gets in this way beyond the data of perception and the powers of imagination, is a fact which comes to the surface more prominently in Theology perhaps than in Science. I am not aware that this is because there is any essential philosophic difference between these two great departments of knowledge. It arises rather from the fact that, for controversial purposes, it has been found convenient to dwell on the circumstance that our idea of the Deity is to a certain extent necessarily anthropomorphic, while the no less certain, if somewhat less obvious, truth that our idea of the external world is also anthropomorphic, does not supply any ready argumentative weapon.

There are, however, further reasons why this side of the case has not received so much attention as the other. One of them is, I think, that any person speculating on this subject is apt to slide away from it into the allied but altogether distinct questions concerning Realism and Idealism. These are problems, however, the solution of which has no direct bearing upon the subject we are now discussing. Whether Realism or Idealism be true, whether either of them or both of them are consistent with Science, this broad fact remains, that the world as represented to us by Science can no more be perceived or imagined than the Deity as represented to us by Theology, and that in the first case, as in the second, we must content ourselves with symbolical images, of which the thing we can most certainly say is that they are not only inadequate but incorrect.

This is not an assertion which in reality requires much argument to support it. Its truth is apparent on simple inspection, and it applies equally to the two main constituents of the external world—to Matter as well as to Force.

To begin with the latter. Force according to Science is the cause of all motion, and its amount in any case is measured by the amount of motion it produces or can produce in a given time. Now, it is evident that we come most closely into contact (so to speak) with Force, *either* when we see one body foreign to ourselves exercising force upon another, as for example, a locomotive engine pulling a coal waggon, *or* when we feel pressure between our bodies and some foreign substance—that, for example, produced by a tight boot—(this pressure not

being the result of energy supplied by our bodies), *or*
when we exercise effort so as to produce pressure
between our bodies and some foreign substance, for
example, by raising a weight ; which pressure *is* the
result of energy supplied by our bodies. If we cannot perceive force in one at least of these cases, we
cannot, I apprehend, perceive it at all ; and if we
cannot perceive it at all, it will probably be admitted
that our ideas respecting it must be purely anthropomorphic, and only symbolical of the reality.

Without wearying the reader by examining these
three cases in detail, it may be assumed, I imagine,
without further discussion that, as a matter of fact,
our idea of force is derived in the last resort entirely
from the second and third : so that if we had never
either felt pressure or exercised muscular effort, we
should be altogether unable to frame a mental
image which should in any way correspond with the
subject-matter of dynamics. Does the idea so derived correspond with the reality ? The common
opinion seems to be that, though it only *symbolises*
the force which acts between inanimate bodies, it
resembles the force which is exerted *by*, or acts *on*,
living organisms. But this, I apprehend, is incorrect.
There can be no resemblance between the mental
images, whether of pressure or of effort, and that
external and independent force which they are employed to represent. Why should the feeling (said
to be) of pressure be like the pressure which pro-

duces it ?   It is not force, it is one of the effects of force acting on our organism : it does not even vary directly with the force which produces it, but depends on the part of the body affected and on other circumstances.   Neither is the feeling of muscular effort, Force ; it is rather one of the mental accompaniments of muscular action when that action is set going by the Will.   I do not even see how it can be accurately called a *cause* of Force : but without going into this question, which is not material to my argument, it seems certain that whether it be cause or merely accompaniment, it must at all events be distinct from that which it causes or accompanies.

If then we try and represent to ourselves in imagination the reality which is expressed by this assertion, ' the inkstand presses on the table with a force of two pounds,' our idea of what is taking place, if we form such an idea at all, will in all probability be entirely false for two separate reasons.   In the first place, we shall introduce notions of pressure and muscular effort, which have no imaginable meaning for us, except as affections of a living organism, into the relation which exists between portions of inanimate matter : and secondly, we shall deal with feelings of pressure and muscular effort as if they were force, or, at all events, resembled force, instead of being only now and then related to force, as causes, as effects, or as accompaniments.

If now from Force we turn to Matter, we find

somewhat similar limits fixed to our powers of imagination. It is true that we find no difficulty in forming an idea of matter as matter appears to us; while in the case of force, since it *never* appears to us, we cannot even do this much. But if, instead of framing an idea of matter as we perceive it, we try to frame an idea of it as Science assures us that it really is, we soon become conscious that we are attempting an impossibility. Of this impossibility there are two kinds or degrees. In some cases, for example, we may be convinced that Matter has certain qualities, because we observe effects which require an hypothesis of this kind in order to account for them. But as to what these qualities may be, apart from their effects, we not only cannot imagine, but we do not even know how to try and imagine. We have nothing to go upon. Our senses and our reason alike fail us; and it would be more accurate perhaps to say that we have no ideas corresponding to them at all than to say that our ideas of them are anthropomorphic. What, for example, is chemical affinity? What is the real nature of the change which takes place in a copper wire when an electric current passes along it? What is magnetism? Science has at present no certain answer to give to these questions: but there are other questions respecting matter to which the true answers are known with a considerable degree of scientific probability, though at the same time they carry us not the less into regions where

the imagination is unable to follow them. For example, we are required to believe (no doubt on
excellent grounds) that the sensation of coloured
light is produced by material particles vibrating with
a certain rapidity, and that the varieties of colour are
the result of differences in the rapidity and combinations of these vibrations when they reach the eye.
It is a necessary consequence of this doctrine, that
the vibrating particles must themselves be regarded
as having no colour : their colour being merely the
effect produced on our particular organism by their
rapid periodic motion acting through space by means
of the diffused ether. But the smallest trial is
sufficient to convince us that to represent in imagination *uncoloured* vibrating atoms is a task altogether beyond our powers. The other senses, touch
or 'the muscular sense,' through which we acquire a
knowledge of material objects, are altogether incapable of supplying the elements necessary for such a
purpose, at least they are so with me ; and it is of
course impossible to bring in the sense of sight to
their assistance without at the same time representing
as coloured the things we are attempting to imagine.
There is no similar difficulty in the parallel case of
heat. Heat, no less than light, exists in the material
world as a mode of motion. Yet it is easy to separate in idea the vibrating particles from the sensation
of warmth, and to consider one as the cause of the
other. We are not compelled, as in the case of

light, by the laws of imagination, to confound the effect with the cause before we can picture to ourselves the cause of all.

This particular weakness or defect in our power of representation affects, it will be observed, our ideas of the whole material universe. There is not a single particle of Matter which we can either perceive or picture to ourselves as it really exists: and as a similar assertion can, as I have shown, be made about Force; and as it can be made with still more obvious truth about the more occult kinds or properties of external objects (ether, magnetism, and so forth), I think I may consider the thesis which in this long digression I set out to prove, as sufficiently established.

Let us now return to the proper subject of the present chapter, namely, Science considered in its most general aspect as a Logical System. We have seen what, according to scientific teaching, is the real nature of the external world (as for convenience I here call it); and we have seen that as it really is, it can neither be perceived nor imagined. It is easy to conclude from this, what indeed is patent to everybody, that we arrive at our actual knowledge of its real nature, not immediately, but by a process of inference. That material objects consist of minute particles; that colour is the effect of the vibration of these particles; that these vibrations are transmitted as through an elastic and imponderable medium:

that, in short, the world is what it is, are truths which, far from being intuitive, must be considered as the most refined deductions, as the latest triumphs, of scientific investigation.

What, then, are these deductions founded on? Men of science, who should be authorities on this point, inform us that they are founded on facts obtained by direct observation; and that the facts obtained by direct observation consist of what we can perceive of the qualities and behaviour of objects whose persistence, for the sake of argument, we are agreed to assume. In other words, our settled view of the universe is inferred from what we know of it *immediately*; and what we know of it immediately is its *appearance*.

Now the singular thing about this sort of reasoning is, that unless the premises be true, there seems no particular ground for accepting the conclusion; while if the conclusion be accepted, it is evident that the premises cannot be entirely true. Unless appearances are to be trusted, why should we believe in Science? If Science is true, how can we trust to appearances?

From the scientific point of view it may possibly be replied, that our immediate knowledge of the external world is in part to be trusted—but only in part. We know by direct observation—and know truly—of the existence of extended, resisting, and moving bodies; and we know, by a process of scientific inference, that the qualities of colour and so forth, which these extended, resisting, and moving bodies appear to possess, are really the subjective effects of the interaction between them and our organism. So that Science may be said to provide us with a criterion by which we may distinguish between that which both seems to be and *is*, and that which seems to be, but *is not*.

Now that we do in practice so use Science to enable us to distinguish between reality and appearance, is undoubtedly the fact. But taken by itself, this circumstance affords no real solution of the difficulty, because the very thing we want more particularly to know is, how we can thus legitimately erect Science into a judge of its own cause.

The precise question which has to be answered, and the insufficiency of this, the first and most natural answer to it, will become obvious to anyone who reflects on the following series of propositions, which extend and define the argument, whose outline I have just indicated :

1st. Scientific knowledge which is not immediate is derived by inference from the immediate knowledge furnished by observations of the external world. (This I apprehend is the view ordinarily taken by men of science.)

2nd. Observations of the external world assure us (if they assure us of anything) that bodies exist which are coloured, extended, resisting, and so forth.

3rd. The assurance we obtain by pure observation that bodies are coloured, is of precisely the same kind as is the assurance we obtain from the same source, that they are extended and resisting. (That this is so cannot of course be proved, but will be evident to everybody on reflection.)

4th. While pure observation shows this, inferences professing to be derived in the main from pure observation show us that bodies are not coloured, but that the appearance of colour is produced by motions or other changes in the uncoloured particles composing the object perceived and the organism of the percipient. (This must be admitted if Science is true, and if it is derived from observation.)

5th. From this it follows that some of the immediate knowledge given in observation is untrustworthy.

6th. According to (4) there is nothing in the observations themselves to suggest any principle of distinction between those which, according to Science *are*, and those which *are not*, trustworthy.

7. Neither is it possible that such a principle of distinction should be furnished by Science, since it is only if the principle of distinction be sound that Science is logically justified. It is not admissible to make Science depend on the principle (whatever it may be), at the same time that we make the principle depend upon Science.

Stated in this form, the exact nature of the difficulty I wish to point out becomes evident ; and if it is not one that forces itself readily on the attention, this is because it does not attach to the received theory of the *causal origin* of our knowledge of the material world (which is the one that habitually regulates our thoughts), but only to the theory of the *logical deduction of scientific doctrine from empirical data*, which is not a subject with which we are usually much concerned. Let me explain. When we are occupied with the consideration of how we come to possess the knowledge we have of the external world, if we are in a scientific rather than in a metaphysical humour, we immediately and naturally look at the question from the point of view of the physiology of perception ; and the physiology of perception, in its most general form, teaches us this—that the immediate antecedent to an act of perception is some definite change in the organism of the percipient ; and that if this change occurs, no matter how it is originated, the particular perception corresponding to it will occur likewise. Now the same kind of change may at different times have different sets of causes. If on any given occasion one of the proximate causes of the physiological change producing the perception is the thing perceived, then perception is said to be *normal.* If, on the other hand, the thing perceived is *not* one of the proximate causes of the physiological change, then we are said to be *deceived by an illusion of the senses.* Supposing, for example, that I see the moon when she is actually in the field of view, and her rays are striking on my retina, then the object seen is one of the causes of my seeing it, and the immediate knowledge conveyed to me in that act of perception is so far accurate. But if (to take the opposite case), I see a ghost, then, on the supposition that there are no such things, I am suffering under an optical delusion, since, whatever may be the causes of the physiological change which results in that act of perception, it cannot at all events be the object perceived, which by hypothesis has no existence.

This is the physiological theory of perception looked at from its causal or physical side. Looked at from its cognitive or mental side, it suggests the idea that there is, on the one hand, a Material Universe, and on the other a Mind ; and that the Mind obtains its information respecting the Material Universe by looking at it through the medium of the five senses,—a medium which altogether excludes a great deal, and distorts much of what it allows to pass. I am not here pretending to criticise this theory. In common with most theories which give an account of the origin of knowledge, it has a logical defect, which I shall attempt to explain in the next chapter. It has also, no doubt, philosophical difficulties peculiar to itself. But what I am concerned to show here is, that so far from presenting any difficulties in the way of a belief according to which a distinction is made between what *appears* and what *is*, it actually suggests such a belief ; and that therefore it is not surprising that since we habitually think in terms (so to speak) of this theory, we should be little troubled by the discrepancy I have shown to exist between the empirical premises of Science and its received conclusions.

It has been already pointed out that this discrepancy cannot be smoothed away by any principle supplied by Science itself, except at the cost of arguing in a circle.   But it may perhaps be thought that the whole scientific doctrine of matter, and of the methods by which the properties of matter become known to us, may be legitimately put forward as a *hypothesis*, and may be capable of verification, like other hypotheses, by an appeal to experience ; and that in this way the objection I have been urging may be successfully evaded.

Let me consider the subject for a moment from this point of view.   The reasoning to which I object asserts that the laws governing material phenomena are inferred from the immediate knowledge of matter given in perception, and at the same time that the laws so inferred show this knowledge to be in certain particulars incorrect.   The reasoning which it is proposed to substitute for this asserts that some at least of the laws governing material phenomena, and more especially those which are included in the physiological theory of perception, are not inferred from the knowledge given in perception, but are adopted as a hypothesis to account for the fact, that such and such perceptions exist,—a function which they perform so successfully that they may be accepted as to all intents and purposes demonstrated truths.

This mode of establishing the laws of matter is identical in its general scope with that adopted by certain philosophers to prove the reality of the external world ; although the difficulty which suggests its adoption is different in the two cases. The philosophers of whom I speak were of opinion that we could perceive nothing beyond our own ideas, and they sought to avoid an idealistic conclusion by supposing that an objective cause was required to account for the fact that our ideas exist. The scientific argument, on the other hand, with which I am at present concerned, is not put forward in order to avoid a psychological difficulty, but a logical one. It is not required because introspective analysis shows this thing or that thing respecting the true nature of perception, but because the conclusions of Science, if made to depend solely on the immediate knowledge given in perception, do not, as a matter of fact, harmonise with their premises.

Now, in order to estimate properly the value of the argument by which this difficulty is sought to be evaded, we must ignore the information given immediately by perception respecting the nature of the external causes by which perception is produced.

This is evident, because the difficulty itself arose from our attempting to rest scientific doctrine on this information.

We are expected, then, to found a theory respecting the true nature of these external causes solely on the fact that their effects, *i.e.*, our perceptions, are of such and such a character. Now this undertaking we may, I think, boldly assert to be impossible; and if there is any doubt about the matter, it may be set at rest by this single consideration, that if two causes capable of producing the effect to be accounted for (namely, our perceptions), be suggested, there is no possible way of deciding between them. Supposing, for example (to revive an old speculation), it was maintained that it is not matter possessed of certain properties which is the required cause, but the Deity acting directly on our minds. What reply could be made to such a supposition? The immediate answer that rises to our lips is, that we know that matter exists, and that we have no such knowledge about the Deity. But how do we know that matter exists? Because we perceive it? This source of knowledge is excluded by hypothesis: nor can I imagine any other, of an empirical kind, except the one we are at the moment discussing. It must further be recollected that we have no reason to suppose that the limits of imagination represent on this subject the limits of possibility. Nor is it practicable, as I pointed out in the chapter on Historical Inference, by the mere contemplation of an effect (and it is to this that we are in the present case restricted) to discover all the causes by which it might conceivably have been produced, or to determine which of these possible causes, known or unknown, actually produced it.

If, then, we cannot argue from the mere fact that perceptions exist to the fact that material objects corresponding to them exist, neither is it possible to argue from the fact that these perceptions are of such and such a kind, to the fact that the objects perceived have such and such qualities.

Before concluding this section, let me point out what it is that I have *not* attempted to do in this last argumentative portion of it. I have not in any way been concerned with theories respecting the real constitution of matter based on metaphysical speculation, nor has any part of the reasoning depended on the truth of a particular doctrine of perception. I have simply assumed that, if as we are told Science is founded upon experience, it must be founded on experience of one of two kinds : either upon that experience which may be described as the immediate knowledge of objects given in perception, or else upon the experience which is nothing else than our knowledge of the fact that we *have* such and such perceptions. On the first of these assumptions, I pointed out that the conclusions of Science contradicted its premises ; on the second, I showed that Science could draw no conclusions at all.

CHAPTER XIII.

THE EVOLUTION OF BELIEF.[1]

EVER since there has been speculation on the subject of varieties of opinion, this fact must have been obvious, that a man's beliefs are very much the results of antecedents and surroundings with which they have no proper logical connection. That the sons of Christians are much more often Christians, and the sons of Mahommedans much more often Mahommedans, that a man more commonly holds the opinions of those with whom he lives, and more commonly trusts the policy of the party with whom he acts, than on the theory of probability could happen supposing that conviction was in all cases the result of an impartial comparison of evidence, must always have been plain to the most careless observer. It other words, it must always have been known that there were causes of belief which were not reasons.

The progress of knowledge has not led us to increase, but rather to diminish, our estimate of the

[1] The substance of this chapter appeared originally in the *Fortnightly Review* of 1877, p. 698. I have attempted to cure the obscurity which some of my friends professed to find in it, at the cost of a little amplification, and I fear a certain amount of repetition.

part which reasons as opposed to other causes have played in the formation of creeds ; for it has shown us that these reasons are themselves the result of non-rational antecedents, so that even when a man attempts to form opinions only according to evidence, *what he shall regard as evidence* is settled for him by causes over which he has no more control than he has over the natural forces by which a particular flora is produced at any particular place and time.

The scientific evidence for this truth is various and overwhelming. It is justified *à posteriori* with regard to individuals by common observation, with regard to races by every improvement in our historic method and every addition to our historic knowledge. Physiology shows it *à priori* by demonstrating the dependence of thought on the organism, and of the organism on inheritance and environment, while finally evolution binds up these detached lines of proof into an imposing and organic whole.

But though, in the face of such evidence, nobody doubts the fact, few people, I should think, contemplate it habitually without now and then suffering under a sort of sceptical uneasiness (if I may so express myself), when they consider its bearing on their own opinions. The multitude of beliefs which, in obedience to a mechanic and inevitable law, sway for a time the minds and actions of men, and are then for ever swept away to the forgotten past, giving place to others, as firmly trusted in, as false, and as transitory as themselves, form a spectacle which is not only somewhat melancholy in itself, but which is apt to suggest uncomfortable reflections as to the permanent character of the convictions we ourselves happen to be attached to. If, indeed, the law obeyed by this intellectual dissolving view applied only to savages, or to the people with whose opinions we disagreed, we might perhaps contemplate its action with a merely speculative interest. Unfortunately, however, this is not so. We are all involved in its operations, from the most ignorant barbarian to the most advanced thinker. The existence of Comtism is explained by it not less than that of fetichism, it accounts for theories of Evolution not less than for Hindoo cosmogonies, and the man of science is as certainly under its control as was the Indian whose superstitions he is making the subject of analysis and classification.

But if these things be so, wherein lies our defence against universal scepticism? It is true that we hear on all sides of the progress of knowledge, that we imagine science to be as it were a fabric of which each generation lays a tier, resting upon that which was laid by its predecessors, and serving for a foundation for that which will be laid by its successors. But after all, this metaphor only represents an opinion—like other opinions. It is the belief of an optimistic age, which may seem to future generations no more than a transitory fashion. The last ground of faith seems cut away from beneath our feet, if no belief is left which can be trusted sufficiently for us to use it as a criterion of immutable truth ; and if our creed be the mere product of irrational law, where is such a belief to be found ?

A train of thought not unlike this must, I should imagine, have been sometimes started in the mind of the reader when he reflects on the evolution of opinion. I propose in this chapter to put in a clear form what I conceive to be the really solid element in such sceptical, if somewhat vague, speculations.

The case may be stated thus :—Since all beliefs are caused, it follows that those fundamental beliefs must be caused which lie at the root of all other beliefs, and which are, as I explained in the first chapter, the rational ground on which we hold them. Now these fundamental beliefs, being the ultimate premises of all knowledge, are themselves, of course, incapable of proof. So that while they resemble other beliefs in being caused, they differ from them in this, that the causes by which they are produced are of necessity, and from the very nature of the case, always non-rational. In ordinary life, when we perceive a non-rational cause for any opinion, as for instance party feeling, or self-interest, or special education, it makes us examine such reasons as there may be for it with more jealous minuteness. In contrast to this, it is curious and interesting to note that the only beliefs of which, according to received scientific theories, we may say with certainty that they *can* have no reason, but *must* have non-rational causes, are those on which the certitude of all other beliefs finally rests. The upholders, however, of the current theory of Evolution are so far from finding any difficulty here, that they even refer triumphantly to this theory of non-rational causation, as supplying a basis of philosophical certitude to these funda-mental beliefs. They hold that though all opinion is the product of natural forces, the general tendency of those forces is gradually to make opinion approxi-mate to truth ; that in particular the opinions which are commonly regarded as ' self-evident ' and ' known by intuition ' are really the result of reiterated and uncontradicted experience acting on successive generations ; and that this theory of their origin supplies a philosophic justification for believing them to be true.

This line of reasoning, however, involves a mani-fest argument in a circle. It cannot be that this interaction between organism and environment is a reason for believing any proposition to be true which is required to prove that interaction. Or (to put it more generally) no argument in favour of a system of beliefs can be drawn from the fact that, according to that system, its fundamental beliefs would be true.

From Evolution, then, no argument can be drawn

in favour of any scientific axiom.   It remains to be
seen whether that theory has any less negative
bearing on the philosophy of belief.

Now the theory asserts this—All phenomena
whatever are evolved by regular laws and groups
of laws from the phenomena next preceding them
in time.   Among other phenomena, beliefs ; among
other beliefs, fundamental beliefs.   All beliefs whatever being caused, the question arises, Is there anything in the nature of the laws according to which
they are caused which should make them true ?   To
which an evolutionist would probably reply that
there *is*, and would mention those causes to which
allusion has already been made, whose tendency is
gradually to make belief correspond with fact.
Then (we may further ask) are these causes of such
a nature as to make *all* beliefs true ?

This question must undoubtedly be answered in
the negative.   If any result of ' observation and
experiment ' is certain, this one is so—that many
erroneous beliefs have existed, and do exist in the
world ; so that whatever causes there may be in
operation by which true beliefs are promoted, they
must be either limited in their operation, or be
counteracted by other causes of an opposite tendency.   Have we then any reason to suppose that
fundamental beliefs are specially subject to these
truth-producing influences, or specially exempt from
causes of error ?   This question, I apprehend, must

be answered in the negative. At first sight, indeed, it would seem as if those beliefs were specially protected from error which are the results of legitimate reasoning. But legitimate reasoning is only a protection against error if it proceeds from true premises, and it is clear that this particular protection the premises of all reasoning never can possess. Have they, then, any other? Except the 'tendency' above mentioned, I must confess myself unable to see that they have; so that our position (as evolutionists) is this—From certain ultimate beliefs we infer that an order of things exists by which all beliefs, and therefore all ultimate beliefs, are produced, but according to which any particular belief, and therefore any particular ultimate belief, must be doubtful. Now this is a position which is self-destructive. No system of beliefs, giving an account of the origin of fundamental beliefs, can be consistent unless those fundamental beliefs are as certain when regarded as the result of antecedent causes, as they are when regarded as the ground of our belief in the existence and operation of those causes. It does not follow (as I pointed out by implication above) that if, according to the account of their origin given by the system, those fundamental beliefs are true, *that therefore they are true*; for the truth of the system is an inference from these beliefs, and cannot therefore prove them. What *does* follow is, that the system has one of the negative conditions of truth, and is (so far at least as this matter is concerned) consistent with itself.

To this criticism it may perhaps be replied, that there is no contradiction involved in considering a proposition from two points of view—from one of which it seems certain, and from the other doubtful. It happens every day in dealing with statements which are established by pieces of evidence of very different degrees of cogency. For example, the fact that the three angles of a triangle are invariably equal to two right angles would be doubtful if we had no better means of demonstrating it than the employment of a pair of compasses. Geometrical proof, on the other hand, makes it absolutely certain. Will it be maintained that such an inconsistency, if it can be called so, suggests any sceptical conclusion ?

Assuredly not. But there is no parallelism between the two cases. Ultimate premises are not shown to be merely probable by one set of proofs, and shown to be certain by another. They are not shown to be certain at all. They are assumed to be so : and the first stage of the difficulty arises from the fact that while they are assumed without evidence to be certain, the evidence we possess as to their origin shows that they are *not* certain.

If this were all, however, the difficulty would be a slight one. We should merely have to modify our original position, and concede to the sceptic that the assurance we possessed respecting the validity of our ultimate premises was not quite so strong as we had supposed. It is at the next stage that the real difficulty arises, when we consider the fact that our whole ground for thinking these ultimate premises doubtful is founded in the last resort upon their certainty. This is a manifest flaw or defect, which must be fatal to the validity of any system from which it cannot be removed.

The difficulty only arises, it may be observed, when we are considering *our own* beliefs. If I am considering the beliefs of some other person—say of some mediæval divine—there is no reason why I should regard them as anything but the results of his time and circumstances. I observe that he lived in such a country, fell under the influence of such and such teachers, came across such and such incidents, and then I infer, with much self-contentment, that his beliefs could not have been other than they were. I may even pay them the compliment of pointing out that they form a necessary stage in the general evolution of humanity. But when I come to consider *my own* beliefs as a stage in the general evolution of humanity, then there emerges the contradiction mentioned above. If they represent such a stage, all of them *may* be, and many of them *must* be, false. Why not the particular belief in Evolution? Because it is scientifically demonstrated? This only removes the difficulty a stage further back. It must be demonstrated ultimately from something which is not demonstrated : and these undemonstrated beliefs are necessarily rendered doubtful by the reflection that they form part of the stage in the evolution of humanity.

'But if this is all,' the advocates of Evolution may be inclined to reply, 'you have proved nothing more than we are quite prepared to grant. We concede, without difficulty, that our theory is not at present rigorously certain ; and even that it can never become so. You have shown that doubt must always attach to our original data ; we will go further, and admit that error may always creep into our most careful deductions. But this only shows— what nobody ever disputed—that we must content ourselves in science, as in everything else, with something short of rigorous demonstration. Unless you can show us that our system has some other defect, not necessarily incident to the work of fallible man, your arguments will be wasted on people who in the main agree with you.' I reply that I *can* show that it has some other defect ; and the defect is this : If we suppose Evolution to become what every evolutionist must wish it to be—though he may admit that it is not—namely, a solid piece of demonstration resting on axiomatic premises, from that moment it becomes self-contradictory. It is impossible as soon as it is certain ; because, by the very fact of its becoming certain, we obtain demonstrative proof that the premises of the system, and therefore the system itself, is uncertain. A system of which this can be said is not merely doubtful, it is incoherent.

The precise nature of this objection will perhaps be more clear if, instead of being put in this its most abstract and general form, a concrete example of it is taken.

We may suppose, then, a conversation between an Evolutionist and an Enquirer, in which, when the former has explained in the usual ways how human beliefs, after passing through infinite gradations of diminishing error, have at length reached the highest development they are now capable of in the opinion he himself professes, the Enquirer continues the dialogue by asking—

Enq.—Do you suppose that this development of beliefs has now reached its limits, or do you anticipate as great a change in the future as has occurred in the past?

Evl.—However great the superiority of my views may be over those of my remote ancestors, or indeed over those of my contemporaries who are still under the influence of tradition, there is every reason to suppose that the causes which have produced this superiority are still in operation, and that we may look forward to a time when the opinion of mankind will bear the same relation to ours as ours bear to those of primitive man.

Enq.—A glorious hope! One, nevertheless, which would seem to imply that many of our present views are either entirely wrong, or will require profound modification.

Evl.—Doubtless.

Enq.—It would be interesting to know *which* of our opinions, or which class of them, is likely to be improved in this way off the face of the earth.   For example, is the opinion you have just expressed, that beliefs are developed according to law—is that opinion likely to be destroyed by development ?

Evl.—To answer your question in the affirmative would appear to involve a contradiction.   If (as we assume) development is truthwards, it is impossible that development should produce a disbelief in development.

Enq.—I understand you to hold then that a belief in development is true, and therefore indestructible, and that in this it differs from many of our other beliefs, of which we cannot, unfortunately, say the same.   It would be important to know the grounds of this distinction, in order that we might see how far it was capable of general application.

Evl.—Evolution is a theory arrived at by received scientific methods.   Doubtless, all results of which the same may be said are equally true, and will be equally permanent.

Enq.—You talk of scientific methods—but a method must proceed on a principle or principles. How do you get at these ?

Evl.—The principles you speak of are, I suppose, the assumptions which every one must start from, who expects to make any progress in knowledge.

Enq.—These assumptions, as I understand you, are what render a scientific method possible They cannot, therefore, be arrived at by a scientific method, nor can they belong to that class of beliefs which, as you just pointed out, the progress of evolution will leave uninjured.

Evl.—Still you must assume something.

Enq.—But the difficulty here, as it seems to me, is, that if you start from your idea of evolution, these assumptions, like all other beliefs not arrived at by 'received scientific methods,' are, or may be, mere transient phases in the development of opinion, like the doctrines involved in ancestor worship or theism. Nevertheless, it is only by starting from these assumptions that you ever get to your theory of evolution at all.   In other words, if Evolution is certain, these assumptions must be certain, when regarded as premises, and uncertain when regarded as products.   This is not easy to believe.

Evl.—Still, you know, you must assume something.

Enq.—Nevertheless, it is a pity you cannot so order your assumptions as to make your system more self-consistent. At present you seem somewhat to resemble an astronomer who should base his whole theory of the real motion of the heavenly bodies on the supposition that his own planet was at rest; but should unfortunately discover that one of the necessary conclusions from his theory was that his planet, in common with all the others, was in motion. Of such a one we should probably say, that if his deductions were correct his premises must have been wrong, while if his premises were correct his deductions must have been wrong.

So far I have only considered this difficulty as it applies to Evolution, because it seemed to me that the issue to which I wished to call attention could be thus most conveniently raised. It is a mistake, however, to suppose that the difficulty necessarily attaches to Evolution alone. Every theory is obnoxious to it according to which all beliefs are supposed to be caused, while fundamental beliefs are caused in such a manner as to make them uncertain. Now it is to be noted that this description is rather a wide one: and must undoubtedly be held to include the world of Science as ordinarily conceived.

For it is plain that current scientific methods can lead to no other result than that belief is a product. If experience can prove anything, it can prove that. There is here none of that doubt which has been thrown on the existence or non-existence of free will by the real or supposed discrepancy between the deliverances of introspective consciousness and the verdict of ordinary historical experience. In this case, whether we consult statistics, whether we interrogate consciousness, whether we judge of the matter on grounds furnished by physiology, or ethnology, or history, or natural selection—whatever scientific doctrine or scientific method be brought to bear on the question, but one result is obtained : beliefs, all beliefs, are the result of the operation of natural causes, and of these alone. And since it is no less certain, I apprehend, that these causes are of a kind to throw doubts on the beliefs they produce, it follows according to our canon, that ordinary scientific methods land us in contradiction. It must, however, be observed that there is a justification, beyond mere convenience of exposition, for making Evolution especially the subject of their criticism, because it is Evolution alone which *necessarily* claims to regulate the whole world of phenomena. The special sciences—physics, chemistry, and so forth—might very well go on, even if their methods were not universally applied, though it must be admitted that it is not easy to find a principle of limitation. But if Evolution is not universal, it is nothing. If certain phenomena are to be left outside it, if it cannot without contradiction and confusion explain, potentially at least, how the whole world as it *is* follows necessarily from the world as it *was*, it certainly appears to me that it ought to modify either its methods or its pretensions.

NOTE.

In the preceding chapter the argument has turned in part on the manner in which the nature of the causes of belief in general (and therefore of ultimate beliefs) may affect their validity. At first sight there may seem to be some contradiction between this portion of the argument and the general principles laid down in the first chapter. For it was there pointed out that no enquiry into the *origin* of ultimate beliefs can be of any philosophic value, and the reader may be tempted to interpret this canon into an assertion that the origin of ultimate beliefs is a matter of absolute philosophic indifference—an interpretation for which my own language offers, perhaps, some excuse. Thus interpreted, however, the doctrine is incorrect. It is true that the origin of ultimate beliefs never can supply any ground for believing them, simply because the fact of their having any particular origin can only be shown by inference founded ultimately on these beliefs themselves. But it is quite possible that the converse of this proposition may be true, and that inference from ultimate beliefs as to their origin may furnish logical grounds for doubting or disbelieving them. The preceding chapter contains an example of this drawn from actual science, and an imaginary instance may perhaps serve to put the matter in a still more forcible light. We might imagine it to be a conclusion demonstrable from our ultimate beliefs, that those beliefs were implanted in us by a being who had the power, and invariably had the wish, to deceive and mislead us. Now I say that under such circumstances we should be compelled either to think that our creed was essentially incoherent, or that we had committed some blunder in our inference ; and this is the dilemma which, though in a less obvious shape, I maintain we are brought face to face with by the doctrine of Evolution when applied, as it must be applied, to our ultimate beliefs.

SUMMARY.

I HAVE now brought to a close the long series of discussions on the speculative foundations of Science, which began with the second chapter of this Essay. It may now be convenient if I endeavour, even at the cost of some repetition, to show by means of a concise summary the main outline of the argument of which these discussions are the essential parts.

However disjointed and fragmentary the general effect of what precedes may be, the attentive reader will not have failed to observe that a kind of unity is introduced into the whole by the common relation which all the other parts bear to the first chapter. In that is laid down with sufficient generality the conditions which any system of thought must satisfy before it can be regarded as reasonable; while the succeeding chapters contain an examination of how far these conditions are satisfied by orthodox Science. If there appears but little unity in this part of the Essay, the fact is only a reflection of the disunion existing between the different systems of Philosophy criticised, which, though they all admit that Science rests on a solid and rational foundation, seem unfortunately able to agree in nothing else.

If there was a single recognised system of scientific philosophy, complete in all its parts—containing, that is, an account of the premises and modes of inference by which every scientific proposition was ultimately established—the task of the critic, so far at least as the arrangement of his work was concerned, would be comparatively easy. This, however, is not so. Existing philosophies are not only various, but they are incomplete. They not only treat the same portions of the problem differently, but they none of them treat of it in all its parts. Their attempts are fragmentary as well as inconsistent.

At what point, then, is the critic to begin ? What system should be examined first, and what parts of that system should be assumed to be provisionally sound while the solidity of the remainder is being tested ? The course that I have adopted in this Essay, whether the most convenient or not, has been to start with the ordinary *Logic* of Science, taking for granted that the view which that Logic takes of the premises of Science is correct, and only modifying the assumption as it was gradually found untenable.

Now the view of the premises of physical science taken by the usual inductive logic is, that they consist of observations of what takes place in the external world. On these is founded everything we know concerning the nature of the laws which obtain in

that world, including the fact that it is governed by
law at all ; so that, as no general principle is given
(except on the transcendental theory which I examined
later), in a single observation, the problem we have
first to consider is, how inference is possible from particulars alone. The result of the discussion on this
point was to show that, so far as at present appears, no
such inference *is* possible ; and for a reason which, in
its most general expression, was given in the first
chapter.[1] I there observed that 'any kind of Logic,
if it is to be philosophical, must be formal. The whole
object of a philosophy of inference being to distinguish valid and ultimate inferences from those which
are invalid or derivative, this can only be done,
either by exhibiting the common forms of such inferences, or (on the violent hypothesis that they have
no common forms), by enumerating every concrete
instance. To enunciate a form of inference which
shall include both valid and invalid examples, can at
best have only a psychological interest.' Now, induction from particulars is a form of inference which
includes both valid and invalid examples, so that, in
accordance with the maxim above enunciated, it is
philosophically worthless. If no attempt is made to
distinguish between the cases where it is legitimate
and those where it is not, then no confidence can be
placed in its conclusions. If such an attempt *is* made,

---

[1] Chap. i. p. 11.

it must be by the help of some general principle, and in that case the inference ceases to be from particulars.

Something, then, must be added to the knowledge we derive from observation to enable us to arrive at a law of Nature : and, further, this additional premiss must be a general proposition. What is it to be ? The reader, recollecting that we wish to keep as close as possible to the ordinary philosophy of Science, and also to make our initial assumptions as few as possible (seeing that we have afterwards to examine their validity), will doubtless approve the choice of the law of causation. In the third chapter, therefore, we enquire how far it is possible to arrive at a knowledge of the special laws of Nature, it being conceded that similar effects always follow similar causes, and that a knowledge of particular sequences and coexistences between phenomena can be derived from observation. The result of this enquiry was to show that, if we take some phenomenon or group of phenomena for investigation, inductive logic is competent under favourable circumstances to prove, with a high degree of probability, that certain of the phenomena preceding it in time *were*, and certain of them *were not*, causally connected with it. But that, on the other hand, inductive logic could not show either of these things respecting that indefinite multitude of phenomena which in experience have always been present, both when the phenomenon under investigation has occurred and also when it has not.

Since there is no apparent method by which the effects of these persistent causes can be eliminated, we are for ever debarred from a theoretical knowledge of any absolute law of Nature : from a knowledge, I mean, of *all* the phenomena required to produce a given result : and since there is no assignable ground for assuming that these persistent objects which have always accompanied, and may possibly have co-operated with, the known cause of any effect, will continue to accompany them whenever they recur, our ground for supposing that these known causes will in the future be followed by their accustomed consequents, seems in a great measure removed.

The principles on which this somewhat unsatisfactory conclusion is based are these two :—First, every phenomenon which invariably precedes another phenomenon may, for anything we know to the contrary, be part of its cause. Second, the present or past existence of a phenomenon furnishes no grounds for anticipating its existence in the future. Of course, in order that these principles may be legitimately applied, we require to assume an absolute ignorance of all the laws of Nature. On the contrary assumption, that some of these laws are known, we may have every reason for thinking that certain antecedents are not causes, and for expecting a continuance of things which have hitherto existed. But since we are examining the methods by which laws of Nature in general are arrived at, we must evidently start by supposing that they are not arrived at yet, and on that supposition the two principles above stated seem to me hard to refute.

In Chapter IV. I took for granted that which in Chapter III. I showed could not be proved, namely, the trustworthiness of our knowledge of the laws connecting phenomena, and enquired how, from laws, we could argue to facts—and more especially to facts that have already occurred.

I pointed out that our knowledge of past events was entirely founded upon reasoning from effect to cause; and that there was a *primâ facie* difficulty attaching to all reasoning of this kind, arising from the circumstance that more than one cause might possibly produce a given effect. The problem, therefore, which required consideration was, how to distinguish from among the causes which are merely possible, the one which was actual or probable. For this problem I could find no solution. The ordinary procedure which is followed by men of science is to estimate the comparative probabilities of the rival hypotheses, on the basis of some theory respecting the condition of things at the time of which they are treating. Now this theory, if it is not a mere figment of their own imagination, must, like any other historical proposition, be itself in the first instance founded upon an inference from effect to cause. But this process of resting successive inferences from effect to cause on historical hypotheses which can only be justified by other inferences from effect to cause, must evidently have a limit. When that limit is reached, what is to be our next ground of belief? On this point Scientific Philosophy is silent, and we are driven to the conclusion, that if two or more explanations of the universe are barely possible, they must, for anything we can say to the contrary, be equally probable ; which is as much as to say, that one version of history need not be less likely than another, merely because it seems in comparison unnatural and extravagant.

These remarks, of course, only hold good as between causes which are *possible*. If a cause *could* not produce the effects which are our sole premises for inferring the existence and character of any cause at all, *cadit quæstio*. Supposing, therefore, it could be shown that at any given time only one set of facts could result in the world as we now see it, we should know the history of that time with a perfect assurance. Can this ever be shown? It cannot. It cannot be shown, I imagine, even if we restrict our attention to those phenomena with whose laws we are acquainted. But, besides these, there may be countless powers with the laws of whose operations we are entirely unacquainted, and by which all that we see may have been produced. If we once admit the possibility of their existence (and I do not know by what authority we are to deny it), all historical inference is thrown into confusion. We can have no ground for supposing these hypothetical powers to begin acting at one time rather than at another, whether they be powers which should be described as metaphysical, theological, or merely unknown. In order, therefore, that a man may have any rational confidence in the history of the Cosmos as revealed in the teachings of Science, he must be something more than an Agnostic. He must have very solid grounds for believing, not only that through the infinite past only one series of phenomena can be assigned capable of having produced the actual universe, but that nothing besides phenomena capable of acting on phenomena have ever existed at all—and these solid grounds of belief or disbelief must *not* be drawn from history; but, if derived from experience at all, must be derived from his own immediate observations.

Here terminated the first part of our enquiry. Its general result is to show (1) that from the particular knowledge obtained by observing the phenomena of a world assumed throughout this part of the Essay to be *persistent*, no scientific conclusions could be drawn : and (2) that even if we suppose these phenomena to be part of a world governed by causation, we were not much advanced, and that therefore, (3) some further principles or modes of inference have need to be discovered before Science is placed on a rational foundation. Of these 'further principles,' since their nature is altogether unknown, no more notice has been taken.

The *second* part of the Essay was principally occupied in discussing various philosophic proofs of two *known* assumptions on which Science proceeds— namely, the persistence of the material universe and the law of universal causation. With regard to the first of them, though not, I think, with regard to the second, two theories have been maintained, either of which, if true, would render any philosophic defence of it unnecessary. According to one, the persistence of the material universe is self-evident; according to the other, it is untrue—though at the same time its untruth has no scientific significance whatever. The first of these statements I gave some reasons for doubting in the Introduction to the second part; the second I discussed at length in Chapter IX.

It will not be necessary to recapitulate the arguments by which I attempted to show that the main systems of speculation which now hold a divided and precarious authority among English thinkers cannot pretend to furnish satisfactory evidence of the trustworthiness of these two scientific assumptions. It will be sufficient to remind the reader that, in the chapters from VI. to XI. inclusive, I dealt more or less fully with (1) The Kantian or neo-Kantian argument which founds knowledge on certain Transcendental necessities of belief. [Ch. VI.]

(2) The system which sets up an internal or subjective authority—called Consciousness—as the final arbiter of Truth. [Ch. VIII.]

(3) The system which finds the highest source of certainty in our original judgments. [Ch. VIII.]

(4) The argument which seeks either in the opinions of mankind in general, or of some selected portion of them, for an ultimate ground of belief. [Ch. VII.]

(5) The argument which infers the truth of an opinion from the fact that it 'succeeds in practice.' [Ch. VII.]

(6) The argument which infers the truth of an opinion from the fact that 'common sense' (in the popular acceptation of that term) supports it. [Ch. VII.]

(7) The philosophy which declares every proposition to be true of which the opposite is inconceivable.

In addition to these discussions on various proposed foundations for a creed, I introduced into the second part two chapters : one devoted to refuting Mr. Spencer's proof of Realism [Ch. XI.], the other to showing that unless Realism be true, Science must be false [Ch. IX.].

I have purposely made these discussions personal, in the sense of fastening them on some particular individual—in all cases, the most distinguished recent exponent of his special views—because this method seems the one most certainly calculated to raise a clear and definite issue. While in regard to the subject-matter of the criticisms, I have attempted to steer between the opposite danger of, on the one hand, dealing with minute or verbal errors, and on the other, of wandering off into comments upon the whole system of an author, instead of confining myself to those parts which are alone relevant to the questions at issue.

Assuming then that the arguments attacked are fairly representative of English Philosophy at the present time—as is, I think, the case—and assuming, as I am bound to do, that the answers here given to those arguments are effective, we may say that Science is a system of belief which, for anything we can allege to the contrary, is wholly without proof. The inferences by which it is arrived at are erroneous; the premises on which it rests are unproved. It only remains to show that, considered as a general system of belief, it is incoherent : and this task is undertaken in the two chapters which together form the Third Part.

The first of these (namely, Chapter XII.) is devoted in the main to showing that there is a discrepancy between the facts which Science asserts to be its (particular) premises and the facts which it puts forward as its ultimate conclusions. But besides this principal contention, it is shown incidentally that the universe, as it is represented to us by Science, is wholly unimaginable, and that our conception of it is, what in Theology would be termed, purely anthropomorphic. It must be noted that the universe here spoken of is not the metaphysical Thing-in-itself, nor is it the Unknowable Reality which we are supposed by some philosophers to arrive at, if we drive our speculative analysis sufficiently deep. On the contrary, it is the subject-matter of all, or almost all, the propositions which are put forward by Natural Science, and which together constitute a large part of what is commonly, though not very happily, described as Positive Knowledge.

The chief argument of Chapter XII. is, however, only indirectly connected with this subject, its principal end being to contrast the world as it *appears* with the world as Science assures us that it *is*, and to show that the scientific reasoning which makes our knowledge of the second depend logically upon our knowledge of the first, is inadmissible.

The fact that the two are in contradiction is flagrant and undeniable—as any one may see who considers that while perception gives us immediate knowledge of the existence of coloured objects, Science tells us that this appearance is really due either to the vibration of uncoloured particles, or to reflection from uncoloured surfaces. It is also, I imagine, evident that no integral part of a system can contradict the premises of that system without introducing confusion and incoherence into the whole: and finally, it must be admitted that since our actual scientific system *does* rest upon the data given in perception, and since its conclusions *are* in contradiction with these data, it must be regarded as incoherent and confused.

Some speculative arguments fail of their effect from their too great subtilty. The argument whose outline I have just briefly indicated is likely to fail from a precisely opposite reason. When once stated it is so obvious, and so readily understood, that it is hard to believe that there is not some recognised and equally obvious reply by which the difficulty it raises may be disposed of. If so, however, I do not know where such a reply is to be found: while, on the other hand, cause may I think be shown (as I pointed out in the chapter under review) why the difficulty itself may easily escape notice. I there explained that in our reflections upon the origin of our knowledge of the external world we habitually take for granted the scientific theory of perception: according to which the perceived object acts upon our organism, which in its turn produces in the perceiving mind what is called a perception of the object. If this theory be true—and I did not dispute it—it is intelligible enough that the object as it is perceived should not exactly correspond with the object as it is, but that (to speak metaphorically) the message sent by the latter should be altered and modified in the course of transmission. But the difficulty is that this theory itself rests entirely on observations of the external world, and therefore, though its existence quite *accounts* for, yet it by no means *justifies* our habitual indifference to the contradiction which lies between the immediate results of these observations and the remote conclusions which Science draws from them. In order to obviate a possible way by which this objection might be met, I showed, at the end of the chapter, that no advantage is gained for the scientific system by supposing that it rests, *not* on the facts given in perception, but (which is quite another thing) on the fact that such and such perceptions occur : *not* on the existence of the various things perceived—crystals, metals, planets, and so forth, but on the fact that *we have perceptions as of* crystals, metals, and planets. It was shortly pointed out that to regard the world of Science as a hypothetical means of accounting for the occurrence of these perceptions—and it is this which we should have to do, if we mean to justify our belief in it merely by an inference founded on the fact that these perceptions exist—would be simply to place it on a level with an indefinite number of other hypotheses, known and unknown, which might be supposed to fulfil the same function.

The Thirteenth chapter, like the twelfth, dealt with an inherent flaw or defect in the scientific system, but one of a much more subtle and difficult character. This flaw is due ultimately to the fact that every belief may be considered from two separate points of view. It may be looked upon as a member of a *logical* series, or it may be looked upon as a member of a *causal* series. If we consider it from the first of these points of view, it appears as a conclusion, as a premiss, or as both a conclusion and a premiss. If we consider it from the second point of view, it appears as an effect, as a cause, or as both an effect and a cause.

Now every belief, without exception, has according to Science got a cause. But every belief has by no means got a reason, and there are some beliefs which cannot possibly have reasons, namely, those ultimate ones on which all others depend ; these, it is evident, must be products, but cannot be conclusions.

Confining our attention, then, to ultimate beliefs considered merely as products, it becomes evident that, *as products*, they are in no way to be distinguished from the infinite multitude of beliefs which rise into notice, become the fashion, fall out of favour, and are forgotten by all but the historians of opinion. Like them, they are the effects of material antecedents, the necessary results of a primeval arrangement of atoms. But these, the reader must note, are causes which unquestionably produce much error, and which it might be plausibly maintained have produced more error than truth. There is consequently a distinct probability—though, of course, one uncertain in its amount—that any belief, and therefore any ultimate belief, which results from their operation will be erroneous.

But if now, from looking at the question exclusively from the causal side, we turn round and look at it from the cognitive or logical side as well, we become conscious of a difficulty. For in so far as Science conforms to the ideal of a rational system, it consists of conclusions certainly inferred from certain premises. But one of the conclusions thus certainly inferred is (as we have just seen), that the premises of all science are doubtful; so that the more certain we choose to consider our inferences, the more we diminish the only ultimate assurance we have for believing them at all.

If it be replied that this consequence may be avoided by considering the scientific system—as all reasonable men do actually consider it—to be merely probable, I answer that we cannot consider any system to be even probable which, if it were suddenly to become certain, would be self-contradictory, and therefore impossible. Such a supposition is absurd. No conclusion less than the recognition of the fact, that there is some fundamental error or omission in the account given by Science, and more especially by the doctrine of Evolution, of the genesis of our ultimate beliefs, will satisfy the argument; though how this error or omission is to be corrected or supplied without entirely altering our ordinary theories about the history of the universe, I am unable to say.

This discussion in the thirteenth chapter concludes the speculative enquiry into the nature and validity of the evidence which can be produced in favour of the current scientific creed. At every point, the results arrived at have been unfavourable to Science. It fails in its premises, in its inferences, and in its conclusions. The first, so far as they are known, are unproved ; the second are inconclusive ; the third are incoherent. Nor am I acquainted with any kind of defect to which systems of belief are liable, under which the scientific system of belief may not properly be said to suffer.

If the reader, in the interests of speculation (the *practical* question will be discussed in the next chapter), feels inclined to complain of the purely destructive nature of the criticisms contained in the preceding pages, I reply that speculation seems sadly in want of destructive criticism just at the present time. Whenever any faith is held strongly and universally, there is a constant and overpowering tendency to convert Philosophy, which should be its judge, into its servant. It was so formerly, when Theology ruled supreme ; it is so now that Science has usurped its place : and I assert with some confidence that the bias given to thought in the days of

the Schoolmen through the overmastering influence
of the first of these creeds was not a whit more pernicious to the cause of impartial speculation than
the bias which it receives at this moment through
the influence of the second.

It is curious to remark how similar are the consequences of this bias in the two cases. Philosophy, or what passed for such, not only supported
Theology in the Middle Ages—it became almost
identical with it; it not only supports Science now,
but it has almost become a scientific department.
To hear some people talk, one would really suppose
that Philosophy consisted either of the more general
aspects of scientific truth or of the results obtained
by applying the 'approved methods of physical investigation' to mind, or even, which is still more extraordinary, to the nervous system! It may be admitted that nothing can well be more interesting than
the treatment of the first of these subjects by such
writers as M. Comte and Mr. Spencer ; though it can
hardly be necessary again to insist on the fact that no
mere generalisations within the sphere of Science,
though they may furnish materials for a 'Positive'
Philosophy, can ever be expected to give us what I
should term a 'scientific' one, any more than a work
which, to start with, assumed the truth of the Three
Creeds, could constitute a rational exposition of
Christian evidences. While, with regard to empirical
psychology and empirical physiology, it is only neces-

sary to remind the reader of what was shown at sufficient length in the first chapter, namely, that no progress made along these very respectable lines of research, however much it may increase our knowledge of mind and of body, can ever produce, or even perhaps suggest, a solid and satisfactory theory of the grounds of belief.

Whatever be the errors and shortcomings of the preceding discussions, I have, I trust, in the course of them avoided this particular confusion (I mean between aspects of Science or parts of Science and Philosophy) which is the fertile cause of so many others. The path of my argument has been a narrow one, deviating neither into Science on the one hand nor into Metaphysics on the other ; and if it seems to run through a somewhat uninteresting region, and to lead to no desirable goal, yet it, or something like it, must, I believe, be traversed before intellectual repose is finally reached. If speculations which do nothing but destroy seem to be, as indeed they are, unsatisfactory even from a speculative point of view, the reader must recollect that definite and rational certainty is not likely to be obtained unless we first pass through a stage of definite and rational doubt.

PRACTICAL RESULTS.

THE reader who has followed the long argument of
this Essay to its termination at the close of the preceding chapter, may perhaps be disposed to ask, what,
if any, is intended to be the practical result of a
piece of criticism so purely destructive in its character.
If it is intended to be a mere dialectical puzzle,
a mere exercise in ingenious objections, or even a
contribution of a somewhat eccentric kind towards
English Philosophy, it cannot be regarded as of much
general interest outside the sphere of speculation. If,
on the other hand, it is intended to influence actual
belief, what effect can it have, except the production of a universal or nearly universal scepticism?
—an object which can scarcely be thought worth the
trouble both writer and reader must undergo in order
to attain it.

Before answering these objections, I must point
out that the word 'scepticism' taken without explanation is ambiguous. It may mean either the
intellectual recognition of the want of evidence, or it
may mean this together with its consequent unbelief.
Now if my supposed critic uses the word in the

second of these senses, it might be well, before asking whether such scientific scepticism is desirable, to
ask whether it is possible ; because if, as I believe,
this question must be answered in the negative—if
scepticism of the far-reaching character required by
the reasoning of this Essay can be produced by no
rigour of demonstration—we may make ourselves
easy as to any ill effect which, did it exist, it might be
expected to produce.   The only persons who might
conceivably be embarrassed by the speculative conclusions I have so far attempted to establish are those
whose devotion to truth takes the form of asserting
that we are in duty bound to make the strength of
our beliefs vary exactly with the strength of the evidence on which they rest.   But this maxim, though
occasionally uttered as if it were a moral law, would
no doubt be found capable of modification in the face
of an imperious necessity.

If, then, scepticism in the second sense be impossible, is scepticism in the first sense—scepticism which
merely recognises the absence of philosophical proof
or other logical defect in a system of belief—of any
but a speculative interest ?   At first sight it would
seem not.   Scepticism which does not destroy belief,
it is natural to suppose, does nothing.   This, however, is by no means necessarily the case.   If in the
estimation of mankind all creeds stood on a philosophic equality, no doubt an attack which affected them
all equally would probably have little or no prac-

tical result.   The only result it could reasonably produce would be general unbelief, and as I have just remarked, general unbelief can hardly be regarded as a possible frame of mind. But if in the estimation of mankind there is the greatest difference in the relative credibility of prevalent systems of belief, if now one system now another is raised to the dignity of a standard of certainty, it is plain that a sceptical attack, especially if it deals with the system which happens at the moment to be in favour, may have considerable consequences—consequences, at least, quite as considerable as any which considerations addressed merely to the reason are ever likely to produce.

To judge, then, of the true bearing of arguments like those contained in the preceding chapters, we must look not merely at the arguments themselves, but also at the general habits of thought which prevail at the time of their publication. We must consider not only the nature of the agent, but the nature of the material on which it is to act.

What, then, is the position actually taken up by various sections of educated men (we may leave others out of account), towards the beliefs by which we find ourselves surrounded? Which do they accept, which do they hesitate about, which do they altogether reject? These are not questions, it is needless to say, to which it is here either necessary or possible to give full answers. But in a sentence or two I can map out in outline the creed secretly or avowedly professed by the two largest and most important classes about whom we need be concerned.

In the opinion of both of these, beliefs tend to assimilate themselves to one of two types. The first type is that presented by established science. The beliefs which conform to it would be described as consistent and positive, as arrived at by recognised methods, and as ultimately resting on primary axioms whose certainty is beyond the reach of scepticism. An example of the second type may be found in any of the superstitions, religious or scientific, which are now by universal consent regarded as the products of fanciful ignorance. Beliefs of this kind form a floating mass of error, unorganised, unproved, and inconsistent, which it is the business of true science gradually to destroy ; a duty which we are given to understand it is rapidly and effectually accomplishing.

Our more advanced thinkers,—those who are of opinion that they have now reached the point of view from which in the indefinite future it will be given to the whole human race to look back on the errors which formerly misled it, deal very shortly with the distribution of beliefs between these two types. Everything which has to do with phenomena, every-thing which they conceive to belong either to recog-nised science or to scientific conjecture, they put in the first class :—it is either certain, or belongs to the type of that which is certain. Everything else they put in the second :—it is either a superstition and untrue, or it resembles superstitions and is beyond the reach of proof.

I do not of course mean by these remarks indirectly to accuse them of classing Ethics among superstitions. This would be unjust. There is no body of men more careful to let it be understood that the course of their speculations is guided by the most elevated morality. But they hold that Ethics either is scientific or might be made so, and they therefore regard themselves as justified in putting it in the first category with the rest of our certain knowledge.[1]

The second class of men whose attitude towards existing beliefs I wish to describe is much more numerous (in England at least) than the first class, but much less definite in its opinions. The people who constitute it are by no means clear that all knowledge excepting that which is ' scientific ' and deals with phenomena is either essentially incapable of proof, or else is mere superstition. On the contrary, they are inclined to admit the existence of a sort of middle ground, a territory where we may provisionally place the beliefs which, in respect of their subject-matter, approach to the type of superstitions, while in respect of their probable truth they resemble science. To this region is consigned Religion. But even of this

---

[1] See Appendix, at the end of the volume, for a more detailed discussion of the subject.

ambiguous position its tenure is insecure. Should criticism succeed in doing to the satisfaction of the people whose opinions I am describing what it has long done to the satisfaction of our advanced thinkers, should it succeed, namely, in demonstrating an essential inconsistency between religious and scientific belief—then, if I understand rightly their canons of judgment, Religion would at once be relegated to the class at present occupied by delusions and detected superstitions.

It is not to be doubted, I think, that most of the persons who speculate at all upon the larger problems now in debate—and in these days everybody dabbles more or less in such speculations—belong to one of the two classes I have just described. But the point I especially desire to insist on is that though in the first class are to be found almost all those who disbelieve in Religion, while the second includes almost all those who believe in it : yet, that however great may be the practical differences between them (and their practical differences are in some cases almost infinite), they nevertheless agree in thinking that no more certain warrant for a creed can be found than the fact that Science supports it ; no more fatal objection to one, than the fact that Science contradicts it.

The result of this is not only that we are expected to interest ourselves in the effect which scientific discoveries have had, or may be expected to have, on the historic evolution of religious thought, but that it seems to be assumed that the logical relation which subsists between the doctrines of actual science and of actual religion is a fact of transcendent theological importance; so that the serious controversies of the day are, in fact, little more than phases of what is called the 'conflict between Science and Religion.' There is no scientific discovery which has not therefore an importance altogether disproportionate to its purely scientific bearing, because there is none which may not suggest or confirm a theory inconsistent with something long held to be an essential part of Religion, and which may not thus become the centre of a bitter controversy, prompted far more by theological or anti-theological zeal than by a dispassionate love of scientific knowledge.

I might insist on the evil done by such a state of things both to Religion and to Science, but at this moment I wish rather to enter my protest against the principle from which the evil itself ultimately springs. Has Science any claim to be thus set up as the standard of belief? Is there any ground whatever for regarding conformity with scientific teaching as an essential condition of truth; and nonconformity with it as an unanswerable proof of error? If there is, it cannot be drawn from the nature of the scientific system itself. We have seen in the preceding pages how a close examination of its philosophical structure reveals the existence of almost every possible philosophical defect. We have seen that whether Science be regarded from the point of view of its premises, its inferences, or the general relation of its parts, it is found defective; and we have seen that the ordinary proofs which philosophers and men of science have thought fit to give of its doctrines are not only mutually inconsistent, but are such as would convince nobody who did not start (as, however, we all do start), with an implicit and indestructible confidence in the truth of that which had to be proved. I am far from complaining of the confidence. I share it. My complaint rather is, that of two creeds which, from a philosophical point of view, stand, so far as I can judge, upon a perfect equality, one should be set up as a standard to which the other must necessarily conform.

I am not insensible that to some of my readers I may now appear to have reached an extremity of paradox far beyond the limits of sober reason. Even the existence of thirteen chapters of argument which, whether good or bad, are undoubtedly serious, may fail to convince them that I am altogether in earnest. It must be admitted that such hardness of belief on their part has some excuse. The vast extension of Science in recent times, its new conquests in old worlds, the new worlds it has discovered to conquer, the fruitfulness of its hypotheses, the palpable witness which material results bear to the excellence of its methods, may well lead men to think that the means by which these triumphs have been attained are above the reach even of the most audacious criticism. To be told in the face of facts like these that Science stands on no higher a level of certainty than what some people seem to look on as a dying superstition, may easily excite in certain minds a momentary doubt as to the seriousness of the objector. Such a doubt is not likely to be more than transient. But if any reader, who has accompanied me so far, seriously entertains it, I can only invite him, since he regards my conclusions as absurd, to point out the fallacies which vitiate the reasoning on which those conclusions are finally based.

I have sometimes thought that the parallel between Science and Theology, regarded as systems of belief, might be conveniently illustrated by framing a refutation of the former on the model of certain attacks on the latter with which we are all familiar. We might begin by showing how crude and contradictory are the notions of primitive man, and even of the cultivated man in his unreflective moments, respecting the object-matter of scientific beliefs. We might point out the rude anthropomorphism which underlies them, and show how impossible it is to get altogether rid of this anthropomorphism, without refining away the object-matter till it becomes an unintelligible abstraction. We might then turn to the scientific apologists. We should show how the authorities of one age differed from those of another in their treatment of the subject, and how the authorities of the same age differed among themselves; then—after taking up their systems one after another, and showing their individual errors in detail—we should comment at length on the strange obstinacy they evinced in adhering to their conclusions, whether they could prove them or not. It is at this point, perhaps, that according to usage we might pay a passing tribute to morality. With all the proper circumlocutions, we should suggest that so singular an agreement respecting some of the most difficult points requiring proof, together with so strange a divergence and so obvious a want of cogency in the nature of the proofs offered, could not be accounted for on any hypothesis consistent with the intellectual honesty of the apologists. Without attributing motives to individuals, we should hint politely, but not obscurely, that prejudice and education in some, the fear of differing from the majority, or the fear of losing a lucrative place in others, had been allowed to warp the impartial course of investigation; and we should lament that scientific philosophers, in many respects so amiable and useful a body of men, should allow themselves so often to violate principles which they openly and even ostentatiously avowed. After this moral display, we should turn from the philosophers who are occupied with the rationale of the subject to the main body of men of science who are actually engaged in teaching and

X

research. Fully acknowledging their many merits, we should yet be compelled to ask how it comes about that they are so ignorant of the controversies which rage round the very foundations of their subject, and how they can reconcile it with their intellectual self-respect, when they are asked some vital question (say respecting the proof of the law of Universal Causation, or the existence of the external world), either to profess total ignorance of the subject, or to offer in reply some shreds of worn out metaphysics? It is true, they might say that a profound study of these subjects is not consistent either with teaching or with otherwise advancing the cause of Science; but of course to this excuse we should make the obvious rejoinder that, before trying to advance the cause of Science, it would be as well to discover whether such a thing as true Science really existed. This done, we should have to analyse the actual body of scientific truth presented for our acceptance; to show how, while its conclusions are inconsistent, its premises are either lost in a metaphysical haze, or else are unfounded and gratuitous assumptions; after which it would only remain for us to compose an eloquent peroration on the debt which mankind owe to Science, and to the great masters who have created it, and to mourn that the progress of criticism should have left us no choice but to count it among the beautiful but baseless dreams which have so often deluded the human race with the phantom of certain knowledge.

Of course a parody—I ought rather to say a parallel—of this sort could serve no purpose but to make people reflect on the boldness of their ordinary assumption respecting the comparative certainty of Science and Religion. But this alone would be no small gain ; since in the present state of opinion a suspicion as to the truth of that assumption seems the last thing that naturally suggests itself. Why should this be so ? That men of Science should exaggerate the claims of Science is natural and pardonable, but why the ordinary public, whose knowledge of Science is confined to what they can extract from fashionable lectures and popular handbooks, should do so, it is not quite easy to understand. Perhaps I shall be told that there is a very simple explanation of this strange unanimity of opinion—namely, the fact that the opinion is true. To this I reply that, even if we dismiss all the reasons I have given for thinking that the opinion is *not* true, the objector will hardly assert that the general public (of whom alone I have been speaking) have ever made themselves acquainted with the sort of reasons by which alone the opinion can be *known* to be true, still less that they have taken the trouble to weigh those reasons with care. While, if it be further suggested that they are guided by an unerring instinct in such matters, I answer that their instinct cannot always be unerring, for history sufficiently shows that it has not always been the same.

Another reason may be given, which in part accounts for the fact, though after all it only removes the difficulty a stage further back. It may be alleged that the popular opinion is merely a reflection of the popular literature, and that the truth of the assumption I am calling in question is generally believed by the many who read, simply because it is constantly asserted by the few who write. This no doubt is accurate, and up to a certain point is an explanation. There exists now a kind of literature, already large and of growing importance, produced by experts for the benefit of those who desire to be 'generally informed'; which, unlike most ephemeral literature, leads public opinion rather than follows it. Of course the greater part of this, whether it consists of handbooks or of review articles, has no bearing whatever on the relation which ought to exist between Religion and Science, or with the positive evidence that may exist for either. But just as popular accounts of chemistry, physiology, or history appear in answer to the natural desire of an educated but busy public for as much knowledge as possible, about as many things as possible, with as little trouble as possible: so there are easily found eminent authors anxious to purvey for that apparently increasing class of persons who aspire to be advanced thinkers, but who like to have their advanced thinking done for

them.   Now the very starting point of these pro-
ductions is the principle that Science is the one
thing certain, that everything which cannot be proved
by scientific means is incapable of proof, and that
everything which is inconsistent with Science is
thereby disproved.   And since this is a doctrine
which is constantly reiterated, since it is one which in
the 'struggle for existence' has the great advantage
of being not only easily stated, but easily understood ; we need not be surprised that a not very
critical public should readily believe it, without taking
any great pains to examine into the nature of its
evidence.   How it comes about that the distinguished
authors who so serenely take for granted this principle of criticism should themselves never be troubled
by any suspicion as to its solidity is, I admit, harder
to understand.   It would have required, I should
have supposed, much less philosophical knowledge
and philosophical acumen than that possessed, for
example, by Mr. Leslie Stephen or Professor
Huxley, to suggest to their minds doubts as to the
rational character of the dogmatic system in which
they so confidently put their trust ; and, once suggested and unanswered, the smallest doubt should be
sufficient to prevent them raising that system into a
standard by which the value of all other systems of
belief might properly be estimated.

Without, however, making any special attack on
individuals, the nature of my indictment against the

general body of anti-religious controversialists may be easily stated. The force of their attack depends in the last resort upon the discrepancy they find, or think they find, between Religion and Science. It must require, therefore, a belief in, at all events, the comparative certitude of Science. On what does this belief finally depend ? Are we to suppose that they rest its whole weight on the frail foundation supplied by the contradictory fragments of Philosophy we have been discussing through all these chapters ? Or are we to suppose that their belief is a mere assumption, with no other recommendation than that it is agreeable to the spirit of the age ? Or are we to suppose that it is established by some esoteric proof, known only to the few, and not yet published for the benefit of the world at large ? The first of these alternatives implies in the thinkers of whom I speak the existence of an easy credulity in singular contrast with the acute scepticism they display when dealing with beliefs they do not happen to share. The second is, I think, hardly worthy of a class of writers who appeal so often and so earnestly to Reason, and who particularly pride themselves on proportioning the strength of their convictions to the strength of the evidence on which they rest. But if the third alternative represents the real state of the case, we have, I think, a right to ask that the conceal- ment which the opponents of Religion are practising with so remarkable an unanimity should come to an end, and that since the philosophy of Science exists, it should forthwith be produced for our enlightenment.

It is but justice, however, to the philosophic and literary advocates of extreme scientific pretensions, to remark that the blame which I have been laying on them should in part be shared by theologians. I do not mean, of course, that many theologians of repute could be found prepared to assert that Religion must either be proved wholly by scientific methods, and be shown to harmonise completely with scientific conclusions, or else be summarily rejected; but I do assert that the extreme anxiety exhibited by certain of them to establish the perfect congruity of Science and Religion—the existence of a whole class of 'apologists,' the end of whose labours appears to be to explain, or to explain away, every appearance of contradiction between the two—are facts which naturally suggest the conclusion that the assumption made by the Free-thinkers [1] is a legitimate one.

Let me not be misunderstood. Truth is one. Therefore any attempt to reconcile inconsistent or

---

[1] It is not easy to find a single word to describe the opponents of Religion which is altogether free from objection. Most of the terms which suggest themselves have either acquired a somewhat offensive connotation, or are inexact. One or both of these defects attaches to the words 'Infidel,' 'Atheist,' 'Agnostic,' and 'Sceptic.' I have pitched upon 'Freethinker' because, if it suggests comparisons not altogether flattering to the modern assailants of theology, on the other hand, this is made up for by the fact that the strict meaning of the word credits them with a virtue to which they have no exclusive title.

apparently inconsistent beliefs is in itself legitimate, and in so far as apologetics aim at this and at nothing more, I have not a word to say against them; but the manner in which the controversy is carried on, even from the theological side, occasionally suggests the idea, not only that a consistent creed embracing both scientific and religious doctrines may be made at some time or other, but that it ought to be made now, and by no process more elaborate than that of lopping off from Religion everything which is not exactly agreeable with Science.

Yet the apologists should be the first to recognise the fact that this Procrustean method of reconciliation is not one which ought ever to be applied to their theological convictions. Its very ground and justification is the idea that enforced consistency is the shortest road to truth. But if this be so, what are we to think of religious mysteries?

Religious mysteries I suppose to be objects of belief which so nearly elude the utmost stretch of our imagination, that they can be only vaguely and imperfectly described in words; or of such a nature that any definite attempt to express their attributes in formulæ results in a contradiction in terms. Brought face to face with such a contradiction, a man may pursue one of three courses: he may reject both contradictories—that is, refuse to believe in the thing described; he may accept one of the contradictories, and thus escape inconsistency at the cost (it may be) of completeness ; or he may accept both contradictories, thinking thereby to obtain, under however unsatisfactory a form, the fullest measure of truth which he is at present able to grasp. This last course is the one which in some cases all (even merely natural) theologians have pursued. It is therefore a matter of surprise that so many of them—thinking, as they must, that religious truth cannot always be so expressed as to be consistent with itself—should argue as if it ought necessarily to be expressed so as to be consistent with Science.

Perhaps the reader may be inclined to object to the foregoing considerations, that if they are adapted to support Religion in its existing shape, they are not less well adapted to support any Religion however absurd, or any superstition however gross. Arguments against one form of belief are rebutted, by rendering argument against any form of belief impossible. Immunity from one kind of criticism is obtained only by the costly process of dethroning all *de facto* authority in the realm of opinion, and introducing into it, thereby, every species of license and confusion.

Before considering the precise extent to which these forebodings as to the consequences of philosophic scepticism are really well founded, I must point out that for the consequences themselves I am in no way responsible. They are the results of an investigation of a purely speculative character conducted with all the impartiality in my power; and though I admit that I should probably never have troubled myself to put them into shape, had I not hoped that they might have some practical results, the thought of those results if it has prompted the commencement of the undertaking has in no way modified its course.   Even, therefore, if my conclusions should tend to foster forms of belief with which neither the Freethinkers nor I happen to agree, I shall expect full absolution from a body of writers who have constituted themselves the especial champions of the doctrine that no enquiry should be discouraged out of mere apprehension of its consequences.

To return to the objection itself.   It must be noted, in the first place, that when I suggest that practically we need not or cannot regulate our beliefs in strict accordance with the results of rational criticism, I am driven to make the suggestion not because I have used reason *less* freely, but because I have used it *more* freely than is usual upon subjects respecting which people, as a rule, accept their opinion without much preliminary examination.   But this unfettered use of Reason need only produce an irrational and therefore unsatisfactory and provisional attitude of mind when we are dealing with Science as a whole, *i.e.* as a single system of belief; and it by no means excludes or tends to exclude the use of Reason within that (or any other) system for the purpose of harmonising or co-ordinating its parts, nor

even from using it to modify details of the system
for the purpose of producing as much consistency
as possible between the different creeds which we
happen to hold.   Any person, therefore, taking my
view of these questions, would be at liberty, nay
would be bound, to regulate his beliefs within the
sphere of Science according to rational principles, to
the same extent and in precisely the same way as
the ordinary man of science does; the only difference between them being that the sceptical philosopher does so in the full consciousness, and the man
of science in utter unconsciousness, that the system
he is dealing with is, as a whole, incapable of any
rational defence. Of course, if Religion is thought
to stand in this respect on a level with Science (a
point which it has not been my business to discuss),
the same remarks, *mutatis mutandis*, may properly
be applied to it.

It appears then that the practical conclusions I
draw from a sceptical philosophy have little or no
tendency to alter the internal structure of any actual
or possible creed.   But it may still be objected that
they give free scope to the simultaneous existence
of any number of creeds, no matter how foolish or
how contradictory these may happen to be.   Now
in considering this question, it must be recollected
that I have not presented or attempted to present
any arguments in *favour* of Theology.   I have
shown indeed, or attempted to show, that the

fundamental assumption of most of its assailants is
altogether baseless. But after such demonstration
the positive motives which produce theological belief
remain precisely what they were—they are not
strengthened because Science is proved to be philosophically unsound, they would not be weakened
if a complete philosophy of Science were to be
produced to-morrow. The extent, therefore, to
which this attack on Science might theoretically
produce a chaos of conflicting creeds is easy to
determine. It will preserve from destruction those
creeds and those only which, while they have a
claim on our beliefs like that possessed by Science
and Theology, are, as Theology is by some supposed
to be, in contradiction with Science. If there be
any system of belief answering to this description,
its adherents are welcome to any assistance they can
derive from the arguments of this Essay. I can
only say, for my part, that if it exists, I know not
where it is to be found.

There is one more question suggested by what
has been said in the course of the preceding remarks,
to which the reader may desire an answer. He
may wish to know what constitute the 'claims on
our belief' which I assert to be possessed alike by
Science and Theology, and which I put forward as
the sole practical foundation on which our convictions
ultimately rest.

In dealing with this subject it can, I suppose, be

hardly necessary to repeat what the whole tenor of
this Essay goes to prove, namely, that these Claims
to Belief do not consist, so far as Science at least
is concerned, in *reasons*. Whatever they may be,
they are not rational grounds of conviction, raised
by their very nature above the reach of criticism.
It would be more proper to describe them as a
kind of inward inclination or impulse, falling far
short of—I should perhaps rather say, altogether
differing in kind from—philosophic certitude, leaving the reason therefore unsatisfied, but amounting
nevertheless to a practical cause of belief, from
the effects of which we do not even desire to be
released. The object of this unreasoning belief is
not, however, as it ought to be if our creeds were
truly rational, the ultimate premises from which all
the other elements of the creed are inferred : it is
rather the cree l as a whole, or even certain arbitrarily
selected parts of it. In the case of Science, indeed,
this can hardly be otherwise, since its premises are
(as we have seen) not yet properly determined ; while
in so far as they *are* determined, they are explicitly
known to but few persons : and of those few there is
probably not one who did not believe in Science before he thought of it in relation to its premises, and
who would not continue to believe in it, if all such
thoughts were obliterated from his mind.

The reader may, perhaps, think that we ought
not to rest content with anything so unsatisfactory

as this 'impulse.'   If so, I am quite of his mind.   It is assuredly unsatisfactory ; and assuredly we ought not to rest content with it.   I know of no means, however, by which the evil can at present be remedied, and I am sure that the discovery of such means is not likely to be hastened by the claims to rationality which the assailants of Religion are accustomed to put forth in favour of their own more limited creed.

But perhaps it will be said, 'Grant that this "impulse" of which you speak is the whole motive on account of which mankind accept their stock of beliefs, still you have not put Science and Religion on an equality, since it is obvious that the "impulse" is much more universal in the case of the former than it is in the case of the latter.'   If the comparative universality here claimed for the Scientific impulse was measured by the comparative number of persons who accepted respectively the general body of Scientific and Religious doctrines, I apprehend that the objection I have just stated would have no standing ground on fact.   There is, however, a better interpretation to be put on it. We may conceive the objection to mean that while nobody does or can possibly exist without believing in *some* scientific doctrines—as that fire burns or food nourishes—we can find plenty of persons among those who have either never heard of Religion, or who have persuaded themselves that

Religion is false—street arabs or advanced thinkers—who do not accept even the smallest and most perverted fragment of religious truth.

The fact in this case is undoubted ; but to bring it forward as an objection to my view implies a double error. It implies, in the first place, that the impulse of which I speak is a logical ground for accepting Religion or Science, as the case may be ; and it implies, in the second place, that this supposed ground is of the kind which I have already sufficiently dealt with,[1] under the name of ' The Argument from General Consent.' My imaginary critic, in short, supposes that I regard an ultimate impulse to believe a creed as a reason for believing it ; and he supposes also that this ultimate ' impulse ' is a better reason, the more people there are who feel its influence. Neither of these opinions is accurate : on the contrary, they imply a total misconception as to the theory I am endeavouring to explain. This theory may be regarded as having two sides—one negative and the other positive. The negative side, the truth of which is capable of demonstration, amounts to an assertion that Religion is, at any rate, no worse off than Science in the matter of proof; that neither from the fact (if fact it be) that Religion only imperfectly harmonises with experience, nor from the fact that while men of science agree substantially with each other in their methods and in their results, theolo-

<hr>

[1] Cf. ch. vii.

gians differ profoundly from each other in both, nor
from any other known difference between the two
systems can any legitimate conclusion be drawn as
to their comparative certitude. The positive side,
on the other hand, which cannot properly be held to
supply any rational ground of assent, and is in no
way capable of actual demonstration amounts to
this—that I and an indefinite number of other persons, if we contemplate Religion and Science as
unproved systems of belief standing side by side,
feel a practical need for both; and if this need is,
in the case of those few and fragmentary scientific
truths by which we regulate our animal actions, of
an especially imperious and indestructible character
—on the other hand, the need for religious truth,
rooted as it is in the loftiest region of our moral
nature, is one from which we would not, if we could,
be freed. But as no legitimate argument can be
founded on the mere existence of this need or impulse, so no legitimate argument can be founded
on any differences which psychological analysis may
detect between different cases of its manifestation.
We are in this matter unfortunately altogether outside the sphere of Reason. It must always be
useless to discuss whether a particular impulse
towards a creed is either of the right strength or
of the right quality to justify a belief in it; because a belief can, in strictness, be justified by no
impulse, whatever be its strength or whatever its

quality. On the other hand, let no man who agrees with the reasoning of this Essay say, 'I cannot believe in any creed which I know to be without evidence, merely because I feel a subjective need for it,' unless he is prepared to limit his beliefs to those detached scientific (or metaphysical) propositions which are, I apprehend, the only ones he must in practice accept whether he likes it or not, or unless he can find some motive for believing in Science which is not an impulse and at the same time is not a reason. Let him, if he will, accept Science and reject Religion, but let him not give as an explanation of his behaviour an argument which would be as appropriate—or inappropriate—if he were engaged in showing why he accepted Religion and rejected Science.

The doctrine that no rational justification exists for adopting a different attitude towards the two systems of belief, depends, it should be noted, not only on the fact that we are without any rational ground for believing in Science, but also on the fact that we are without any rational ground for determining the logical relation which ought to subsist between Science and Religion. The Freethinkers habitually assume that this relation is one of dependence on the part of Religion, and that if there exist any reason for believing it at all, these reasons are to be found scattered up and down among the doctrines of Science ; confusing apparently the historic reasoning by which particular religious truths are established, with the deeper sentiments by which Religion itself is produced, and in the light of which these historic reasonings are conducted. Those, however, who make this assumption offer no proof of it, nor do they, so far as I know, even indicate the kind of proof of which they conceive it to be susceptible. They accept it, as they accept so many other assumptions, not only without having any evidence for it whatever (which I should not complain of), but without being apparently conscious that any evidence whatever is required.

In the absence then of reason to the contrary, I am content to regard the two great creeds by which we attempt to regulate our lives as resting in the main upon separate bases. So long, therefore, as neither of them can lay claim to philosophic probability, discrepancies which exist or may hereafter arise between them cannot be considered as bearing more heavily against the one than they do against the other. But if a really valid philosophy, which would support Science to the exclusion of Religion, or Religion to the exclusion of Science, were discovered, the case would be somewhat different, and it would undoubtedly be difficult for that creed which is not philosophically established to exist beside the other while in contradiction to it—difficult, I say, not absolutely impossible. In the meanwhile, unfortunately, this does not

seem likely to become a practical question. What
has to be determined now is the course which ought
to be pursued with regard to discrepancies between
systems, neither of which can be regarded as philosophically established, but neither of which can we
consent to surrender ; and on this subject, of course,
it is only possible to make suggestions which may
perhaps commend themselves to the practical instincts of the reader, though they cannot compel his
intellectual assent. In my judgment, then, if these
discrepancies are such that they can be smoothed
away by concessions on either side which do not
touch essentials, the concessions should be made ;
but if, which is not at present the case, consistency
can only be purchased by practically destroying one
or other of the conflicting creeds, I should elect in
favour of inconsistency—not because I should be
content with knowledge, which being self-contradictory must needs be in some particulars false, but
because a logical harmony obtained by the arbitrary
destruction of all discordant elements may be bought
at far too great a sacrifice of essential and necessary
truth.

It is not probable that to these opinions (whose
correctness is, from the nature of the case, altogether
incapable of demonstration) I shall obtain the assent
of many scientific philosophers ; still less is it likely
that I shall convert any of those more declared
assailants of Theology to whom I have alluded

several times in this chapter. But if the arguments of this Essay prove insufficient (as they doubtless will) to induce these writers to agree with the Theological opinions to which I adhere, perhaps they may effect some alteration in the mode in which a perfectly legitimate disagreement is at present expressed and defended. I do not, of course, see any reason why the Freethinkers should not continue to derive what advantage they may, from the use of these convenient phrases, by a judicious employment of which it is possible to imply that they are in possession of the last secrets revealed by Time, while their adversaries are still struggling in the toils of ancestral prejudice. There need be no objection taken, for instance, to their advertising their opinions as the indications of 'progress,' the results of 'culture,' or the offspring of 'advanced thought.' The direct facts so stated are in a sense true, and the implications intended are not, perhaps, very damaging to their opponents. But it would be well, I think, if the sanction of Reason were less often and less loudly invoked in favour of opinions with which, so far as at present appears, Reason has very little to do. It would be well if an appeal to the religious need, instinct, impulse—call it what you will—were no longer openly asserted to be an argument in favour of Theology so weak that it practically concedes the whole case, by writers who would be puzzled if they were required to produce anything better in favour of Science.   And it would be well if an examination into the truth of Religion were less persistently inculcated as a moral duty, incumbent on all believers, by philosophers, to whom it never seems to occur that Religion is not the only creed to which a rule of that kind, if valid at all, would necessarily apply.

It is not necessary, I think, that I should add anything more in explanation of my attitude towards those positive beliefs which I hold in harmony with, though not as conclusions from, the negative criticisms contained in the body of this Essay.   I am painfully aware of how few there are, even among those few whom the dry and abstruse character of the argument does not repel, who are likely to be the least in sympathy with the point of view I have been trying to defend.   It will hardly find favour either with the ordinary believer or with the ordinary unbeliever. As regards the former, indeed, I console myself by thinking that the only practical end I desire has been in their case already attained.   But as regards the latter, I am afraid that I have said nothing which they will even consider relevant to their own difficulties—if they have any—respecting the choice of a creed.   They either ignore or are without that religious impulse, in the absence of which it is useless to clear away, by any merely dialectical process, the obstructions that, did it exist, would hinder its free development. Their case is not one that can be reached by argument, and argument is all I have to offer. Even could I command the most fervid and persuasive eloquence, could I rouse with power the slumbering feelings which find in Religion their only lasting satisfaction ; could I compel every reader to long earnestly and with passion for some living share in that Faith which has been the spiritual life of millions ignorant alike of Science and Philosophy, this is not the occasion on which to do so. I should shrink from dragging into a controversy pitched throughout in another key, thoughts whose full and intimate nature it is given to few adequately to express, and which, were I one of those few, would seem strangely misplaced at the conclusion of this dry and scholastic argument.

In any case, however, such a task is beyond my powers, and therefore I cannot hope that my reasoning, even could I suppose it to be unanswerable, will produce any but a negative effect on those who approach the question of religious truth in that indifferent mood which they would perhaps themselves describe as intellectual impartiality. There may, however, be some of another temper, who would regard Religion as the most precious of all inheritances—if only it were true ; who surrender slowly and unwillingly, to what they conceive to be unanswerable argument, convictions with which yet they can scarcely bear to part ; who, for the sake of Truth, are prepared to give up what they had been wont to think of as their guide in this life, their hope in another, and to take refuge in some of the strange substitutes for Religion provided by the ingenuity of these latter times. It is not impossible that to some of these, hesitating between arguments to which they can find no reply and a creed which they feel to be necessary, the line of thought suggested by this chapter may be of service. Should such prove to be the case, this Essay will have an interest and a utility beyond that of pure Speculation ; and I shall be more than satisfied.

NOTE ON THE DISCREPANCY BETWEEN RELIGION AND SCIENCE.

IN the preceding chapter there was a good deal of reference to the discrepancy which exists, or is supposed to exist, between Religion and Science. To determine the actual amount of such discrepancy, or even to decide whether it has any reality or not, was in no way necessary to my main argument; but it may be convenient to indicate in a note the general view which I should be disposed to take of a question which, though its importance has been greatly exaggerated, is not without interest.

The discord between Science and Religion has reference chiefly, if not entirely, to the interference by the supernatural with the natural, which Religion requires us to believe in; and the amount of this discord may be measured by the importance of the scientific doctrines which such a belief would require us to give up, if we were determined at all hazards to make the two systems consistent with each other. In discussing this subject, I shall assume, for the sake of argument, that this interference is not, as has been often suggested, produced immediately by the operation of some *unknown* though *natural* law; but that the common opinion is correct which attributes it to the direct action of a Supernatural Power. The question therefore we have to ask, is this : What scientific beliefs do we contradict if we assert that a Supernatural Power has on various occasions interfered with the operation of natural laws? 'We contradict,' it will be replied, 'the belief in the uniformity of Nature.' Is the belief which is thus contradicted particularly important then to Science? 'So important,' many people would answer, ' that it lies at the foundation of all our scientific reasoning, as well as all of our practical judgments.' This I understand to be the opinion of the two most recent assailants of Theology who, so far as I know, have touched on the subject—namely, the author of ' Supernatural Religion ' and Mr. Leslie Stephen. The former of these, whose treatment of the whole question suggests a suspicion that he is hardly equal to dealing with the profounder problems which he has undertaken to solve, I need not further allude to. Mr. Stephen, however, may be quoted with advantage. 'If it is not contrary,' he says, 'to the laws of Nature that the dead shall be raised, or one loaf feed a thousand men, the occurrence of the fact does not prove that an Almighty Being has suspended the laws of Nature. If such a phenomenon is contrary to the laws of Nature, then a proof that the events had occurred would establish the inference. But, on the other hand, it must always be simpler to believe that the evidence is mistaken ; *for such a belief is obviously consistent with a belief in the uniformity of Nature, which is the sole guarantee (whatever its origin) of our reasoning.* Really to evade Hume's reasoning is thus impossible,' &c.[1]

From the sentence in this extract which I have put in italics, it would appear that Mr. Stephen holds, and thinks that Hume implicitly held, the doctrine that a belief in occasional Divine interference is inconsistent with that belief in the uniformity of Nature which is ' the sole guarantee of our reasoning.' I doubt whether this was Hume's opinion ; in any case it is incorrect.

[1] ' English Thought in the Eighteenth Century,' p. 341.

The scientific belief which, with least impropriety, may be termed the 'sole guarantee' of our reasoning, is *that* belief in the uniformity of Nature which is equivalent to a belief in the law of universal causation ; which again is equivalent to a belief that similar antecedents are always followed by similar consequents. But this belief, as the least reflection will convince the reader, is in no way inconsistent with a belief in supernatural interference.

A belief in the uniformity of Nature, which is equivalent to a belief that natural effects are uniformly preceded by natural causes, no doubt *is* inconsistent with supernatural interference ; but of what pieces of reasoning it is our sole guarantee, except those directed to show that in any given case the hypothesis of supernatural interference must be rejected, I am not able to say.

It is clear, then, that the most important discrepancy which has been, or could be, alleged to exist between Science and Religion has no real existence. The only great general principle on which scientific philosophers have as yet been able to rest their scientific creed is untouched. Let us therefore now turn our attention to the more special and derivative doctrines of Science, and consider how far they are affected by a belief in supernatural interference.

In this enquiry it will be convenient to keep in mind a distinction drawn in the fourth chapter of this essay, between what were there called the *abstract* and the *concrete* parts of Science. By the abstract parts of Science were meant the general laws by which phenomena are connected ; by the concrete parts were meant (what may be sufficiently described as) particular matters of fact.

Does, then, Theology require us to modify in any way our beliefs concerning the abstract part of Science? I apprehend that **it does not.** Such beliefs are in themselves **as true** and as fully proved if supernatural interference be possible as they are if such interference be impossible. A law does not do more than state that under certain circumstances (positive and negative) certain phenomena will occur. If on some occasions these **circumstances,** owing to supernatural interference, **do** *not* occur, the fact that the phenomena **do** not **follow proves nothing as to the truth or falsehood of the** law. If we believe that oxygen and hydrogen will combine under given conditions to produce water, we believe so none the less because we happen also to believe that some Supernatural Power may interpose, or has on certain occasions interposed, to prevent that result. I need not further insist on this point, which is obvious enough in itself, and on which I believe I am in agreement with Mr. Mill and others who are not commonly suspected of a theological bias.

There remains then the concrete part of Science : the matters of fact which compose history in its widest sense, or which belongs to that fraction of the future which Science can pretend to foresee. Now with regard to the former of these the question is complicated by a consideration which does not affect us when we are dealing with other portions of the scientific system— by the consideration, namely, that it is a matter of controversy *what*, in certain very pertinent particulars, the scientific version of history really is. For the Theologians usually maintain that the kind of scientific inference which I call Historical, compels a belief in the intervention on certain **occasions of supernatural** causes : a great part of **what are** commonly called Christian evidences being indeed nothing more than a detailed attempt **to** prove this thesis, **just** as most of the direct attacks on Christianity **are attempts** to prove the precise opposite. Now, if the Theologians are right in their opinions on this point, there can be no discrepancy whatever between Religion and Science as regards matters of fact, because it is Science itself which compels us to accept the account of miracles in which Religion teaches us to believe. Before, therefore, discussing the nature and magnitude of the discrepancy which is supposed to exist between them, it would seem necessary to enter fully into all the disputes respecting the authenticity of documents, the credibility of witnesses, the interpretation of texts, the growth of myths, the natural history of religions, the abstract question as to the possibility of inferring supernatural facts from natural data, and, in short, all the topics which supply theological and anti-theological writers with so much material for discussion. Such a task is of course impossible. But it may be worth while to note the conclusions that would have to be faced if on all these disputed questions the Theologians are wrong and the Anti-theologians are right ; if known natural causes are able in all cases, without straining, to account for the historical facts which both sides allow to have occurred, and if, either for this, or for some more abstract reason, only natural causes can rationally be admitted to have been in operation. On such a hypothesis theological beliefs would, without doubt, modify opinions framed out of purely scientific materials, though the modification may easily be exaggerated. Regarded in their relation to us as men, the facts which Theology asserts to have happened are unquestionably of transcendent importance. Regarded in their relation to Science, this can hardly be maintained. *As phenomena*, the few events which are said to have occurred in Palestine and elsewhere of a supernatural character are scarcely worth noting. Being supernatural, they furnish no grounds either for believing in any new law of Nature or for disbelieving any which we had before supposed to be established; and being few, they are lost in the mass of facts which have succeeded each other since the earth came into being. 'Is the supernatural creation of the world, then, nothing?' the reader may be tempted to exclaim. I have always understood[1] that this is a subject on which men of science professed to be altogether out of their sphere. 'What, then, do you say about a belief in Providence, and in the possible interference of Supernatural Power in answer to prayer?' These, again, are not convictions which require us to modify our adherence to known laws. They may cast, indeed, an additional shade of doubt over our expectation of the events which are to occur in the future, as well as over the explanation of the events which have occurred in the past; and if our actual scientific inferences were (as I have shown in the fourth chapter that they are not) of a satisfactory character on these points, this might prove a matter of some, though not, I think, of very great importance. As it is, however, the Supernatural Power is only one of an indefinite number of known and unknown natural powers, which we never have seen, and perhaps can never hope to see, reduced to law, and which even if we leave miraculous interference out of account would suffice to make demonstrative prophecy or retrospection an absolute impossibility.

It would appear then that the discrepancy between Religion and Science which vanishes altogether if we take

---

[1] If the literal interpretation of the Mosaic account of the creation is to be accepted as an essential part of religion, no doubt the discrepancy between Religion and Science will be greater than that stated in the text. I have, however, assumed (in accordance with what I understand to be the opinion of theological experts) that this is not the case.

the hypothesis most favourable to the Theologians is comparatively insignificant in its amount even on the hypothesis most favourable to the Freethinkers : and if many writers who certainly know a great deal about Science, and may be supposed to know something about Theology, are of an altogether different opinion, this may, I apprehend, be attributed to the fact that they approach the question with their minds completely saturated with a theory of the logical relation which ought to subsist between Religion and Science, according to which the grounds, if any, for believing the first, are to be found, if anywhere, among the doctrines of the second. It is not hard to see that on any presupposition of this sort (combined as it is with the assumption that Science is philosophically established), the smallest want of harmony between the two systems may, or rather must, lead to the most important consequences : since the mere discovery that they are not rationally connected would remove all ground for accepting the dependent creed ; while the least appearance of contradiction would supply a positive ground for rejecting it. As, however, I have in the preceding chapter sufficiently expressed my dissent from this view, it is not necessary that I should here any further allude to it. I merely desired to point out the principal reason which I believe exists for the great exaggeration which is occasionally to be observed in the estimate of the importance of the contradiction between current Religion and current Science put forward by thinkers of reputation.

APPENDIX.

ON THE IDEA OF A PHILOSOPHY OF ETHICS.

IN this Appendix I propose to extend and apply the remarks on the Idea of a Philosophy in general contained in the first chapter of the Essay, to the Philosophy of Ethics in particular. But, in order to do so, it is necessary, in the first place, to correct an error which, in these days when Science and the Knowable are supposed to be co-extensive, is natural though not the less mischievous :—the error I mean by which Ethics is degraded to a mere section or department of Science. At first sight, and from some points of view, the opinion seems plausible enough. That mankind have passed through many ethical phases (for example) is a fact in history, and history belongs to science : that I hold certain moral laws to be binding is a fact of my mental being ; and, like all other such facts, is dealt with by Psychology,—also a branch of science. Physiology, Ethnology, and other sciences all have something to say concerning the origin and development of moral ideas in the individual and in the race ; it is not unnatural, therefore, that some men of science, impressed by these facts, have claimed, or seemed to claim, Ethics for their own.

To hold such a view would be a most unfortunate error ; not to hold clearly and definitely its contrary may lead to much confusion ; for though, as will appear, scientific laws form necessary steps in the deduction of subordinate ethical laws, and though the two provinces of knowledge cannot with advantage be separated in practice, still the truth remains that scientific judgments and ethical judgments deal with essentially different subject-matters.

Every scientific proposition asserts either the nature of the relation of space or time between phenomena which have existed, do exist, or will exist ; or defines the relations of space or time which would exist if certain changes and simplifications were made in the phenomena (as in ideal geometry), or in the law governing the phenomena (as in ideal physics). Roughly speaking, it may be said to state facts or events, real or hypothetical.

An ethical proposition, on the other hand, though, like every other proposition, it states a relation, does not state a relation of space or time. 'I ought to speak the truth,' for instance, does not imply that I have spoken, do speak, or shall speak the truth ; it asserts no bond of causation between subject and predicate, nor any co-existence nor any sequence. It does not announce an event ; and if some people would say that it stated a fact, it is not certainly a fact either of the ' external ' or of the ' internal ' world.

One cause, perhaps, of the constant confusion between Ethics and Science is the tendency there appears to be to regard the psychology of the individual holding the moral law as the subject-matter of Ethics, rather than the moral law itself ; to investigate the position which the belief in such a proposition as 'I ought to speak the truth ' holds in the history of the race and of the individual, its causes and its accompaniments, rather than its truth or its evidence ; to substitute, in short, Psychology or Anthropology for Ethics. The danger of such confusion will partly be shown by the few remarks which, in order to carry out the train of thought begun in the first chapter, I have to make on the

Idea of a Philosophy of Ethics : that is, on the *form which
any satisfactory system of Ethics must assume, or be able to
assume, whatever be its contents.*

The obvious truth that all knowledge is either certain in
itself, or is derived by legitimate methods from that which
is so, has been already, perhaps, more than sufficiently
insisted on ; and this, which is true of knowledge in general, is of course also true of ethical knowledge in particular.
A little consideration will enable us to go on, and state this
further fact, which is peculiar to Ethics. *The general propositions which really lie at the root of any ethical system
must themselves be ethical, and can never be either scientific
or metaphysical.* In other words, if a proposition announcing obligation require proof at all, one term of that proof
must always be a proposition announcing obligation, which
itself requires no proof. This truth must not be confounded
with that which I have just dwelt upon, namely, that
Science and Ethics have essentially different subject-matters.
This might be so, and yet Ethics might be indebted for all
its first principles to Science.

A concrete case will perhaps make clearer this axiom
of ethical philosophy. A man (let us say) is not satisfied
that he ought to speak the truth. He demands a reason,
and is told that truth-telling conduces to the welfare of
society. He accepts this ground, and apparently, therefore, rests his ethics on what is a purely scientific assertion.
But this is not in reality the fact. There is a suppressed
premiss required to justify his conclusion, which would run
somewhat in this way,—' I ought to do that which conduces
to the welfare of society.' And this proposition, of course,
is ethical. This example is not merely an illustration, it
is a typical case. There is no artifice by which an ethical
statement can be evolved from a scientific or metaphysical

proposition, or any combination of such ; and whenever the reverse appears to be the fact, it will always be found that the assertion, which seems to be the basis of the ethical superstructure, is in reality merely the 'minor' of a syllogism, of which the major is the desired ethical principle.

If this principle be as true as it seems to me to be obvious, it at once alters our attitude towards a vast mass of controversy which has encumbered the progress of moral philosophy. So far as the proof of a basis of morals is concerned it makes irrelevant all discussion on the origin of moral ideas, or on the nature of moral sentiments ; and it relegates to their proper sphere in Psychology or Anthropology all discussion on such subjects as association of ideas, inherited instincts, and evolution, in so far, at least, as these are supposed to refer to *ultimate* moral laws. For it is an obvious corollary from our principle, that the origin of an ultimate ethical belief never can supply a reason for believing it ; since the origin of this belief, as of any other mental phenomenon, is a matter to be dealt with by Science ; and my thesis is, that (negatively speaking) scientific truth alone cannot serve as a foundation for a moral system ; or (to put it positively), if we have a moral system at all, there must be contained in it, explicitly or implicitly, at least one ethical proposition, of which no proof can be given or required.

In one sense, therefore, all Ethics is ' *à priori.*' It is not, and never can be, founded on experience. Whether we be Utilitarians, or Egoists, or Intuitionists, by whatever name we call ourselves, the rational basis of our system must be something other than an experience or a series of experiences ; for such always belong to Science.

Limited indeed is the number of English Moralists who have invariably kept this in view. However foreign it may be to their various systems, an enquiry into origin or into the universality of moral ideas always appears to slip in—not in its proper place, as an interesting psychological adjunct, but—as having an important bearing on the authority of their particular principle. And the necessary result, of course, of these efforts to support ultimate principles is, that they cease to be ultimate, and become not only subordinate, but subordinate to judgments which, if explicitly stated, would very likely appear far less obvious than they.

There is a whole school of Moralists, for example, who find or invent a special faculty, intellectual or sensitive, by which moral truth is arrived at ; who would regard it as a serious blow to morality if the process by which ethical beliefs were produced was found to be common to many other regions of thought. Oddly enough, these are the very people whose systems are often called ' *à priori.*' Now if by this term be meant that the ordinary maxims of morality are (according to these systems) independent of experience, it is appropriate enough ; but if it be meant that they are self-evident, it is a singular misnomer. For it is clear that on their systems rigidly interpreted those maxims derive their evidence, not from their own internal authority, but from the fact that they bear a certain special relation to our mental constitution ; so that the ethical proposition which really lies at the root of their ethics is something of this sort :—' We ought to obey all laws the validity of which is recognised by a special innate faculty, whether called Conscience or otherwise.' Now, I do not deny that from a philosophical point of view such propositions as these are possible foundations of morals ; but what I desire to point out is that such a phrase (to take a concrete case) as ' I ought to speak the truth because conscience commands it,' may have two widely different meanings, and may belong to two different systems of Ethics, not commonly distinguished. According to the first and most accurate meaning, ' I ought to speak the truth ' is an inference, of which the major premiss must be, ' I ought to do what conscience commands,' and being an inference, cannot obviously be an *à priori* law. According to the second and inaccurate meaning, ' I ought to speak the truth ' is in reality received on its own merits, and conscience is very unnecessarily brought in, either to add dignity to the law, or to account for its general acceptance among mankind, or for some other extra-ethical reason. The first of these views is open to no criticism from the point of view of ethical philosophy ; so far as form is concerned it is unassailable. But I greatly suspect that most people who nominally found their morality on conscience really hold the second theory ; and in that case, as I think, their statement is misleading, if not erroneous.

So far I have only given a negative description of the nature of an ethical proposition. I have said, indeed, that it announces obligation, but this statement is tautological ; for if we knew in what obligation consisted there would be no difficulty in stating the meaning of ethical. Beyond this I have only said that an ethical judgment deals with an essentially different subject-matter from either Science or Metaphysics. Is it possible to say more than this ? Is it possible to give any description of ethical propositions which shall add to our knowledge of their character ? On general grounds it is plain that this can only be done, supposing that what are *commonly* called ethical propositions form part of a larger class of judgments which resemble them in being neither scientific nor metaphysical, but differ from them in some other respect. I myself hold this to be the case. I hold not only that the judgments commonly called ethical (but which, in spite of the clumsiness attendant on changing the meaning of a word in the middle of a discussion, I shall henceforward call *moral*) have the two negative characteristics above mentioned in common with a larger class of judgments ; but that the distinction between the two classes should be ignored by ethical philosophy, since it depends not on 'form' but on 'matter.' All judgments belonging to either of these classes I shall henceforth call ethical. Those commonly called ethical I shall describe as moral ; the rest are either non-moral or immoral. Every possible judgment, then, is either ethical or non-ethical ; and every ethical judgment is either moral or non-moral or immoral. The terminology thus being defined, let me explain it, and at the same time my view on the subject.

If a man contemplates any action as one which he chooses to perform, he must do so either because he regards the action as one which he chooses for itself, or because he expects to obtain by it some object which he chooses for itself. And similarly, if he contemplates any object as one he chooses to obtain, he must do so either because he regards that object as chosen for itself, or because it may be a means to one that is. In other words, deliberate action is always directed mediately or immediately to something which is chosen for itself alone ; which something may either be itself an action, or what I loosely term an object. Including both, then, under the term 'end,' I define an ethical proposition thus :—*An ethical proposition is one which prescribes an action with reference to an end.* Nobody will deny that this definition is true of all moral propositions (most people, indeed, will think that it is too obvious to need stating) ; but they will probably say, and say truly, that it is also true of a great many propositions which are not usually called moral. Now my object is to show that the distinction between what are usually called moral propositions and that larger class which I have defined above, has no philosophic import, has nothing that is to do with the grounds of obligation. And for this purpose, let me analyse more carefully this larger class (which I call ethical) from a philosophic point of view, that is, with reference to the rational foundation and connection of its parts.

(1) Every proposition prescribing an action with reference to an end, belongs either explicitly or implicitly to a system of such propositions. (2) The fundamental proposition of every such system states an end, which the person who receives that system regards as final—as chosen for itself alone. (3) The subordinate propositions of that system are deduced from the fundamental proposition by means of scientific or theological minor premises. (4) When two such systems conflict, their rival claim can only be decided by a judgment or proposition not contained in either of them, which shall assert which of these respective fundamental 'ends' shall have precedence. [Ethics, then, rests on two sorts of judgments, neither of which can be deduced from the other, and of neither of which can any proof be given or required. The first sort declares an end to be final, the second declares which of two final ends is to be preferred, if they are incompatible. This second sort, of course, is not essential to an ethical system, but can only be required when an individual regards more than one end as final.] (5) No other sort of proposition can possibly lie at the root of an ethical system. [This is merely a restatement of the law dwelt on at the beginning of this discussion.]

Now in so far as this is a complete philosophical diagram of every ethical system, it must show the sort of authority on which every ethical proposition—every imperative—must rest. Yet since it is plain that this diagram takes no account of the differences there may be between *moral* and *immoral* ethical systems, how (it may be asked) can we account for the wide-spread delusion, that these differences affect the authority of the former?   This question takes us far afield into the regions of Psychology and Anthropology, but the answer to it may perhaps be suggested as follows. The main reason for this error appears to be, false analogy, unchecked by any clear apprehension of the nature of the rational or philosophical peculiarities of an ethical system. And in order to illustrate this, and at the same time to place the theory I am defending under as strong a light as possible, it may be as well to examine the exact bearing which 'Universality' and the approval of 'Conscience' (two of the chief characteristics of moral as opposed to non-moral or immoral systems) have on obligation.

My position, of course, is that they have *no* bearing— and in order to show this I offer the following analysis to the reader—taking Universality first.   A law may be said to be Universal in one of four senses.   It may mean (first) that all intelligences regard themselves as bound by it. This meaning we need not further consider, not only because it is a scientific assertion, and therefore, as I have shown, incapable of becoming the foundation of an ethical system, but also because it is a scientific assertion now entirely discredited.   It is quite out of fashion to maintain that Morality is the same in every race and every country, and therefore till, in the revolutions of thought, some one is found to re-assert this doctrine, we need not further discuss it.

The second possible meaning is, that by a universal moral law we mean one by which all intelligences *ought* to regard themselves as bound. This also we may dismiss because it amounts to saying that there is a moral law which obliges all intelligences to be bound by other moral laws. Is then *that* moral law Universal *in the sense we are discussing?* If it is, we are committed to an infinite series of moral laws, each commanding us to be bound by the preceding one. If it is not, then there can be a moral law which (in this sense) is not universal.

In the third place, by a universal moral law we may mean one which *we* think all men ought to obey. That we do think this of most moral laws, and that we do not think it of the other ethical laws, namely, the non-moral and the immoral ones, is tolerably certain. It remains to enquire whether the difference bears on obligation ; and this enquiry, as it seems to me, may be settled by a very simple consideration. All intelligences means Me and all other intelligences. The first of these constituent parts would be bound by a law held by Me whether it were universal (in this sense) or not. The second would *not* be bound by a law held by Me whether it were universal in this sense or not. In other words, to be bound by a moral law (and this, by the way, brings out very clearly the difference between being ethically bound and legally bound) is exactly the same thing as to regard it as binding on you ; it is not to regard it as binding on someone else ; and it is not for someone else to regard it as binding on you ; it has therefore, and it can have, no connection with Universality in this third sense.

It is, of course, open to anyone to assert that he recognises no imperative which is not universal (in this sense). This may very well be the fact, and I have no wish to deny it.   What I deny is, that the connection between the two is other than empirical and accidental, or that it has any place in the philosophy of obligation.

The fourth and last meaning which I am able to attach to the word Universal, when used of a law, is that it signifies that all people of 'well-constituted minds' do, as a matter of fact, regard themselves as bound by a law so qualified.   Now, if 'well-constituted' is defined with reference to morality, and means 'holding the one true moral system,' a proposition that all true or right moral laws are universal, is frivolous and merely verbal.   If it be defined with reference to something else—if it means, for instance, sane, or well-educated, or Christian, or scientific, or anything non-moral, then the same arguments may be used to show that universality in this sense cannot be a ground of obligation, as I used when speaking of the first sense.   For a proposition asserting that any considerable body of men, distinguished from the rest of mankind by some non-moral attribute, hold the same moral code, is very likely to be questionable, and being a scientific assertion, is quite certain to be irrelevant.

So much, then, for Universality.   As regards Conscience, I have shown before, that to assume a special faculty which is to announce ultimate moral laws can add nothing to their validity, nor will it do so the more if we suppose its authority supported by such sanctions as remorse or self-approval.   Conscience regarded in this way is not ethically to be distinguished from any external authority, as, for instance, the Deity, or the laws of the land.   Now, it is plain that no external authority can give validity to ultimate moral laws, for the question immediately arises, why should we obey that authority?   Only two reasons can be given.   The first is, that it is *right in itself* to obey; the second is, that (through a proper use of sanctions) it will be for our happiness to obey. Now, the first of these is a moral law, which obviously does *not* derive its validity from the external authority, because the external authority is an authority only by means of it. And the same may be said of the second reason, substituting the words 'ethical but non-moral' for the word 'moral.' In neither case, then, is the external authority the ultimate ground of obligation.

The inevitable ambiguity which arises from the sudden extension of the meaning of the word 'ethical' to imperatives which are immoral or non-moral, makes it, perhaps, desirable that I should very concisely re-state, from another point of view, the main position I have been attempting to establish.

All imperatives, all propositions prescribing actions, have this in common:—That if they are to have any cogency, or are to be anything but empty sound, the actions they prescribe must be to the individual by whom they are regarded as binding, either mediately or immediately desirable. They must conduce, directly or indirectly, to something which he regards as of worth for itself alone. The number of things which are thus in themselves desirable or of worth to somebody or other is, of course, very great. Pleasure or happiness in the abstract, other people's pleasure or happiness, money (irrespective of its power of giving pleasure), power, the love of God, revenge, are some of the commonest of them, and every one of these is regarded by some person or other as an end to be attained for its own sake, and not as a means to something else. Now, it is evident that to every one of the ultimate propositions prescribing these ends, and for which, as the ends are ends-in-themselves, no further reason can be given, there will belong a system of dependent propositions, the reasons for which are that the actions they prescribe conduce to the ultimate end or end-in-itself.

If, for instance, revenge against a particular individual is for me an end-in-itself, a proposition which prescribes shooting him from behind a hedge may be one of the subordinate or dependent propositions belonging to that particular system. But whereas the indefinite number of such systems is thus characterised by a common form, it is divided by ordinary usage into three classes, the moral, the non-moral, and the immoral, about the *de*notation of which there is a tolerable agreement. It would be universally admitted, for instance, that a system founded on the happiness of others was a moral system, while one founded on revenge was immoral : and, though there would be more dispute as to the members of the non-moral class, this is not a question on which I need detain the reader. The denotation then of these names being presumably fixed, what is the connotation ? or to limit the enquiry, what is the connotation of a *moral* system ? The apparent answers are as numerous as the number of schools of Moralists. But however numerous they may be, they can all be divided into two classes. The *first* class merely re-state the denotation ;—in other words, announce the ultimate end-in-itself of the system, and so, properly speaking, give no answer at all. A Utilitarian, for example, may simply assert that the greatest happiness of the greatest number is for him the ultimate end of action. If he stops there he evidently shows no philosophic reason for distinguishing the system he adopts from the countless others which exist, or have existed. If he attempts to give any further characteristic of his system, he then belongs to the *second* class, who do indeed explain the connotation of the word 'moral' according to their usage of it, but whose explanations have, and can have, nothing to do with the grounds of action or the theory of obligation.   The sanction of conscience, the emotion of approval, the expectation of reward, the feeling of good desert, glow of conscious merit— these are all most undoubtedly marks or characteristics of moral actions : how they came to be so, whether by education, association of ideas, innate tendency, or howsoever it has happened, matters nothing whatever, except to the psychologist ; that they are so is certain, but the significance of the fact is habitually misunderstood.   Are they simply the *causes* of good action ?   Then they have nothing to do with Ethics, which is concerned not with the causes but with the grounds or reasons for action, and would remain wholly unchanged if not a single man ever had done or could do right.   Are they the *ends* of action ?   Is the fact that they are obtained by a certain course a valid reason for pursuing that course ?   In that case they stand to a person holding that opinion in precisely the same relation as money does to the miser, or revenge to the savage.   They are the groundwork of an ethical system, and to state them is simply to denote *what* ethical system it is which is being alluded to.   Are they, finally, not ends of action, but merely marks by which certain actions may be known to belong to a particular system ?   In that case, and for that very reason, they can have nothing to do with the grounds or theory of obligation.   Therefore, I am justified in asserting that though under the general name 'ethical' are included not only moral, but also non-moral and immoral systems, the distinctions regarded from the outside between these subdivisions are not essential, and has no philosophic import—which was the thing to be proved.

Before concluding these remarks, I would point out three corollaries that may be drawn from them, which are not without interest. The first corollary is—that no instructive analogy exists between Ethics and Æsthetics. It is true, no doubt, that philosophers have talked about the Good and the Beautiful, as if they were co-ordinate subjects of investigation, and that in ordinary language we say both that a picture 'ought' to be admired, and that an action 'ought' to be performed. Nevertheless, reflecting on actual or possible æsthetic systems, it would seem clear that they must be included under one of four heads. They must belong either (1) to Ethics, or (2) to Psychology, or (3) to Metaphysics, or, lastly (4) to Metaphysics with an ethical or psychological element superadded. And in none of these cases can Æsthetics be said to rank as a parallel subject of enquiry with Ethics.

The first of these possibilities, namely, that Æsthetics belongs to, or is included in Ethics, I mention chiefly for the sake of completeness. Even those art-critics whose denunciations of bad taste approach most nearly to the level of moral reprobation, hardly maintain that it is our *duty* to admire the Venus of Milo in the same sense as it is our *duty* to love our neighbour. If any do hold this view, the conclusion to be drawn is, not that their Æsthetic code stands on a different, but similar platform to their Ethical code, but that their Ethical code is larger than that of ordinary people, by the whole amount of their Æsthetics.

According to the second of these possibilities, namely, that Æsthetics belongs to Psychology ; Æsthetics is merely the investigation of the nature and causes of peculiar emotions—chiefly secondary—produced in us by certain external causes, objects, or representations, and has no more to do with Ethics, either by way of resemblance or contrast, than any other part of the science to which it belongs.

The third possibility, namely, that Æsthetics belongs to Metaphysics, includes all such theories of the Beautiful as deal exclusively with 'objective standards,' 'ideas,' or 'archetypes,' 'the evolution of the Idea,' or 'the Perception of the agreement of the Subject and Object,' and the like. Taken by themselves, theories of this kind belong to Metaphysics; but if there be added any consideration of the relation such ontological entities or processes bear to the individual, these considerations must belong either to the first or the second of the above-mentioned possible treatments of Æsthetics, and must, therefore, be either ethical or psychological. This is the fourth possibility.

From this concise analysis then, it would seem clear that no analogy exists between Ethics rightly understood and any system right or wrong of Æsthetics. But if that be so, how comes the existence of any analogy even to have been supposed? The reply to this is, that there does exist an analogy between some theories of Æsthetics and Ethics *wrongly* understood. Some moralists, for example, have dwelt largely on the emotion excited in us by virtuous actions. And if the scientific examination of these emotions really constitute the essence of Ethics, there is unquestionably an analogy between theories of the Good and some theories of the Beautiful. Again, if ethical enquiries are thought to resolve themselves into researches concerning the existence and nature of some objective standard of right, it is inevitable that they should suggest, and it is probable they would resemble, those other metaphysical enquiries concerning the objective standard of beauty. Now it must not be supposed that I pronounce either of these investigations irrational; all I contend for is that they are not ethical ; or, rather (to avoid a dispute about words), what I contend for is that they have nothing, and can have nothing, directly to do with Obligation.

The second corollary concerns the functions of the Moral Philosopher. It is clear from what precedes, that it is *not* the business of the moral philosopher to account for the origin of moral ideas, or to analyse and explain that growth of sentiment which collects around the time-honoured maxims of current morality. These are topics which belong to Psychology. Neither is he expected to prove the propositions which lie at the root of any system of morals ; for these are incapable of proof. Nor, for the same reason, can he justify the judgments which declare which of two final ends is to be preferred in case of conflict, or how much of one is to be preferred to how much of the other. Nor, in reality, has he any but a subordinate part to play in expounding or deducing the derivative rules of morality ; and for this reason.

The deduction of any derivative rule is always necessarily in this form : ' the happiness of mankind ought to be promoted ' (this, let us say, is the ultimate unprovable foundation of the system) : ' monogamy promotes the happiness of mankind ' (this is the scientific [in another system it might have been theological] minor premiss) : ' therefore monogamy is a system which ought to be supported.' This is the required derivative rule. Now the only difficulty in deducing this conclusion from the first principle of the system lies in the difficulty of demonstrating the minor premiss ; in other words, it lies in the difficulty of a certain sociological investigation, which the speculative moralist as such cannot be expected to undertake.

The important duties of the moralist, for he has important duties, arise from the confused state in which the greater part of mankind are with regard to their ethical first principles. The two questions each man has to ask himself are—What do I hold to be the ultimate ends of action ? and—If there is more than one such end, how do I estimate them in case of conflict ? These two questions, it will be observed, are questions of fact, not of law ; and the duty of the moralist is to help his readers to discover the fact, not to force his own view down their throat by attempting a proof of that which is essentially, and by its very nature, incapable of proof. Above all, he must beware of substituting some rude simplification for (what may perhaps be) the complexity of nature, by deducing (as the Utilitarians do) all subordinate rules from one fundamental principle, when, it may be, this principle only approximately contains actual existing ethical facts.

Since these two questions can be answered, not by ratiocination, but only by simple inspection, the art of the moralist will consist in placing before the enquirer various problems in Ethics free from the misleading particulars which surround them in practice. In other words, his method will be casuistical, and not dogmatic.

It may perhaps seem strange that, after commenting at some length on the prevailing confusion between Ethics and Psychology, I should now have to announce that the business of the Ethical Philosopher (at least, so far as first principles are concerned) is as purely psychological as, according to the two preceding paragraphs, I make it out to be ; and it may seem, therefore, as if the difference between my view and that of the Philosophers whom I have attempted to criticise is by no means essential or important. This, however, is not the case. My complaint against these philosophers is that they appear to suppose that a psychological law can serve as a rational basis for an ethical system ; so that their chief aim often seems to have been the establishment of their own particular views on the origin and nature of our moral sentiments. I, on the other hand, altogether deny the possibility of such a basis, and maintain that all that a moralist can do with regard to ethical first principles is, not to prove them or deduce them, but to render them explicit if they are implicit, clear if they are obscure. To do this effectually he must, of course, treat of ideas and motions, and his work will, therefore, in some sense be undoubtedly psychological. To make this statement complete, I should add, that (as appears by my next paragraph) there is no absurdity in supposing that a moralist may in the course of his speculations hit on some entirely new first principle which he has not held even obscurely before, but which commends itself to his mind as soon as it is presented to him.

The third corollary I draw is this—that there are only two senses in which we can rationally talk of a moral system being superior to the one we profess. According to the first sense, superior means superior in form, more nearly in accordance with the ideal of an ethical system just sketched out. According to the second sense, in which the superiority attaches to the *matter* of the system, it can only mean that the system is one of which we are ignorant, *but which we should adopt if presented to us.* The superiority indicated is a hypothetical superiority.

Now it must be observed that the sense in which we speak of other hypothetical systems as being superior to our own, is by no means identical with that in which we speak of our own as being superior to that of other people. Looking back over history, we perceive a change and development of the moral ideas of the race in the direction of the systems which now prevail ; and this change we rightly term an improvement. But if, arguing from the past, we suppose that this improvement will continue through the indefinite future, we are misled by a false analogy. The change may very well continue, the improvement certainly will not. And the reason is clear. What we mean, or ought to mean, by an improvement in the past, is an approach to our own standard, and since any change at all corresponding in magnitude to this in the future must involve a departure from that standard, it must necessarily be a change for the worse.

In other words,—when we speak of another system as being superior (in matter) to our own, we speak of a possible system which we should accept if we knew it. When we speak of our own system being superior to that of some other person, we assert the superiority unconditionally, and quite irrespectively of the possible acceptance of it by that other person, supposing him to be acquainted with it. If then we believe that development will proceed in the future as it has done in the past, we must suppose that a time will come when the moral ideas of the world would be as much out of our reach, supposing them presented to us, as ours would be out of reach of primitive man. This is also true of scientific ideas : but there is this difference between them, that whereas the change in scientific ideas may be an improvement, that in moral ideas must be a degradation. The grounds of this distinction of course are obvious, viz., that the standard of excellence in the case of scientific ideas is, or is supposed to be, conformity to an infinitely complex external world :— a conformity which may *increase* with every change in the ideas. The standard of excellence, on the other hand, in moral ideas must necessarily be conformity to our actual ideal, and this conformity must *diminish* with every change in the ideas.

This point would not perhaps have been worth dwelling on, if it was not that the discussion brings into strong relief the nature, so far as form is concerned, of the criterion of right, and also has some bearing on current theories of optimistic evolution, with which I confess it does not seem possible easily to reconcile it.

LONDON : PRINTED BY
SPOTTISWOODE AND CO., NEW-STREET SQUARE
AND PARLIAMENT STREET